The Siege of Brest
1941

The Siege of Brest 1941

A Legend of Red Army Resistance on the Eastern Front

Author
Rostislav Aliev

Russian text by
Sergei Anisimov

Translated by
Stuart Britton

Maps by
Igor Savin

Pen & Sword
MILITARY

First published in Great Britain in 2013 by
Pen & Sword Military
an imprint of
Pen & Sword Books Ltd
47 Church Street
Barnsley
South Yorkshire
S70 2AS

ISBN 978-1-78159-085-0

A CIP catalogue record for this book is
available from the British Library.

Typeset in 10/12 Ehrhardt by Concept, Huddersfield, West Yorkshire
Printed and bound in England by CPI Group (UK) Ltd, Croydon, CRO 4YY

Pen & Sword Books Ltd incorporates the imprints of Pen & Sword Archaeology, Atlas, Aviation, Battleground, Discovery, Family History, History, Maritime, Military, Naval, Politics, Railways, Select, Social History, Transport, True Crime, Claymore Press, Frontline Books, Leo Cooper, Praetorian Press, Remember When, Seaforth Publishing and Wharncliffe.

For a complete list of Pen & Sword titles please contact
PEN & SWORD BOOKS LIMITED
47 Church Street, Barnsley, South Yorkshire, S70 2AS, England
E-mail: enquiries@pen-and-sword.co.uk
Website: www.pen-and-sword.co.uk

Contents

Maps

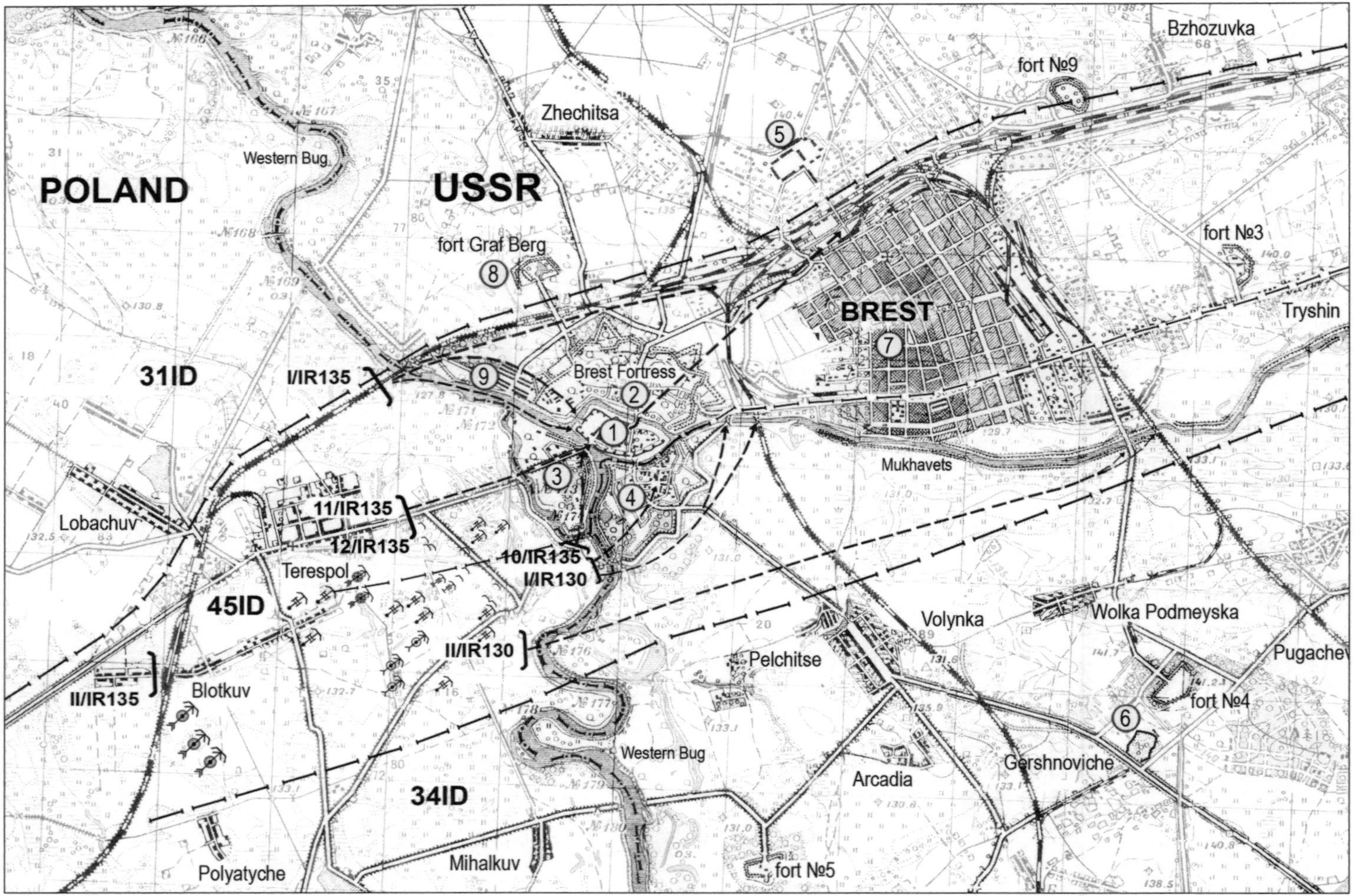
POLAND
USSR
Western Bug
Zhechitsa
fort Graf Berg
8
5
fort №9
Bzhozuvka
fort №3
BREST
7
Tryshin
31ID
I/IR135
9
Brest Fortress
2
1
3
4
Mukhavets
Lobachuv
11/IR135
12/IR135
10/IR135
I/IR130
Terespol
45ID
II/IR130
II/IR135
Blotkuv
Volynka
Wolka Podmeyska
Pugachev
Pelchitse
fort №4
6
Western Bug
Gershnoviche
Arcadia
34ID
Polyatyche
Mihalkuv
fort №5

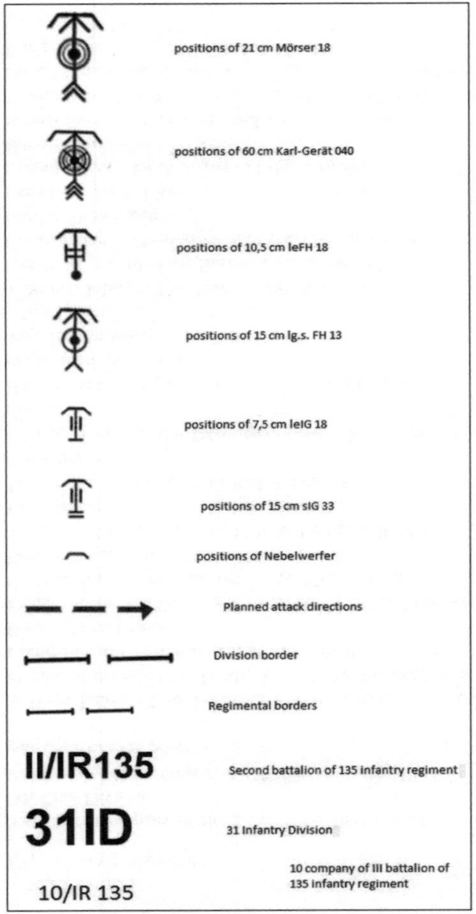

Map 1: The Brest Fortress

The array of opposing forces and the 45th ID's plan to seize the fortress and the town

1. The Citadel (The Central Island)
2. North Island (The Kobrin Fortification)
3. West Island (The Terespol Fortification)
4. South Island (The Volyn Fortification)
5. The North Military Encampment
6. The South Military Encampment
7. Brest
8. Fort 'Graf Berg'
9. The Proviant Magazines

The positions of the Red Army's forces in Brest (keyed to circled numbers)

1. The Citadel (The Central Island)

2nd Rifle Co., 132nd Separate NKVD Military Escort Battalion

3rd Rifle Co., 132nd Separate NKVD Military Escort Battalion (by 22 June its personnel were carrying out the assignment to escort prisoners into the Soviet interior, and were not located in the fortress)

Headquarters and specialized elements of the 132nd Separate NKVD Military Escort Battalion

9th Line Border Post of the 3rd Border Commandant's Headquarters of the 17th Red Banner Border Detachment

3rd Reserve Border Post of the 3rd Border Commandant's Headquarters of the 17th Red Banner Border Detachment

3rd Border Commandant's Headquarters of the 17th Red Banner Border Detachment

31st Separate Motorized Transport Battalion of the 6th Rifle Division

333rd Rifle Regiment of the 6th Rifle Division (some of its elements by 22 June had been moved out to build fortifications of the fortified district)

84th Rifle Regiment of the 6th Rifle Division (the 1st and 2nd battalions by 22 June had been moved out to build fortifications of the fortified district, while a portion of the regimental artillery had been moved out to the 4th Army's artillery firing range)

75th Separate Reconnaissance Battalion of the 6th Rifle Division

33rd Separate Engineering Regiment of the Western Special Military District (part of it was away, building fortifications of the fortified district)

455th Rifle Regiment of the 42nd Rifle Division (the 1st and 2nd battalions by 22 June had been moved out to build fortifications of the fortified district)

7th Separate Signals Battalion of the 6th Rifle Division (by 22 June it had been moved out to a camp near the village of Plosk, and only its alert force remained in the Citadel)

Headquarters (headquarters elements) of the 44th Rifle Regiment of the 42nd Rifle Division

School for the junior command staff of the 44th Rifle Regiment of the 42nd Rifle Division

Residents of Brest Oblast who'd been summoned to conscript muster points

2. North Island (The Kobrin Fortification)

44th Separate Field Mobile Bakery of the 6th Rifle Division

98th Separate Anti-tank Artillery Battalion of the 6th Rifle Division

393rd Separate Anti-aircraft Artillery Battalion of the 42nd Rifle Division (by 22 June its 2nd and 3rd batteries had been withdrawn to the 4th Army's artillery firing range)

Specialized elements of the 44th Rifle Regiment of the 42nd Rifle Division

1st Rifle Battalion of the 44th Rifle Regiment of the 42nd Rifle Division

125th Rifle Regiment of the 6th Rifle Division (the 3rd Battalion by 22 June had moved out to build fortifications of the fortified district)

Transport Company of the 333rd Rifle Regiment of the 6th Rifle Division
Residents of Brest Oblast who'd been summoned to conscript muster points

3. West Island (The Terespol Fortification)
Details of the 9th Line Border Post of the 3rd Border Commandant's Headquarters of the 17th Red Banner Border Detachment
Details of the 3rd Reserve Border Post of the 3rd Border Commandant's Headquarters of the 17th Red Banner Border Detachment
Transport Company of the 17th Red Banner Border Detachment
Sapper Platoon of the 17th Red Banner Border Detachment
Driving School of the Belorussian SSR NKVD's Border Forces
Border Guards at gatherings of light machine-gunners, cavalrymen and athletes
Veterinarian clinic

4. South Island (The Volyn Fortification)
Details of the 9th Line Border Post of the 3rd Commandant's Headquarters of the 17th Red Banner Border Detachment
Details of the 3rd Reserve Border Post of the 3rd Commandant's Headquarters of the 17th Red Banner Border Detachment
School for the junior command staff of the 84th 'Comintern' Rifle Regiment of the 6th Rifle Division (by 22 June it had moved out to the 4th Army's artillery firing range)
95th Medical-Sanitary Battalion of the 6th Rifle Division
Brest Military Hospital
Military Hospital of the 28th Rifle Corps

5. North Military Encampment
111th Separate Sapper Battalion of the 6th Rifle Division (by 22 June it had been moved out to build fortifications of the fortified district)
246th Separate Anti-aircraft Artillery Battalion of the 6th Rifle Division
84th Separate Reconnaissance Battalion of the 42nd Rifle Regiment
18th Separate Signals Battalion (by 22 June it had been moved out to the camp near the village of Plosk, and only its alert force remained)
17th Howitzer Artillery Regiment of the 42nd Rifle Division
158th Separate Motorized Transport Battalion of the 42nd Rifle Division
447th Artillery Regiment of the 28th Rifle Corps
District Courses for junior political officers of the 4th Army

6. South Military Encampment
Units of the 22nd Tank Division

7. Brest
Headquarters of the 28th Rifle Corps
Headquarters of the 6th 'Orel' Red Banner Rifle Division
Headquarters of the 42nd Rifle Division
Elements of the 60th Regiment of the 9th Division of NKVD Forces, guarding the railroad facilities (field command, headquarters, political unit, 2nd Battalion headquarters, and a reserve company)
Headquarters of the 17th Red Banner (Brest) Border Detachment of the Belorussia SSR NKVD Border Forces
Commandant's platoon of the 17th Red Banner (Brest) Border Detachment of the Belorussia SSR NKVD Border Forces

8. Fort 'Graf Berg'
2nd Battalion of the 131st 'K.E. Voroshilov' Light Artillery Regiment (one battery by 22 June had been moved to the Brest artillery firing range)

9. Proviant Magazines
1st Battalion of the 131st 'K.E. Voroshilov' Light Artillery Regiment (one battery by 22 June had been moved to the Brest artillery firing range)
3rd Battalion of the 131st 'K.E. Voroshilov' Light Artillery Regiment (one battery by 22 June had been moved to the Brest artillery firing range)
Headquarters of the 131st 'K.E. Voroshilov' Light Artillery Regiment
Headquarters battery of the 131st 'K.E. Voroshilov' Light Artillery Regiment
Headquarters elements (surveying platoon, signals platoon, intelligence platoon, anti-aircraft platoon) of the 131st 'K.E. Voroshilov' Light Artillery Regiment
Specialized elements (school for junior command staff, transport platoon, ammunition support platoon, logistics platoon, musicians' platoon, sanitary unit, veterinarian unit) of the 131st 'K.E. Voroshilov' Light Artillery Regiment)
Residents of Brest Oblast who'd been summoned to conscript muster points

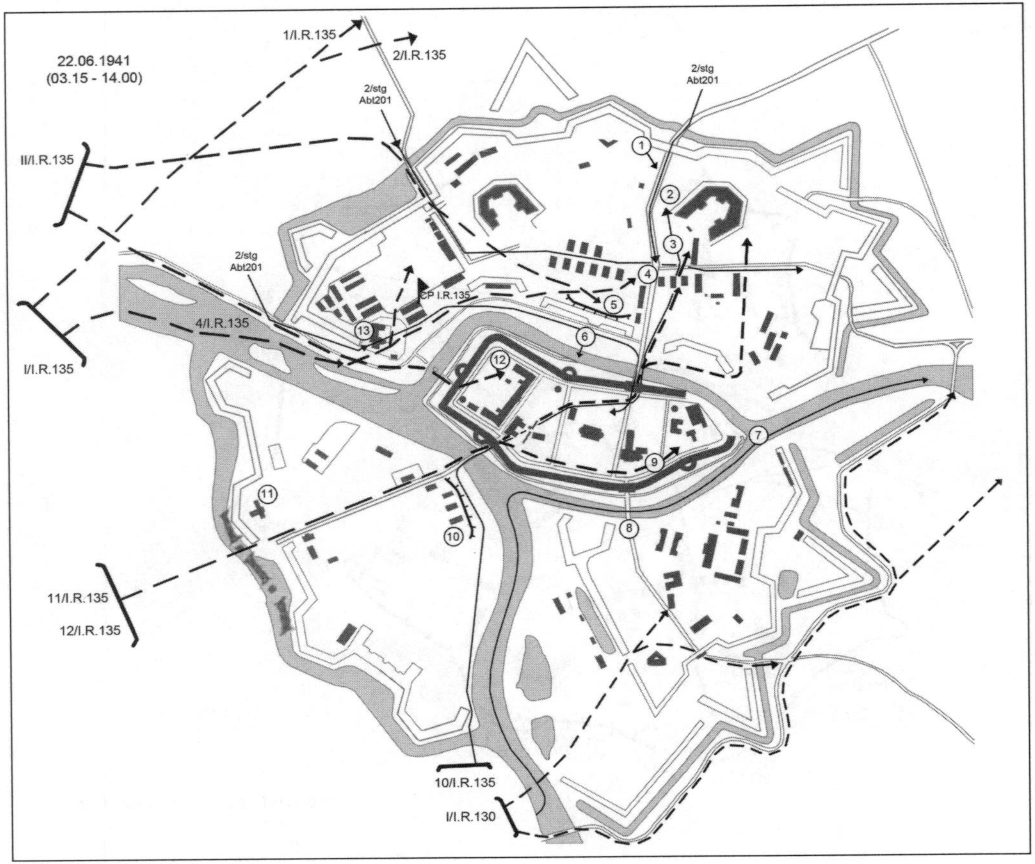

Map 2: Brest

Positions and actions of the Soviet and German troops between 3.15 and 14.00 22 June 1941

1. Place where Teuschler's assault team came under fire
2. Place where Teuschler was wounded
3. Places where Praxa, Oeltze and Kimberger were killed
4. Position where German assault gun was knocked out
5. Position of Orbach's 8/I.R. 135
6. German assault gun's firing position
7. Route of Kremers' detachment. Point marks the spot where one of his boats sank
8. Place where Kremers' detachment, having struck a sandbar, was fired upon
9. Spot where Soviet troops under the command of Matevosian counter-attacked the assault group of III/I.R. 135
10. The position of 12/I.R. 133 (*Oberleutnant* Loertzer's company in which Lozert served)
11. The Driver's School, in the proximity of which many soldiers of III/I.R. 135 were killed
12. The attack of two of III/I.R. 135's assault groups, which crossed the Brigidki Bridge
13. The buildings of Brigidki jail

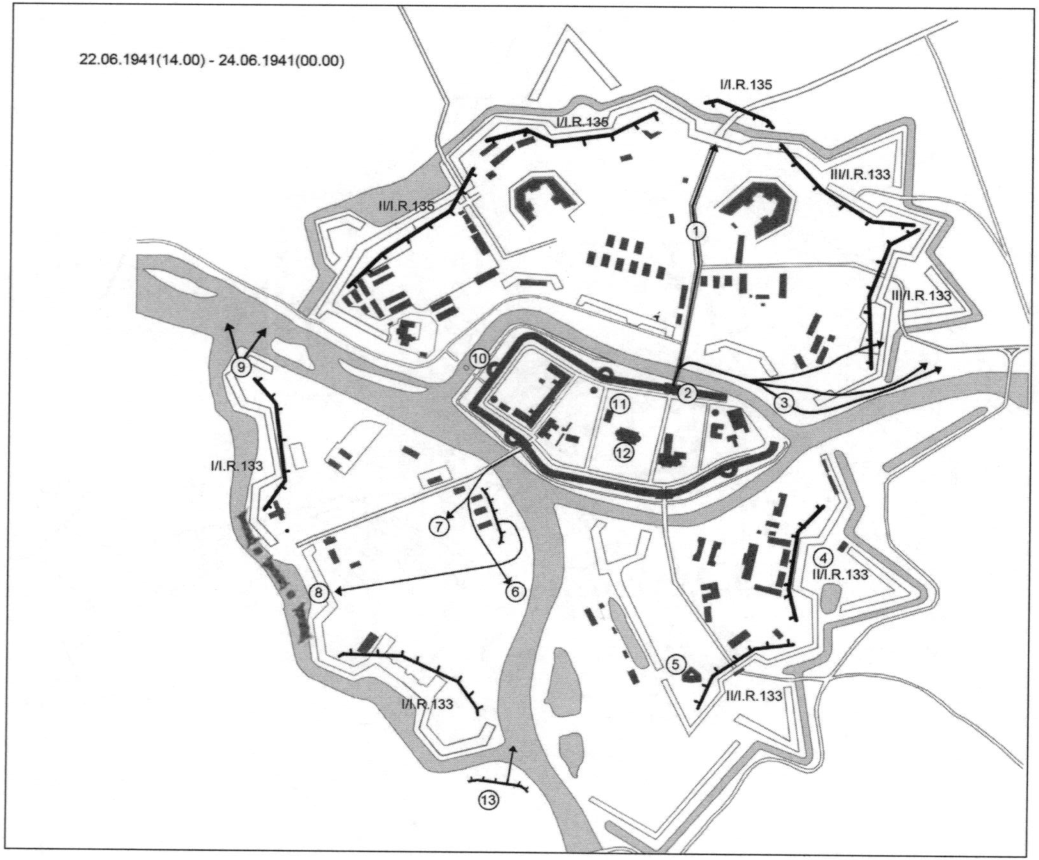

Map 3: The Fortress

Positions and actions of the Soviet and German troops between 14.00 22 June and 00.00 24 June

1. Direction of Lieutenant Bytko's break-out
2. Mess hall of the 33rd Separate Engineering Regiment, where an assault group of III/I.R. 135 was isolated
3. The direction of attempts to break out of the Citadel on the night of 22–23 June 1941
4. The position for cover against friendly artillery fire
5. The building of the 84th Rifle Regiment's junior command staff (a defensive strongpoint)
6. The attempt by Potapov's group to break out (with it went the schoolboy Petia Klypa)
7. The place where those of Potapov's group that were breaking out came under fire
8. The positions of 12/I.R. 133 and I/I.R 133 for cover against friendly artillery fire
9. Pillbox No. 3 (a Border Guards defensive strongpoint)
10. The place where those who were surrendering under the partial capitulation emerged from the Citadel on 23 June
11. The officers' mess hall where a group of 10/I.R. 135 was isolated
12. The Church of Saint Nikolai
13. Machine-gun position nailing down Soviet soldiers attempting to force the Bug

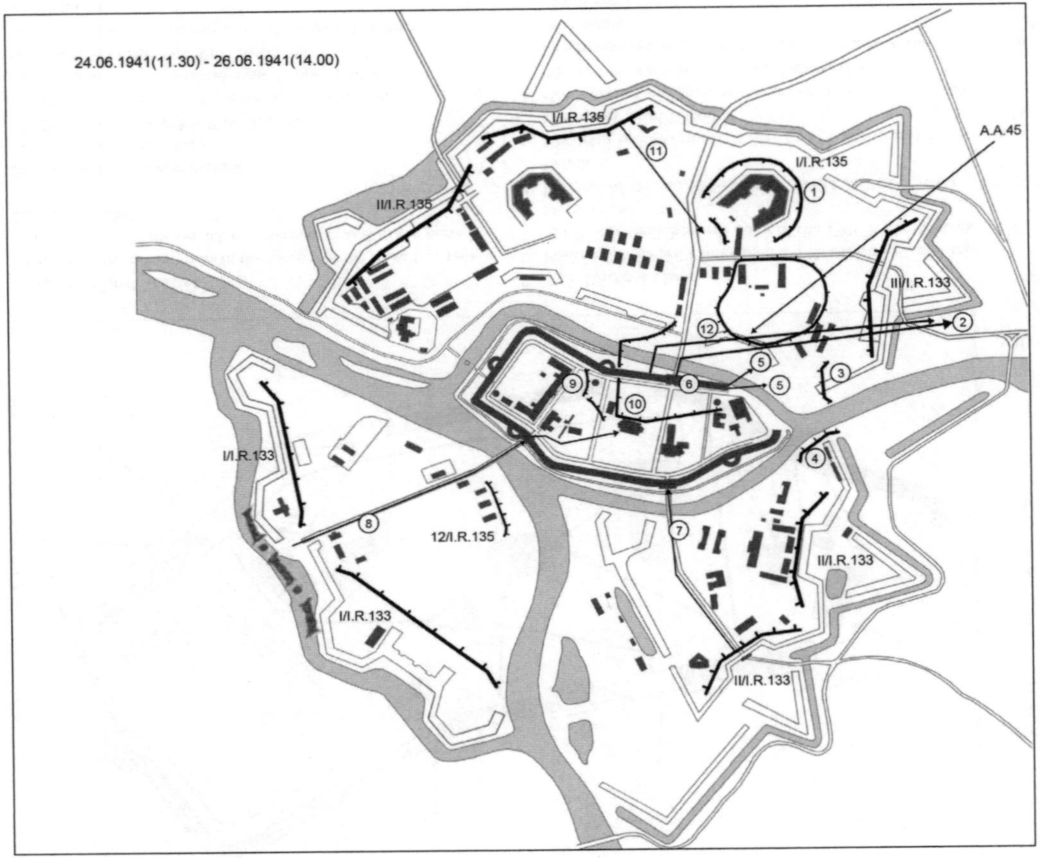

Map 4: The Fortress

Positions and actions of the Soviet and German troops between 11.30 24 June and 14.00 26 June

1. The cordon of I/ I.R. 135 and II/I.R. 130 around the East Fort
2. The break-out direction and the place where the break-out group under the command of Lieutenant Vinogradov were captured
3. & 4. I.R. 133's machine-gun positions, which blocked break-out attempts. Traces of the machine-gun nests are still visible
5. The direction of the break-out attempts on the night of 23–24 June
6. The place where the Zubachev – Fomin group was captured
7. The route taken by the guns of 14/I.R. 133 (Watzek, Schneiderbauer) into battle
8. The relief of the isolated Germans in the Church of Saint Nikolai by *Feldwebel* Lozert's group
9. The positions of I/I.R. 133 before taking the 455th Rifle Regiment's sector
10. The positions of I/I.R. 133 before taking the Officers' House
11. The attack by 2/I.R. 135 on the morning of 24 June 1941. It was precisely this moment that was captured in the frames of *Die Deutsche Wochenschau*'s film chronicle
12. Point 145 – the least studied defensive strongpoint of the fortress's defenders

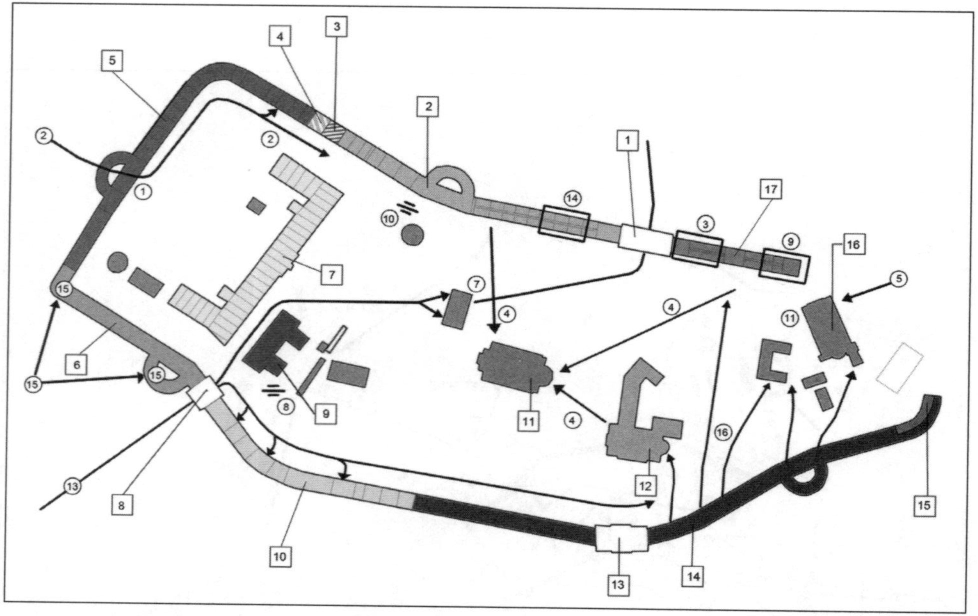

Map 5: The Citadel

Positions of the Soviet units in the Citadel of the Brest Fortress and the actions of the Soviet and German troops in the period 22–26 June 1941

Positions (boxed numbers)

1. The Trekharoch Gate
2. Position of the 455th Rifle Regiment
3. Position of the 37th Separate Signals Battalion
4. Position of the 111th Separate Sapper Battalion
5. Position of the 44th Rifle Regiment
6. Position of the 31st Separate Motorized Transport Battalion
7. Position of the 333rd Rifle Regiment
8. The Terespol Gates
9. Position of the 3rd Commandant's Headquarters, and the 3rd Reserve and 9th Line Posts of the 17th Border Guards Detachment
10. Position of the 132nd Separate NKVD Military Escort Battalion
11. The 84th Rifle Regiment's Red Army Club (formerly the Church of Saint Nikolai)
12. Headquarters and men of the armored car company and the armorer's workshop of the 75th Separate Reconnaissance Battalion (formerly the Engineering Directorate)
13. The Kholm Gates
14. Position of the 84th Rifle Regiment
15. The armored car park of the 75th Separate Reconnaissance Battalion (winter school of boxing)
16. Storage facilities, club and mess hall of the 75th Separate Reconnaissance Battalion (the so-called 'White Palace')
17. Position of the 33rd Separate Engineering Regiment (the so-called 'Officers' House')

Actions (circled numbers)

1. Firing position of Paternola's 20mm anti-aircraft guns
2. Route of advance of the two assault groups, which penetrated across the Brigidki Bridge and through the Brigidki Gates
3. Kitchen of the 33rd Separate Engineering Regiment, where a group of III/I.R. 135 was isolated and captured
4. The assault on the Church of Saint Nikolai
5. Here the Germans from Kremers' sinking boat came ashore
6. The fight for the position of the 132nd Separate NKVD Military Escort Battalion
7. The position of an assault gun of 2/StgAbt 201 covering the volleyball court
8. The firing position of the Soviet gun, which fired on the Church of Saint Nikolai on the evening of 22 June
9. The final defensive pocket of resistance within the Citadel
10. The firing position of the Soviet gun, which had been set up to fire at the church and to cover the Trekharoch Gate
11. The White Palace, where during an explosion of a shell fired by a Karl siege mortar, wounded men located in the cellar were buried by rubble
12. & 13. Directions of attack by the assault groups of III/I.R. 135 at 04.00 on the morning of 22 June
14. Here, under shelling of the Ring Barracks from a German assault gun, wounded men located in the basement (in the garage pit) were burned alive
15. Storage facilities of the 333rd Rifle Regiment, from where attempts were made to fire upon the Germans' temporary bridges across the Bug River
16. The withdrawal from the Ring Barracks of elements of the 84th Rifle Regiment to the position of the 33rd Separate Engineering Regiment

Translator's Note

The author Rostislav Aliev presents a detailed study of the assault on the Brest Citadel in June 1941. Using the records of the Russian Federation's Central Archives of the Ministry of Defence, as well as official German records, as well as what are of possibly even greater value, the recollections of veterans and civilians who were there, Aliev analyzes the combat operations of the German 45th Infantry Division [formerly the Austrian 4th Infantry Division] as it tackled the bastion at Brest as part of Operation Barbarossa. Encountering unexpectedly tough resistance, combat operations continued for a week, by which point the 45th Infantry Division had lost heavily in officers and men, and now stood far behind its neighboring divisions of General Schroth's 12th Army Corps. Tormented by thirst, the heroic defenders literally fought until the final round of ammunition in many instances. Even after the capitulation of the last defending fortification, the East Fort, on 29 June, the Germans spent the month of July dealing with individual and small groups of defenders who continued to lurk in the ruins of the Citadel.

Because the author offers numerous German recollections and reports, the translation presented a particular problem. Naturally, translation of German text via a Russian translation leads to a loss of verbatim accuracy, but I trust that the essence of what the speaker said has been preserved. I was aided considerably by the fact that Aliev took many of the German recollections from Robert Kershaw's *War Without Garlands* (De Capo Press, 2000), so in those instances I have used Kershaw's translation. However, even in that case, Aliev sometimes presents additional statements by the German participants that were not included in Kershaw's text. I have had to offer my own translation.

Throughout the study, Aliev occasionally employs the reference numbers for specific buildings and fortifications that can be found on German maps. For example, one fortification that became critical to the fighting was the gorge barracks on North Island that defended the approaches to the Trekharoch Bridge, which led from North Island into the Citadel. On German maps, this was designated as Point 145, which the author also uses at times. I have preserved these numerical designations as 'Points', but the readers should be aware that they refer to specific buildings, fortifications or sections of walls. In the narrative, the author did make clear which particular building or fortification lay behind the numerical designation for it. In addition, because the Citadel was laid out in the nineteenth century, the text sometimes uses French military engineering terms for specific types of fortifications, such as reduit, gorge barracks, lunette, barbican [which I have translated as semi-tower] and caponier. I have sought to explain these to the reader when they occur. Note that the author often uses conventional references to the two opposing sides as 'Germans' and 'Russians'. Readers should keep in mind that the 45th Infantry Division was composed of Austrians primarily recruited from Upper Austria, while the defenders were of many different nationalities that were once part of the Soviet Union.

The fighting, especially on 22 June, swirled around numerous bridges, gates, buildings, mess halls and sections of barracks, and in addition some of these locations received nicknames before or during the battle, such as the 'Officers' House', which was actually a section of the Ring Barracks that was occupied by the 33rd Engineering Regiment and the 75th Separate Reconnaissance Battalion, where as it happened, several leaders of the Citadel's defense came together. It can be difficult to track the fighting without the aid of a map. Readers are thus advised to bookmark the map section, at least until they have a firm image of the Brest Fortress and the Citadel in their mind's eye.

Note regarding the designation of German units:

The *Wehrmacht*'s system of organizing infantry regiments (I.R.) in 1941 was as follows. Each regiment had three subordinate infantry battalions, expressed in this text with Roman numerals as I Battalion, II Battalion and III Battalion. Each infantry battalion consisted of three rifle companies and a machine-gun company. Within the regiment, these rifle companies were numbered consecutively 1 through 12, with the 4th, 8th and 12th companies being the machine-gun companies. Companies 1 through 4 were assigned to I Battalion, 5 through 8 to II Battalion, and 9 through 12 to III Battalion. The regiment had two additional companies that were directly subordinate to regiment headquarters, the 13th and 14th companies. The 13th Company was a howitzer company, while the 14th Company was an anti-tank company.

Because the company's number made its battalion affiliation obvious, it rendered the battalion designation superfluous when referring to the company. Rather than 11/III I.R. 135, the author shortened this to 11/I.R. 135. Thus, an Arabic number prefix to the regiment's designation refers to a company, while a Roman numeral refers to a battalion. For example, 3/I.R. 130 refers to the 3rd Rifle Company (of I Battalion) in the 130th Infantry Regiment, while III/I.R. 130 refers to the 130th Infantry Regiment's third battalion.

Introduction

On 22 June 1941, the German army crossed the Soviet Union's western border along its entire length. The swift advance of the *Wehrmacht*'s panzer groups led to the encirclement and dismemberment of the Soviet units and formations in close proximity to the border, which frequently entered the fighting without any sort of preparation. They were quickly crushed – one after another. Their fate remained unknown; communications with them were lost almost immediately after the invasion began, and at times there weren't even any rumors which might have said something about what happened.

... However, in the spring of 1942 on one of the sectors of the Soviet-German front, an 'Account of the taking of Brest-Litovsk', which had been written by the commander of the German 45th Infantry Division Major General Fritz Schlieper, fell into the hands of the Red Army command. A year before, Schlieper's Austrian division had crossed the border on the axis of the German army's main attack in the vicinity of the Belorussian city of Brest. Its objectives were the city and its old fortress, which had been built by Russian czars back in the nineteenth century, which provided sufficient quarters for major formations of Soviet troops right on the very border of the Soviet national boundary. There were not even rumors about their fate after the German invasion ...

Yet when studying the captured German 'Account of the taking of Brest-Litovsk', the Red Army command discovered with surprise that the resistance of Brest lasted for more than a week, while this hopeless battle was fought by isolated groups of the fortress's defenders that were scattered throughout its casemates and underground bunkers and tunnels. During the assault on the fortress, the 45th Infantry Division suffered heavy casualties, and its commander specially noted the courage and tenaciousness of the Red Army men that were battling with his battalions.

For the anniversary of the start of the war, in June 1942 the official newspaper of the People's Commissariat of Defence *Krasnaia zvezda* [*Red star*] took a rare step for those times and published the 'Account of the taking of Brest-Litovsk'. Although many details, which didn't answer to the propagandistic task, were removed from the text and the document was supplied with bombastic comments, its publication nevertheless had a significant impact. It turned out that the resistance of the Soviet troops that had been encircled a year before was far more savage than had been assumed by the Soviet citizens, who'd been stunned by the *Wehrmacht*'s rapid advance toward Moscow.

The *Krasnaia zvezda* article laid the basis of the 'Brest legend', which quickly became thanks to official Soviet propaganda a symbol of June 1941 and which mollified the bitterness of the defeats. However, initially this was still only a legend – not a single name of one of the defenders of Brest was known (though much was being said about their heroism), nor was anything known about their fate or the details of the fighting.

This situation began to change only in the early 1950s – at the time, during the clearing away of rubble in the fortress, traces were found of the bitter fighting, which had erupted here a decade before: the remains of defenders, their weapons, but most importantly, documents that allowed some of the names of the defenders and certain details of the events to be established. However, these documents (several decomposed pages) were nevertheless insufficient at least to picture what had happened in Brest in 1941 with a sufficient amount of confidence.

A fundamental change in the study of the 'Brest legend' occurred in the mid-1950s, when the Soviet writer Sergei Smirnov took an interest in this subject. He exerted much effort to create a more real picture of what had happened out of the complex of hazy myths and rumors. Over the years of research work, the author located dozens and hundreds of the defenders and established the identities of the defense's leaders. The collected stories provided the basis for the book written by Smirnov at the end of the 1950s, *Brestskaia krepost'* [*Brest Fortress*], which became one of the more celebrated events in the public life of the post-Stalinist USSR and gained cult-like status for many generations of Soviet youth.

However, simultaneously one of the main research problems connected with the Brest events arose. The point is that a so-called 'official version' of the events, tightly adapted to propaganda aims, was created on the basis of the picture of events as created by Sergei Smirnov. Despite the fact that over the passing decades quite a few facts appeared that contradicted it, the 'official version' remained unaltered. For example, its main tenet remained the supposition of 'a struggle to the last soldier', although the majority of the defenders were taken as prisoners already in the course of the first two or three days of fighting. The dating of any sort of events, connected with the defense of the fortress, was also not subjected to re-examination; this concerns first of all the duration of the defense, both of separate sectors and of the fortress as a whole.

The turbulent events that led to the collapse of the USSR changed much. By this time almost none of the participants of the events remained alive, but interest in the history of 1941, which had become one of the questions of Russian society's self-identification, flared up anew. Sergei Smirnov's *Brestskaia krepost'* and the official version of events connected with it came to be re-examined.

So I headed to Brest, in order to find out on the spot just what happened in June 1941. My first guide around the fortress became a man of indefinite age, but of a fully identifiable profession – Kolia collected empty bottles for recycling. Combining the excursion with his work, he escorted me along his most profitable paths. Bottles love remote places, and that's how I entered the Brest Fortress through the 'back door', avoiding the set itineraries of formal excursions. However, I was quickly detained by Belorussian border agents, who took me as a potential border violator . . . They were mistaken – I had no intention to cross the border, but I wanted to violate the official version of events. For this purpose I had decided to move along a fresh path and to enter the history of Brest Fortress from an unexpected direction – from the west.

The holdings of the German Federal Military Archive in Freiburg provided a heretofore unseen evidential foundation confirmed by documents. More than 3,000 pages of the most diverse documentation enabled at last the creation of a study that has been maximally purged of myth-making. The history of the defense of the Brest Fortress was gradually cleansed of the tarnish of propaganda and became a real historical event. However, my 'approach from the west' didn't supersede the 'eastern view': one distinction of this book from the work of Western authors is the comparison of Soviet sources with German documents and memoirs, which provided both the possibility to fill in the date of many episodes mentioned by defenders of the fortress and to indicate the location of the events or the *dramatis personae* on both sides more accurately.

This book is a reconstruction of the events. Despite the fact that I was able to draw upon a multitude of sources, which often successfully added to one another, enormous pieces of the history of the defense of the Brest Fortress and the interrelationship between events still remain as 'blank spots'. Although many of the details seem not so important, in the first place I have given myself a rather ambitious task – to lay bare the events in Brest as fully as is possible; secondly, it was precisely the inductive method that permits in the given case the restoration of some insignificant episode and to make it a basis for the reconstruction of the course of events, which determined the history of the defense of Brest and its fortress.

However, each new step forward only expands the horizon. Then it becomes obvious that it can scarcely be reached.

Part I

Thunderstorm is Approaching

Chapter 1

'Gentlemen, our objective is Brest-Litovsk'

Three assaults

Brest-Litovsk is a city which by 1941 had already become a victorious symbol of German arms. Despite the fact that prior to the First World War, the high command of the Imperial Russian Army had placed a lot of hopes on the Brest Fortress, in 1915 the powerful fortress was abandoned by the Russians to the attacking Germans without a fight, and the fortifications which had taken decades to complete were demolished.

However, in March 1918 Brest-Litovsk quickly became better known in history with the signing in its fortress of the Brest Peace Treaty, which was a humiliation for Russia. This was the final victory of Imperial Germany over the already collapsing Russian Empire.

Brest-Litovsk also became an important symbol in the pre-war Soviet-German relationship. However, even by the start of the 'military relations', it just as before remained not simply a border city, but a complex of fortifications now being occupied by the Russian People's Army, the unpredictability and ferocity of which in fact had to a great degree brought about the 1918 Brest-Litovsk Treaty.

By 1939 Brest was now part of Poland, having been ceded to it under the terms of the 1921 peace treaty between the young Soviet republic and Poland. Thanks to the fact that Brest (which before 1939 was known as Brest-on-Bug) now lay rather distant from the German borders, in the years prior to the Second World War the *Wehrmacht* showed little interest in it.

During the 1939 campaign in Poland, on 13 September 1939 German forces arrived on the outskirts of Brest-on-Bug. Polish units of Group 'Brest' under the command of the previously retired 49-year-old General Konstantin Plisovsky were occupying the city, primarily ensconced in the fortress. According to various data, they numbered between 2,500 and 4,000 men – primarily soldiers of march and sentry units and elements, which had a total of 18 field guns, 8 anti-aircraft guns, 36 French Renault FT-17 light tanks and a platoon of TKS tankettes.

On 14 September, units of the 10th Panzer Division (its reconnaissance battalion and Panzer Regiment 8) breached the outer perimeter of fortifications. Corps commander Heinz Guderian ordered the entire corps to attack Brest as quickly as possible in order to exploit this unexpected success. However, the Germans failed to take the city from the march. In the period between 14 and 16 September, the Poles repulsed seven German infantry attacks that had been supported by panzers, artillery and the *Luftwaffe*, while in the process losing approximately 40 percent of its personnel in killed and wounded. Considering the casualties, the dwindling amount of ammunition, and the fact that in certain sectors the Germans had nevertheless been able to penetrate the Main Wall and to push the Poles back into the Citadel, at 1700 on 16 September, General Plisovsky decided to abandon the Citadel.

In 1941, Guderian's divisions again faced assaulting the Brest Fortress. Later he would write:

> The fortifications of Brest-Litovsk were out of date, it is true, but the combinations of the Bug, the Muchavec and water-filled ditches made them immune to tank attack. Tanks could have only captured the citadel by means of a surprise attack, as had been attempted in 1939. The requisite conditions for such an attack did not exist in 1941.

Guderian understood that his forces might get bogged down seizing the fortress, in the process losing both strength and time – factors that would prove decisive in Russia.

The Fortress

Situated at the confluence of the Bug and Muchavec Rivers, the Brest-Litovsk Fortress was founded in 1833. Its construction developed on the territory of medieval Brest, which was demolished to make way for the fortress. Using branches of the Muchavec and canals that were dug to link with the river, the designers planned for the fortress to consist of four fortified island areas – a central, northern, southern and western – that would be created by the rivers and canals. The fortress was surrounded by an undulating plain that varied in elevation by no more than 15 meters. It was cut by river branches and streams, often with boggy bottomlands, which to the south-east merged with the swampy Polesia Forest. The soil in the area, as a rule, is a mixture of sand and clay, but predominantly sandy. The approach to the forest depends totally upon the weather. The broad meadows surrounding it during a prolonged dry spell become passable for vehicles even in the swampy places. In contrast, rains create wide, swampy areas that are difficult to access, and make the roads in the south-east virtually impassable. The entire fortress is surrounded by several belts of forested tracts, which in swampy areas are replaced by patches of alder. The Bug River bisects the fortress, flowing generally from east to west; to the north it is joined by the Lesna River. In the center, the Citadel stands on the Central Island, which is skirted by a ring of two-story brick barracks (referred to subsequently as the Ring Barracks) approximately 11 meters high and with a perimeter of 1.8 kilometers. The thickness of the outer walls, which contain embrasures, reached 2 meters, while the window-lined inner walls were up to 1.5 meters thick. The Ring Barracks consist of 500 casemates, with embrasures for guns and small-arms fire. A most important circumstance is the fact that data about the thickness of the walls of the buildings on the territory of the Central Bastion, which were built in the mid-nineteenth century cannot be found in any of the available German documents. In contrast with the fortifications of the inner and outer fortified belts (for which certain, albeit sparse measurements were available), they probably were considered to have lost completely any military significance and were interesting only as barracks facilities. It is assumed that in the extreme case, they might have only caught the Germans' attention when being assaulted by the infantry and heavy infantry weapons. With the application, for example, of aircraft and heavy artillery, the fortifications lost their significance.

The entire Ring Barracks (as well as all the buildings within the Citadel) had cellars, which were used as storage areas. It is important to note that there was no passageway through the interior of the Ring Barracks or its cellars. This meant that the enemy, having seized any particular casemate of the barracks and its accompanying cellar still had no available interior access to the adjacent casemates of the Ring Barracks. The enemy would have to emerge back into the courtyard or climb onto the roof, and while under fire from every direction, launch a new assault on the neighboring sector, or else blow holes through the walls that divided the casemates, which given their thickness, was rather problematic. However, the absence of passageways presented a problem to the defenders as well – they had nowhere to retreat, so their only options became to die in place or to surrender. Of course, the buildings of the fortress were linked by a network of underground tunnels.

The approaches to the walls of the fortress were guarded by branches of the Muchavec River, as well as by four semi-towers, which provided the opportunity for flanking fire. Access to the grounds of the Citadel was given via four gates – the Trekharoch and Brigidki (from North Island), the Kholm (from South Island), and the Terespol (from West Island).[1] A bridge of the same name led across the branches of the Muchavec River to the corresponding island and gateway. In addition, a causeway ran alongside the Terespol Bridge. It is important to note that by 1941, a portion of the Ring Barracks on the eastern side of the Citadel, where the Muchavec River forks, had been destroyed, creating a gap which both the defenders and attackers sought to use. It still isn't known whether this section had been destroyed by a German barrage in 1939, or, what is more likely, the Poles themselves had demolished it even earlier, with the aim of obtaining a perspective and beautiful view of the fork of the Muchavec River.

There were other buildings in the Citadel, some of which (as in the case of other portions of the fortress) had as their basis buildings of medieval Brest. One of its strongest buildings, the two-story Arsenal, which covered a rectangular area of nearly 3,000 square meters, lay in its western area next to the Terespol Gate. Among the buildings of the Citadel in 1939 was the Orthodox Church of Saint Nikolai, which had been transformed by the Poles into the Roman Catholic Church of Saint Kazimir. Nearby were the Rectory building, an old building of the Engineering Directorate (which had been the headquarters of the Polish 9th Army) and the spacious 'White Palace', which served as an officers' club and contained a casino, hotel and ballroom. There were numerous other structures in the grounds of the Citadel. Altogether according to German estimates, the Citadel could accommodate 12,000 to 15,000 soldiers together with their ammunition and provisions.

North Island, which actually lies to the east of the Citadel on the Central Island, had the housing for the families of the officers and career sergeants, as well as a post office, shops, a stadium and the powder depots. There were two two-story barracks on its western side. A road ran from the Trekharoch Gate across North Island to its Northern Gate. On opposite sides of this road were the Western and Eastern Casemate Redoubts. Entering history as the West and East Forts, they were earthen lunettes, each of which contained a smaller, but taller crescent-shaped embankment. Within the earthworks, as was practically the case everywhere else in the fortress, were fortified chambers that could shelter defenders; within the inner lunettes, these were two-tiered. The approach to the Trekharoch Gate from the direction of North Island was also guarded by bulwarks, with gorge barracks concealed within them that offered shelter to defending troops and served as reduits (inner redoubts built within enclosed fortifications for combat within the latter and for strengthening the inner defenses in case the outer walls are breached). No less strong were the fortifications on the West and South Islands, which faced to the west, since that was the direction from which the architects anticipated an enemy attack would come. All four fortified areas, covering a total area of 4 square kilometers, were enclosed by a strong, 10-meter-high wall (which henceforth will be called the Main Wall), within which there were more fortified barracks designed as reduits. In front of the Main Wall was a moat (henceforth referred to as the Forward Moat), which is often referred to as the Bypass Canal. The Main Wall, which had a thickness of up to 8.5 meters, had four entrances – the Northwestern, Northern, Eastern and Southern Gates. Narrow, paved embankments led across the Forward Moat to each of them.

At the end of the 1860s, the Warsaw–Moscow railroad was laid down north of the fortress. The railroad embankment partially blocked fire from North Island, creating a dead zone that enemy troops could exploit. As a result, Fort 'Graf Berg' was built on the opposite side of the railroad embankment, 850 meters from the Main Wall, and in front of this fort was an earthwork for artillery (on the German maps it is designated as an infantry fortification). From this moment it would be more correct to call the Brest Fortress the 'Central Bastion', which became surrounded by a string of forts, the construction of which took place in the years 1878–87. At a radius of 3–4 kilometers from the Central Bastion, nine brick-and-earth forts were constructed, which created a planned inner auxiliary ring, and in 1910, Fort X was built in order to guard a new railroad track. In 1913 work began on an outer auxiliary ring, which lay 4–5 kilometers beyond the inner ring of forts. At that time, while the brick masonry work in the Central Bastion and the inner auxiliary ring was almost finished, the work on the outer auxiliary belt was being done in compressed concrete over wire netting. The finished brickwork in the inner auxiliary ring was also strengthened by an applied coating of reinforced concrete with a thickness of 1.5 to 2 meters.

The Array of Forces

It is still unknown who, how or when the planning for the capture of Brest-Litovsk and its Citadel in 1941 was done, whether in army headquarters, army group headquarters or even higher, in the headquarters of the OKH [*Oberkommando des Heeres*, or High Command of the Army]. One thing is clear – from the moment when the decisions were taken for Operation Barbarossa, the city lay in the direct path of the main attack. On one hand this dictated the increased focus on its capture, and on the other hand – the prompt initiation of working out all the details of the assault.

The key figures in the fight for Brest began to assemble already in the second half of 1940. Soon after the conclusion of the campaign in France, the headquarters of General Field Marshal Fedor von Bock's Army Group 'B' was transferred to Poznan. At the end of December 1940, the headquarters of General Field Marshal Gunther von Kluge's Fourth Army was located in Warsaw.

Prior to January 1941, neither von Kluge nor his headquarters had received any directions about preparing for a war with the Soviet Union. Then an order was received from the headquarters of Army Group 'B': as the former Fourth Army chief of staff General Gunther Blumentritt recalls in his post-war account of the Moscow campaign, it was a 'cautiously worded order . . . which discussed the possibility of a campaign in the East. It was vaguely phrased in general terms.' It isn't clear what Blumentritt had in mind in January 1941, if the task of the Army Group had been clearly stated in a directive from the Army Group 'B' command back in December 1940 on the strategic deployment for Barbarossa – attacking to the north of the Pripet Marshes, employing major mobile formations, it was to break through the Russian front with attacks from the areas of Warsaw and Suwalki and to develop the offensive in the general direction of Smolensk. Having assembled its main forces on either side of Brest and acting in concert with Panzer Group 2 (which was under its temporary command), the task of the Fourth Army (VII, IX, XII, XIII and XXXXIII army corps) was to seize a crossing of the Western Bug River. Then, in the OKH directive from 31 January 1941, the army's task was further clarified – to launch its main attack on both sides of Brest-Litovsk, force a crossing of the Western Bug, and then open the road to Minsk for Panzer Group 2.

From this moment, it was already necessary to begin preparations for the offensive. On 10 February 1941, Gunther Blumentritt asked the chief of staff of the XXXIV Army Corps Colonel Sicht to give a short, detailed outline of a proposal on the subject 'The Assault on Brest-Litovsk' for working out details of the tactical assignment. Sicht's headquarters faced the task of determining the quickest way of seizing the fortress, in order to open the important highway leading to Kobrin. The corps' headquarters and three subordinate infantry divisions were committed to the operation. The objective was the Central Bastion. In particular, it was necessary to calculate the minimum number of supplemental artillery and combat engineering units required to take the objective, as well as the *Luftwaffe* support that would be needed. The assignment stated, 'Any initiative and repeat reconnoitering of the area are only welcome.'

The key elements (assignments, forces and means) had already been determined by the Fourth Army command. The task given to Sicht and the staff of the XXXIV Army Corps was to elaborate them into specific orders and to select the units that would carry them out. The latter would have to force a crossing of the Bug River, breach the line of defending pillboxes, and to pursue the retreating enemy rapidly, striving to cut off the possibility of escape in order to encircle and destroy them close to the border. Accordingly, the troops selected for this mission had to have experience in quickly and successfully crossing a river, breaking through a line of concrete fortifications, and making rapid marches. Moreover, it was namely they that would have to serve as the spearhead of the main attack, which at a minimum would decide the outcome of the border battle and in essence the fate of the campaign in the East. Who could accomplish all this? Likely the answer was found in March 1941 in the divisions of Major General Hans Behlendorff (the 34th Infantry Division) and Major General Gerhard Körner (the 45th Infantry Division), which both had previous experience as participants in the forced crossing of the Aisne River in June 1940 in France. General of Artillery Rudolf Kämpfe's 31st Infantry Division was also well-known to von Kluge after its superb performance on the Loire River while part of his Fourth Army. At this moment Kämpfe's division (on 22 May he was replaced by Major General Kurt Kalmukoff) was serving in the XII Army Corps. Thus, the Fourth Army command pondered the choice between the latter and General of Infantry Friedrich Wilhelm 'Fritz' Koch's XXXXIV Army Corps for a long time. The initial plan for the offensive in the Brest sector had been prepared precisely by Koch's headquarters, and for a certain time the 31st Infantry Division was placed under his command. However, the final choice fell upon General of Infantry Walther Schroth's XII Army Corps, in no small part because he was one of the *Wehrmacht*'s most experienced corps commanders. Schroth had been commanding the XII Corps back on 1 September 1939 and had led it through the campaign in Poland, then (9 April 1940) having turned command of it over for a short time to Gotthard Heinrici, Schroth resumed command of the XII Corps and concluded the campaign in France in charge of it. Schroth ultimately decided to give the task of seizing Brest to Körner's 45th Infantry Division, which had previously been the Austrian 4th Division prior to Hitler's 1938 annexation of Austria.

Why was it the 45th Infantry Division that was given this role? Firstly, as already mentioned, it had the experience of forcing the Aisne River in 1940 in the Neufchâtel sector, which involved the successive forced crossing of several water barriers, with the additional task of breaching a belt of concrete fortifications that lay between them. Secondly, one can also assume an element of propaganda behind the decision – it would be the *Führer*'s 'fellow Austrians' who would be assaulting in the center of the main attack. Moreover, skipping ahead a bit in our narrative, they were due to be almost the first, on the entire Eastern Front, to launch an attack even before the start of the preparatory artillery barrage (which is to say practically even before the war's start) in order to seize an objective that was key for Army Group Centre – the railroad bridge just north of Brest at Terespol. The fact that correspondents of all the *Wehrmacht*'s main journals – *Die Wehrmacht* and

Signal, as well as operators of the *Reich*'s newsreel journal *Deutsche Wochenschau* – were assigned to the 45th Infantry Division during its assault also emphasizes the propaganda significance attached to the operation.

At the same time, from a military, not a propaganda viewpoint, it was Heinz Guderian's Panzer Group 2 that would resolve Army Group Centre's main tasks. In the initial phase of the offensive it was to cross the Bug on both sides of Brest and breach the Russians' defenses, before advancing along the Roslavl'–El'nia–Smolensk axis without delay. The aim of this impetuous attack, which was to serve as the basis for a victory already in 1941, was to prevent the enemy from regrouping and consolidating on a new defensive line. In the opinion of Panzer Group 2's commander, in the interests of a swift advance, it was necessary to pass the panzer forces quickly through wherever a breach in the defenders' lines began to appear. Infantry would handle the other tasks, such as the assault on the fortress.

When preparing to assault the fortress, the 45th Infantry Division command began to gather information on Brest-Litovsk in its role as a constituent element of the Russians' border fortifications. Despite the fact that in 1939 the fortress was in the Germans' hands for several days, they of course had no anticipation of the need to assault it again. No close inspection or survey of the defenses was conducted. As a result, by 1941 the visualization of the Brest fortifications was based on an outdated 1916 study of them, Polish plans that were seized in 1939, and aerial reconnaissance. On 13 April 1941, a reconnaissance team of Pioneer Regiment 507 made an extremely detailed study of the shore line and surface flows of this section of the Bug River (which based on the experience of the Aisne, seemed to be a much more serious obstacle to the attackers than the fortress). The sections of the river confronting all three of the XII Infantry Corps' divisions (the 31st, 34th and 45th) were studied.

A rather extensive report on the fortified structures of the Brest area was prepared, based on a study of the fortifications. Giving an assessment of the possible enemy, it was noted that the Central Bastion, based upon the 1916 data, could possibly accommodate 12,000 to 15,000 troops. A similar estimate of the number of troops that could be manning the forts of the inner and outer auxiliary defensive belts was not made. However, probably assessing the possibility of launching an attack against them during an artillery barrage, it noted that in the inner ring, only a portion of the shelters for the troops were made of reinforced concrete, while in the outer ring they were given shelters that were designed only to protect against shell splinters.

The report stressed:

> In general, it must be said that the fortifications don't present any sort of special obstacle for us; however, in the dry season an attack is easier, since in the muddy season the well-known Russian swamps are passable only with the help of sufficient engineering equipment, thus presenting a definite obstacle.

However, when discussing the Citadel, the study's author cautiously, but significantly noted, 'Even today the defensive fortifications in the bridgehead give the possibility to an energetic defender to hold up an aggressor with insignificant forces and means.' Indeed someone (probably in the headquarters of the 45th Infantry Division) prudently underlined these words.

Army Group Centre's intelligence organs noted that first and foremost, Brest-Litovsk was one of the lynchpins of the belt of border fortifications being constructed by the Soviet Union. Intelligence quite accurately established the number and location of the existing border fortifications, as well as approximate data on their strength. It was emphasized that the degree of completion of the fortifications on the Soviet-German border in individual sectors varied rather significantly, but on the whole, 'only approximately 20 percent of the structures that were initiated by 1 February 1941 have been completed.'

New fortifications of the Soviet period in the Brest-Litovsk sector, closely linked to the fort's original fortifications, supplemented them. In descriptions of the old fortifications of the Citadel that were supplied to the German divisions, it is noted that they 'encompass 17 forts, strengthened before the world war with reinforced concrete.' It is again stressed that 'it is not necessary to ascribe much combat significance to the old fortifications. Together with the recent fortifications, they can be treated more like reinforced field defensive works.'

Summing up, the report concluded that

> 'the greater portion of the new fortifications surrounding the old permanent fortifications still consists of half-finished works. Thus, their present combat significance is nominal'; however, 'on the whole, when viewing this sector it must be said that the Bug and the fortifications give the defender the possibility at the very least of significantly delaying the vitally important crossing in this sector and the capture of the 3 important highways (leading to Kovel', Kobrin and Pruzhany).'

It is understandable that the troops attacking Brest were required not only to take the fortifications, but they also had an incommensurately more important task on the scale of the Fourth Army's sector. That was to secure a crossing for the motorized and panzer units and to enable their subsequent advance along the highways leading into the Soviet interior.

Note

1. All but one of these bridges and gates were named after the Belorussian or Polish town to which they led. The exception was the Brigidki Bridge and Gate, named after the Brigidki prison on North Island, which prior to early 1941 had been the Brigitt Monastery.

Chapter 2

King Tiger

On 27 April 1941, Major General Körner was killed in an automobile accident near Hannover, Germany. Was this an omen of future misfortune? However, just a day later the first echelons of the 45th Infantry Division began to load aboard trains: the division was heading to Poland, leaving behind 462 of its soldiers and officers in graves in Corbigny, Saint-Quentin and Ardres (just outside Calais).

In the new billeting area of Warsaw and its environs, the construction of barracks and roads was proceeding at full speed. Knowing that the appearance of a new formation wouldn't go unnoticed by the Soviet radio intelligence services (of the Western Special Military District) and network of agents, nevertheless measures were undertaken to keep the division's arrival concealed. The total ban against the use of radio communications dictated a reliance on the public telephone system. Therefore on 30 April, in order to disguise the telephone communications, code names were given to the division's units down to the battalion headquarters inclusively. Each was given a secret, specific code name. From this point on, the 45th Infantry Division became 'King Tiger'. The departments of its headquarters would now be referred to as, for example, 'King Tiger, business office I-a.'

By the beginning of May, supply and communications were being organized. The first training exercises specified by higher command were designed around the tasks the troops would face in Russia. Among the exercises were small unit assaults against fortified strongpoints, and also to handle the poor road conditions and the lack of adequate maps. Countermeasures against chemical warfare acquired particular significance for the purposes of the future operations, and emphasis was placed on the air defense assets of small infantry units.

On 9 May 1941, the new commander arrived in the division – the 48-year-old Major General Fritz Schlieper. Born on 4 August 1892 in Koldromb, Posen, Fritz Schlieper began his military service in the artillery. In 1912, serving in the 17th Field Artillery Regiment, he acquired the rank of lieutenant. In the interwar period he commanded the 17th Artillery Regiment and Arko [*Artilleriekommando*, or Artillery Headquarters] 24. In 1939 Colonel Schlieper was performing as the chief of staff of the XIII Army Corps, and from 23 October, chief of staff of Army Group Centre's border sector. On 1 November he became the quartermaster of 18th Army, while simultaneously being promoted to major general. Schlieper worked in this post until 25 November 1940, after which he was assigned to the OKH reserve command staff. It wasn't the most glittering career, and despite the fact that new formations were being created, Fritz Schlieper remained on the sidelines for a full six months. Of course, even though General Schlieper had never received public acclaim as a 'celebrated commander' and had never proven himself as an experienced commander, nevertheless he could hardly have remained unassigned. Sooner or later the general would have found a role somewhere in an army headquarters. However, Körner's death changed everything – on 1 May 1941, Fritz Schlieper was appointed commander of the 45th Infantry Division.

Schlieper lacked the experience of division command, and had no experience with operations to force a crossing of a river or to take a major city. Moreover, Schlieper's closest assistant, Ia [operations chief] Major Armin Dettmer had also occupied his current post for less than three months.

In order to prepare the division for the tasks it would face, General Schroth ordered the division to organize practical training of the infantry and combat engineers for the rapid crossing of rivers and moats (sometimes with a subsequent assault against a fortress wall) while under enemy fire. There was also training to prepare for the assault against the previously-mentioned bunkers and casemates of the Brest-Litovsk Citadel on a duly handy training ground – the fortifications of the Warsaw Citadel. With the approval of corps' headquarters, the Warsaw commandant's office and the commandant of the airfield, Fort VI of the old Warsaw Fortress (on the south-western outskirts of the city) was handed over to the division's control. General Schroth likewise emphasized that it was also necessary to search for additional beneficial opportunities for training exercises, in order to train as many soldiers as possible to handle the most diverse situations within the time remaining.

Fort VI had adequate conditions for the simultaneous training of at least two companies: a water-filled, 12- to 15-meter-wide moat extending for 250–300 meters with a depth of 3 meters, and in the northern part – an unused casemate. The training, considering the tasks to be faced and using all the results of reconnaissance, was planned to be as realistic as possible, so that the division, using its entire means (small and large inflatable rafts, expedients, implements, temporary bridges, etc.), supported by the infantry's and engineers' heavy support weapons, could quickly overcome the water obstacles at Brest-Litovsk. For some reason, there was no emphasis on what might take place once the water obstacles were crossed or on other matters.

The 45th Division was given temporary command of the headquarters of Nebelwerfer Regiment 4 (NbwRgts.Stab z.b.V. 4) located in Gultowy, Nebelwerfer Battalion 8 (Nbw.Abt. 8) in Rozalin, and the 105th Decontamination Battalion (Entg.Abt. 105) in Posen. In the month of May, planning sessions were actively conducted by the German headquarters. Training was in full swing (including practice assaults against fortified strongpoints), as were engineering work and camouflage measures. The division was assessed by its headquarters as a fully combat-effective formation, although the report mentioned problems connected with the lack of fuel and automobile tires.

On 20 May 1941, the commander of the Fourth Army von Kluge held a meeting with the subordinate corps and division commanders at the Fourth Army headquarters in Warsaw. Simultaneously, the Fourth Army's chief of staff Blumentritt conducted a meeting with all the corps' chiefs of staff and the operations chiefs of the corps and divisions. At the meetings, all the main problems of preparing for the operation were discussed, including questions of intelligence, border surveillance, and camouflage; the stockpiling of ammunition for the initial attack; the tasks of the combat engineers, artillery and the armored train; the forming and composition of the forward detachments; and so forth. In particular, mention was made of bringing up supplementary artillery (including captured guns), such as 210mm howitzers (for the attack against the Brest Citadel) and one heavy, long-range 283mm railroad cannon, the Krupp K5. It is noteworthy that here, for the first time at the army level, a month before the start of combat operations, there was talk about attaching heavy artillery to the 45th Division – a recognition that the seizure of the Brest Citadel posed a particular challenge, distinct from the tasks given to other divisions while breaking through the line of border fortifications. Prior to this meeting, there had only been talk of giving the 45th Division rocket-launchers and heavy 600mm Karl siege mortars.

The German command attached great attention to all the aspects of personnel training. However, it was reported that sometimes (of course, when the command wasn't watching), these exercises were more like holidays at the beach – the constant frolicking and splashing in the water meant that not only the rafts, but also the swimming trunks of the division's soldiers got a lot of use. Training with the inflatable rafts often turned into merry splashing and clowning around with races in the rubber boats. When testing the custom-made rafts fabricated by Pioneer Battalion 81, rocks were tossed into the water around the rafts, probably in the attempt to simulate a crossing under fire – to the great amusement of the local onlookers. The soldiers and officers had only a vague idea about the purpose of the training. At the same time, the pioneer battalion conducted genuinely serious work to test the still not widely known miraculous instrument, water skis, as well as flotation rafts, inflatable boats and various types of life preservers. Walter Loos of I.R. [*Infanterie Regiment*, or Infantry Regiment] 130 wrote:

> At the time many, especially the reasonable, thoughtfully shook their heads and believed that we could have engaged in this 'cascade of waterworks' back in France. However, it gradually became increasingly obvious that all this training was for a final and conclusive fight with our powerful eastern neighbour, the Soviet Union. We didn't talk openly about this though; in the depths of our hearts we believed – or speaking more accurately, didn't want to believe, this.

On 28 May, the Fourth Army headquarters ordered increased patrolling and reinforcement of the combat outposts on the Russian border. Pickets and roving patrols, in order to blend in with the regular border guards, moved with rifles in trail position and wore forage caps rather than helmets whenever proximate to the posts that marked the border. A day before, the division had begun to move out to its assembly area prior to the invasion, which was perceived by many as a momentous event. For example, I.R. 133 left Warsaw to the accompaniment of the regimental band.

The division's march went according to orders, without any noteworthy events. Gerd Habedanck, a correspondent with *Die Wehrmacht* who'd been assigned to the 45th Infantry Division accompanied I.R. 135 on its march from Warsaw 'through heat, dust and jam-packed roads to the Bug. We passed tracts of woodland bristling with vehicle parks, artillery batteries in villages and radio relay stations and headquarters staffs under tall fir trees.'

The heat and dust was not a bother to *Leutnant* Michael Wechtler, who was marching along together with his 5th Company in the columns of I.R. 133:

> A downpour at the start of the march soaked the entire regiment, but the mood rose again when it was replaced by the heat, with the opportunities of bathing in the lakes along the way. The march was rather difficult, but we scrupulously adhered to the 40-kilometre stages.

XII Corps headquarters kept an eye on the departure of the divisions to the assembly area. Thorough camouflaging of the movement was emphasized. The scene at the border had to remain unchanged! It was stressed that the premature delivery of ordnance, the preparation of assault-crossing equipment in the border zone, and so forth were strictly forbidden. Artillery and heavy weapons of the infantry could only be in positions that were previously foreseen for 'Case Berta' (an alternative plan for the assault). Von Kluge's Fourth Army headquarters would authorize and issue the order to move up and deploy the artillery as late as possible, so the guns wouldn't all be standing out in the open in firing position for weeks! It was planned that the OKH would arrange a mission by a special *Luftwaffe* reconnaissance squadron for photographing the Soviet positions screening the border.

The general principle was as follows: all 'paper' preparations on the map and ground, invisible or inconspicuous, would begin as soon as possible. In contrast, all the visible and conspicuous measures would be taken at the last possible moment.

On 29 May, Major General Schlieper returned from the planned area of the offensive. In order to establish cooperation between the arms, *Hauptmann* Hans Meesmann, the commander of a battery of heavy artillery of the OKH reserve, reported to him. Thus, the second means of reinforcement after the *nebelwerfers* had arrived, though standing first by the measure of its impact: the 2nd Battery of the 833rd Heavy Artillery Battalion – two 600mm Karl self-propelled siege mortars.

The question about involving heavy artillery in the assault on the Brest fortifications had already been discussed weeks before. Back on 7 March 1941 at a morning conference with the commander-in-chief of the OKH, General Inspector of Artillery Brandt had suggested that it was possible to employ 'Battery K' against the Brest Fortress – probably having in mind a battery of railroad artillery. However, they decided to settle upon the 600mm Karl siege mortar (*Gerät* 040), which in the *Wehrmacht* was second in its power only to the 800mm Dora heavy guns.

On 3 June 1941, the order came down about transferring the 45th Infantry Division from XXXV Corps Command at 00.00 4 June to the XII Corps. On this same day, the last units of the division were completing their march. Michael Wechtler writes:

> The regiments were billeted in comfortable village homes, 27 kilometres from the border. With pleasure we drank up the last of the captured French champagne. The last letters were written home. 'Search lights' appeared among us – resplendent groups of fellows with bare pates, who had shaved their heads for the forthcoming campaign (and who had received the nickname 'Shiny Noggins'). In the well-hidden forest bivouacs, the final group photographs were taken before the campaign. Everyone recognized that few of them would ever gather again in their full complement of men.

By 10 June, a draft order with the invasion plan was ready and was sent to XII Army Corps headquarters. Even though the order was dated 16 June, judging from all the evidence there were no substantial changes to the plan after 10 June. The essence of the plan was as follows: in consideration of the major Russian forces that were positioned behind the Bug River (especially in Brest-Litovsk), the 45th Division would attack with I.R. 130 on the right and I.R. 135 on the left, with I.R. 133 held back in corps reserve. The division's own reserve would consist of II/I.R. 135. The main change in the order, compared with previous draft plans, was to launch the attack not with the emphasis on the left, but on the right. It was planned that I.R. 130, now responsible for the main effort, would cross the Bug with the support of 2/Pioneer Battalion 81, seize South Island, and prevent the demolition of bridges on the Muchavec River on the east side of the fortress; then, it was to bypass the southern outskirts of the city itself and advance to its eastern outskirts. On the left, I.R. 135, having prepared a surprise attack, would seize the railroad bridge across the Bug and prevent its demolition; once across the Bug, it would assault and take the North and West Islands, as well as a portion of the center of the fortress. It would then penetrate through Brest-Litovsk itself and link up with I.R. 130 on the eastern outskirts of the town.

Not much is known about I.R. 135's plan of attack: on 20 June, the regiment had 61 officers, 423 non-commissioned officers, 2,293 enlisted men and 3 clerks reporting for duty, for a total of 2,780 (90 percent of the table strength of an infantry regiment of the first-wave divisions in 1941, which was 3,049 men). It had 80 percent of its authorized officers, 85 percent of its authorized non-commissioned officers and 92 percent of its authorized enlisted men. The regiment was equipped with 151 machine guns, 18 heavy machine guns, 27 light machine guns, 6 light and 2 heavy infantry guns, and 9 37mm anti-tank guns. The numerical strength of the machine-gun and infantry companies (their percentage of authorized manpower could differ from that of the regiment as a whole) is not known precisely. However, judging from the number of officers and men reporting for duty in the regiment as a whole, the machine-gun and infantry companies might have averaged 160 men each.

For example, III/I.R. 135 (commanded by *Hauptmann* Praxa), which was to advance across West and Center Islands and seize the Trekharoch Bridge, had 520 men. Together with the temporarily attached machine-gun company 12/I.R. 133, it had approximately 650 men. Praxa planned to conduct the attack in two waves, with approximately 200 men in the first echelon.

It should be noted that back in December 1940, three battalions of the 45th Infantry Division had been removed from it in order to form a new division, the 100th Light Division. It isn't known how they were replaced – possibly from march replacements. As a rule in the *Wehrmacht*, departing units were replaced by newly-formed units that had poorly-trained personnel and officers without combat experience. In this case, one-third of the attacking battalions may have been green and perhaps unready for such a challenging assignment.

Major Oeltze's I/I.R. 135, which was to attack North Island and the west side of the city of Brest, had 750 men. Oeltze's plan of attack isn't known – it is possible that some of the companies were held back in reserve, or his plan might have been to attack with the full battalion, but in waves. On the basis of the field manual, according to which an infantry battalion with supported flanks was to attack on a sector between 400 and 1,000 meters wide, it can be assumed that in this respect, the composition of I.R. 135's attack groupings corresponded to the assignment.

The strength of the defenders wasn't known. With the aim of neutralizing possible surprises, the division commander ordered the regiment to keep a significant reserve. Judging that the reserve consisted of II/I.R. 135, it was precisely in Infantry Regiment 135's sector that surprises were anticipated. At the same time, the assignment of attachments to Oeltze is evidence that I Battalion's advance was of critical importance – by a rapid envelopment of the fortress, it was to block the retreat of the Russian units from it and the evacuation of equipment and supplies.

The Russians would be caught in a pincer – their retreat to the east would be barred by Oeltze, while Praxa would be attacking from the west. Considering that the strength of the enemy grouping in the fortress was not known, this was a rather risky decision. The Germans planned that the element of surprise and their superior firepower would be the decisive factors.

More is known about I.R. 130's plan of attack. The regiment would attack with two battalions, keeping the third in reserve. On the left of the advance would be *Oberstleutnant* Naber's I/I.R. 130, which was to take South Island and capture the first two bridges on the Muchavec. Major Hartnack's II/I.R. 130 advancing on the right was to seize the next two bridges. Major Ulrich's III/I.R. 130 was temporarily to mark time in place ... Ulrich, it seems, had only two companies under his command, the 9th and 12th (320 men). The 14th Company had been broken up and its elements assigned to the attacking battalions as reinforcements. The river crossing would be supported by machine-gun fire of 4/I.R. 133 and assisted by a combat engineer detachment of Reconnaissance Battalion 45.

The possibility that the Russians would blow up the bridges on the Muchavec presented a serious problem for I.R. 130. This would immediately and sharply bog down the offensive of the entire right flank of the division and corps. Therefore, in addition to the fact that it was precisely on this axis that the main attack of both the 45th and 34th Infantry division was aimed, it was decided (on the basis of a proposal from *Oberstleutnant* Masuch, the commander of Pioneer Battalion 81), to conduct a special operation using nine assault boats. Command of this detachment was given to *Leutnant* Josef Kremers, a platoon commander in 3/Pioneer Battalion 81. The assignment was to move out along the southern branch of the Muchavec after the completion of the artillery preparation on the Bug and seize the four bridges across the Muchavec. Seven of the boats (without navigators) would carry men from I/I.R. 130, while the other two would carry assault pioneers of 2/Pioneer Battalion 81 and all the navigators. Squads of 3/I.R. 130 were assigned to deliver the boats to the bank of the Bug in the sector of I/I.R. 130's offensive, from which point the assault teams were to set out at the designated time.

The regiment's assignment was not only to take, but also to hold the bridges – this would deprive the Russian 22nd Tank Division (which was positioned to the south of Brest) of the possibility of retreat or of rushing to aid the defenders of the Brest Citadel, which together with the artillery preparation, would immediately ensure the successful start of the offensive.

Assessing the German plan of attack, it is possible to come to the conclusion that on one hand, Schlieper's division had the task of overcoming the resistance of a foe that was numerically stronger than his attacking regiments, and on the other – to accomplish this within the shortest timespan necessary for the successful development of the corps' offensive. Yes, the numerical strength of the Soviet defenders might be greater than that of the German attackers in certain sectors – for example, I.R. 130 would not only have to repel possible counter-attacks by the 22nd Tank Division, which would be trying to break through to the bridges from the South Training Ground, but also possible counter-attacks from the east. On 19 June, the 22nd Tank Division had 148 T-26 regular tanks, 81 T-26 tanks equipped with radios, 6 twin-turreted T-26 tanks, 16 flame-throwing T-26 tanks, and 5 light T-37A/38 tanks, for a total of 256 armored vehicles. In addition, it had 14 armored cars (6 BA-20 and 8 BA-10). If all of this equipment had moved against Naber's and Hartnack's battalions, then the latter ultimately would simply not have had enough shells for the defense . . .

It is also necessary to talk about the command staff of the division that had been called upon to resolve these tasks. Colonel Helmut Hipp, the commander of I.R. 130, was the most experienced of the 45th Infantry Division's regiment commanders; moreover, he was the only one to have led his regiment into combat as part of this division. For that reason, he had been given the primary responsibility – the seizure of the bridges on the Muchavec and the envelopment of Brest from the south. The battalion commanders of I.R. 130 were in no way inferior to Hipp – Major Hartnack had commanded the II Battalion back in the Polish campaign, while Naber had marched through France with his III Battalion. Hipp was practically assured that they would handle the capture of the bridges and South Island. Ulrich, the commander of I Battalion, was younger, but his battalion was in the regiment reserve.

Oberst Friedrich John, the commander of I.R. 135, lacked combat experience, but he could rely upon his battalion commanders Majors Oeltze and Parak, who had both gone through the campaign in France. Praxa, the commander of III Battalion, was still only a *hauptmann* and had only recently assumed command of his battalion.

Judging from the division's combat assignment, its first order of business was to seize and hold the bridges on the Muchavec. Second, it was to eliminate any interference, which was to be assured by the presence of sufficiently experienced and powerful units in reserve (Parak's battalion, and if necessary, *Oberst* Fritz Kühlwein's I.R. 133). Lastly, it was to encircle the Brest-Litovsk Fortress from the south. Seemingly, the option of seizing the Citadel by direct assault was either viewed as dubious, regarded as a possible option, or was a gross miscalculation in the assessment of the enemy, which led as a result to an underestimation of the forces and means required for the task.

On these days orders were given about positioning the ammunition dumps, and the delivery and unloading of ammunition. Staff exercises were held. The headquarters of XII Corps issued special orders regarding the conducting of reconnaissance patrols. The headquarters' logistics department issued addenda to the special orders within the area of operation: the regiments and separate battalions were to create and prepare forage teams, which were to include a commander (a food supply officer), a veterinarian officer, a pay clerk, technical supply clerks and security. Great attention was given to questions related to the guarding and transportation of future captured equipment and prisoners-of-war.

On 12 June, the neighboring 34th Infantry Division on the right provided a copy of its attack order to the 45th Infantry Division for familiarization purposes. Concerning observations of the Russian side, reports dated on this day indicated: 'Outposts: The strength of outposts and patrols is unchanged. Railroad traffic: Unchanged. Situation in the air: Unchanged.' and so forth. The most important comment in this document is Item K: 'Russian preparations for an attack: No signs!'

Two days later, on 14 June, Schroth conducted a staff exercise with the command staff (including the commanders of the regiments and separate battalions) – it focused primarily on the planned actions when crossing the Bug. That evening, Schlieper held a meeting with the regiment commanders and shared the date and time of the invasion with them: 22 June, 0330 (which was subsequently altered to 0315). An order arrived from XII Corps headquarters about moving up into the jumping-off areas.

Schlieper reported to corps headquarters that the final preparations for the attack had been completed: the artillery had been prepared for deployment and action; local roads had been improved and the engineers were ready; training of the units had been conducted, with the exception of drills with pneumatic pontoons (due to their unavailability). It was anticipated that the supply of ammunition to the division and its attached units would be completed on 17 June and to the units of Nebelwerfer Regiment 4 – probably on 20 June.

The 2nd Battery of Heavy Artillery Regiment 833 had still not yet shown up; however, a provisional report indicated an expected arrival date of 18 June. The positions prepared for the Karl siege mortars proved unsuitable due to the delayed transmission of firing tables, because some of the targets were at excessively short ranges. It was hoped to complete the preparation of the new positions located further to the rear before 20 June. The 45th Infantry Division's additional attached mortar batteries (682, 683 and 684 – 'Galle's mortar battalion') were fully staffed and combat-ready.

Oberstleutnant Masuch, the commander of Pioneer Battalion 81 reported that although six of the assault boats for Pontoon Park 'B' had been assigned and were to be delivered to the army engineering equipment and materials depot at Legionovo near Warsaw, they hadn't yet arrived. Engineers had assembled temporary bridges on the northern road, while the delivery of the fascines had been designated to take place on the following nights. The saw mill at Bialy on 16 and 17 June was also supposed to supply boards for the temporary bridges. Everything else was ready.

The commander of the divisional artillery regiment (Artillery Regiment 98) *Oberst* Karl Welker was in a better situation – he was only lacking the due supplementary load of 300 shells for the light artillery battalion. All the other preparations had been completed: positions had been laid out and were masked by cut branches stuck into the ground, and had been prepared for bringing to full readiness at night. The battalion commanders had been briefed about the attack; the commanders of the batteries and of other services would receive their briefings on 16 June.

The artillery regiment's ammunition had been distributed to the battalions. Its distribution and delivery to the firing positions themselves would take place on the night of X-2 as foreseen by I.R. 130. The ammunition for 13/I.R. 133 would be delivered before daybreak on 16 June. The conditions for laying down lines of communication (arranged for the night of X-1) had been reconnoitered. I.R. 135 was reporting that it was ready: it only had to complete some trenching and complete the laying of the planned lines of communication.

The nights were growing shorter. Only a week remained until the shortest night of the year.

Chapter 3

The Brest Fortress

In April 1941, the USSR People's Commissar of Defence S.K. Timoshenko and the Red Army's Chief of the General Staff G.K. Zhukov ordered D.G. Pavlov, the commander-in-chief of the Western Special Military District to set to work on an operational deployment plan. With regard to this work, the directive particularly pointed out:

> It can be assumed at the present time that the non-aggression pacts between the USSR and Germany, and between the USSR and Italy, secure a peaceful situation on our western borders. The USSR is not contemplating an attack against Germany and Italy. These states, plainly, also have no intention to attack the USSR in the near future. However, considering ... the assembly of significant forces by Germany on the USSR borders ... and the conclusion of the Germany-Italy-Japan military alliance ... it is necessary while working on the USSR's plan of defence to have in view ... even such possible adversaries as Germany ... It can't be excluded that the Germans are concentrating their main forces in East Prussia and on the Warsaw axis in order to launch and exploit an attack through Lithuania ... towards Riga or towards Kovno, Dvinsk. Simultaneously it is necessary to expect secondary strong attacks from the direction of Lomza and Brest with a subsequent effort to exploit them in the direction of Baranovichi and Minsk.

The main tasks for the Western Special Military District, which became the Western Front with the initiation of combat operations, were to conduct a stubborn defense of the fortified region in order to cover the mobilization and assembly of reserve forces, and to prevent an incursion into Soviet territory. Further, in conjunction with the Southwestern Front's offensive, it was to contribute to the destruction of the enemy's Lublin–Radom grouping with an attack by its left wing toward Sedlets [Siedlce].

By June 1941, Major General A.A. Korobkov's 4th Army (chief of staff – Colonel L.M. Sandalov, Military Council member – Divisional Commissar F.I. Shlykov) was covering 150 kilometers of the USSR national border on the Brest–Minsk axis. It consisted of the 28th Rifle Corps (6th, 42nd, 49th and 75th Rifle divisions), the 14th Mechanized Corps (22nd and 30th Tank divisions and the 205th Motorized

Rifle Division), the 10th Composite Air Division, the 62nd Brest Fortified District, the Kobrin Brigade Anti-Aircraft Region, and the 120th Howitzer Artillery Regiment of the Supreme Command Reserve. By 22 June, Korobkov had been commanding the army for two and a half months. As Sandalov recalled, the army commander himself acknowledged that he was better suited to command a rifle corps.

The main forces of the 4th Army (which later became the Belorussian Front) arrived in the area of Brest back in September 1939: on 22 September, Brigade Commander S.M. Krivoshein's 29th Tank Brigade had entered the city. After *Wehrmacht* units abandoned Brest, one of the best divisions of the Red Army, the 6th Orel Red Banner Rifle Division was billeted in the town. It had been formed back on 23 May 1918 (as the Gatchina Infantry Division) from volunteers of P.E. Dybenko's detachment, Petrograd Red Guard detachments, and workers of the town of Narva. Having served throughout the Russian Civil War, the division (which in 1921 received the honorific 'Orel' and in 1928 was awarded the Honorary Revolutionary Red Banner of the USSR Central Executive Committee) in 1939 took part in the campaign in western Belorussia. In June 1941, its commander was Colonel M.A. Popsui-Shapko.

On 13 June 1940, the 42nd Rifle Division, the second of the divisions stationed in Brest by June 1941, arrived in Belorussia from the Baltic area. It had been formed on 17 January 1940 in the Leningrad Military District as a light motorized rifle division. The 42nd Rifle Division, unlike the 6th Rifle Division, had recent combat experience. Immediately after its creation, under the command of Colonel I.S. Lazarenko, the division had taken part in the war with Finland as part of the 7th Army. Despite the fact that the 42nd Rifle Division's combat path in the war with Finland did not bring it the glory of celebrated victories, the command staff received combat seasoning. Strongly-knitted at the front, the division became one of the Red Army's most combat-capable divisions, and after the war continued to be based in the western part of the country: for example, on 17 June 1940 the 42nd Rifle Division had been sent to the Baltics to take part in the occupation of Estonia. In June 1941, the same I.S. Lazarenko was still commanding the 42nd Rifle Division, but now as a major general.

In September 1940, soon after the arrival of the 42nd Rifle Division in the Brest area, an inspection of the units of the Western Special Military District was conducted by a commission of the USSR People's Commissariat of Defence. Based on the results of the conducted exercises and drills, it was noted that units of the 42nd Rifle Division (probably because of its combat experience) had demonstrated the greatest improvement in combat training, while the units of the 6th Rifle Division stood out more negatively in every category of the assessment. The district was ordered to implement a fundamental change in the entire system of combat training by making the training of each soldier, each element and each unit in the field closer to real combat conditions. As People's Commissar of Defence S.K. Timoshenko directed, 'The troops must be instructed to act in war and only that which will be called for in time of war.' Meanwhile it was noted in the Red Army's Main Military Council that 'the lag in the training of the individual soldier, the squad, and the platoon in a number of divisions and regiments, especially in the Western Special Military District, reaches 1.5 to 2 months.' Despite the intense training, the professional qualities of a significant portion of the Red Army enlisted men were not high. The simultaneous formation of a multitude of units and formations in the Workers' and Peasants' Red Army also affected the overall level of combat competence, as well as did the departure of soldiers with a moderate level of education from the rifle units at the beginning of 1941 to serve in more technical types of forces. Despite all this, in 1941 the regimental schools that produced sergeants accelerated the course of training (for example, the 1 October graduation date was moved up to 1 July, while the 15 June graduation date was moved up to 14 May); even so, the rifle divisions of the Western Special Military District continued to be understaffed with commanders; they had only 60 percent of the requisite number of non-commissioned officers and only 86 percent of the authorized number of mid-level and higher command staff. The quality of the troops was also affected by the departure into the reserve at the end of 1940 and the beginning of 1941 of those Red Army men who had been called up in 1937 and who'd served out their term of compulsory military service (the majority of which had combat experience). They were replaced by young conscripts, including those of the supplementary draft of April–May 1941, who were sent directly into combat units, bypassing the training companies. At the start of the war many of them, who hadn't even gone through basic training or had yet taken the military oath, amounted only to a mass of unprepared, disarmed men in Red Army uniforms. In addition, the presence in the rifle divisions of a significant portion of Red Army men of the autumn 1940 call-up from the Central Asian republics, who had little or no understanding of the Russian language, sharply and negatively affected their level of training, as well as the combat-readiness of the units as a whole. The fact that the soldiers were often diverted to building fortifications, billets, supply dumps, mess halls, stables, rifle ranges, shooting galleries, armor training grounds, sports facilities and so forth also weighed heavily on their level of combat-readiness. Moreover, after the forces were moved up to the new western borders, soldiers were often diverted from combat training in order to guard the numerous military supply depots and to perform daily detail duties. Despite the threatening situation, there was no change in routines – for example, on 10 June several additional rifle battalions were detached for construction work in the fortified district.

The construction of defensive works in the 4th Army's first (and main) line of defense – pillboxes and additional field-type positions in the Brest Fortified District – began back in 1940 at the beginning of summer. Its forward line (and by June 1941 only it had been completed; work in depth had not even begun), ran along the eastern bank of the Bug River. Only on West Island were pillboxes positioned directly at the water's edge. North of Brest they stood back from the Bug, for example, along the Lesnaia River. However, there has been no explanation for the unsatisfactory placement of the pillboxes in such an exposed, forward position on West Island.

The pillboxes of the Brest Fortified District were two-tiered concrete blocks; the embrasures of the upper casemate, divided by a wall into two caponiers, were almost at ground level. The layout of each level was identical: a gallery, separated from an armored door by a blast-proof antechamber; a gas lock; an ammunition stockroom; a barracks with several bunks; enclosed rooms for radios; an artesian well; and a toilet. In one of its compartments was an electrical generator and filtration plant. The upper level had casemate guns with shortened barrels or machine guns in the caponiers. The pillboxes as constructed were primarily of a single- or twin-embrasure machine-gun, artillery machine-gun or artillery style. Key positions were guarded by pillboxes with three to five firing ports. The walls were 1.5 to 1.8 meters thick, while the roofs were up to 2.5 meters thick (calculated to withstand a direct hit by a 250kg bomb). Certain pillboxes contained one 76mm gun and two heavy machine guns each, while others had a 45mm gun with a tandem DS-39 machine gun. The pillbox garrisons consisted of 8 to 9 men or 16 to 18 men.

Altogether by 21 June, 128 concrete pillboxes had been built in the Brest Fortified District. Some of them had fittings for weapons that had been sent from the Mozyrsk Fortified District. However, only twenty-three of the pillboxes were combat-ready (furnished with garrisons, weapons and ammunition, but without technical means of communication between themselves or with troops outside the pillbox). Eight of these were in the Brest area, primarily within the fortress. In all, each of the battalion sectors had four to six prepared pillboxes with weapons and garrisons. The main shortcoming of the pillboxes was their positioning – they were plainly visible from the German observation posts and were vulnerable to destruction with the very first artillery barrage. Meanwhile, the lighter weapons mounted within them lacked the range to strike back.

A serious problem for the Brest Fortified District was one of personnel – the command staff of the Fortified District's separate machine-gun–artillery battalions by the start of the war had extremely few artillery commanders, primarily from the rifle units, who were poorly trained for conducting fire from pillboxes and showed extremely poor results in weapons proficiency. By the start of the war, not a single one of the District's separate machine-gun–artillery battalions was fully staffed according to TO&E [Table of Organization and Equipment], averaging only 34 percent of the authorized number of commanders, 28 percent of the authorized noncommissioned officers and 47 percent of the rank and file. Incidentally, why create units that lack weapons and equipment? However, of the five planned separate machine-gun–artillery battalions (each with 1,500 men), they organized three (each with 350–400 men). Their personnel had only just begun to arrive, while the command staff came from artillery units of the Western Special Military District. The untrained personnel that arrived, which still hadn't received either weapons or uniforms, were in the meantime placed in the 16th, 17th and 18th Separate Machine-gun–Artillery battalions.

In addition to the pillboxes, the Brest Fortified Region consisted of fieldworks that were located between them, which in response to an alarm were to be manned by units of the 4th Army. They were designed in the form of strongpoints and battalion boxes and consisted mostly of earth and timber structures and a few made of rubble, as well as entrenchments (which as a rule were rectangular rifle pits designed for one or two men, without communication trenches or any camouflage) and a few obstacles (anti-tank only in the form of ditches and log post obstacles in individual sectors, while the anti-infantry obstacles were not mined). There were few command posts, observation posts and shelters.

For the construction of the positions, the entire frontier belt was divided into battalion areas. At first, all of the completed works were to be occupied in response to an alarm, but later only those depending upon their importance in the defensive scheme. From May 1941, a rifle battalion from each regiment of every division, all combat engineer elements, the main force of the District's 33rd Engineer Regiment and a battalion each from the artillery regiments were working on the construction of the fortified district. As a result, 9 of the 27 rifle battalions of the 4th Army's first-echelon divisions (the 6th, 42nd and 75th Rifle divisions), 3 artillery battalions, and 5 construction companies of the 62nd Fortified Region's 74th Construction Command were constantly at work in the sector of the 62nd Fortified Region. The 62nd Fortified Region's 21st Construction Command was stationed in Brest.

Work on the District's fortifications progressed slowly and could not be completed by 1941. The positioning of the units assigned to man them, which were frequently based 15–50 kilometers away from their designated sectors, discounted the possibility of a surprise attack. After all, in the first place their 'neighbor' Germany was busy with the campaign in the West; in the second place, a non-aggression pact had been signed between the two countries, and there apparently were no disagreements; and thirdly – how could forces be assembled on the border unnoticed?

As a result, the stationing of the troops in Western Belorussia was dictated not by any operational reasons, but by the availability of accommodations: when entering this territory after it was forcibly annexed by the Soviet Union, the Red Army had collided with a shortage of barracks – there was no place to billet the troops. An enormous number of troops had accumulated in Brest, simply because it alone offered an ample amount of the necessary living accommodations. In order to house the Red Army men, some of the warehouses had to be adapted for this use, while stockades of the Brest Fortress, which had been blown up in 1915, had to be re-built. The Central Bastion became the primary place for stationing the troops of the 4th Army, but even in its accommodations they had cramped billets where the soldiers had to sleep in multi-tiered bunks.

Such overcrowding was undesirable; however, the District commander D. Pavlov, when billeting the troops in this way, planned to create the greatest possible conveniences for them to compensate for the overcrowding. Otherwise, the units would have found themselves in barracks and dugouts. Thus, Pavlov's utilitarian ideas overcame his operational ideas. Later, the chief of staff of the 4th Army L.M. Sandalov would self-critically note: 'The 4th Army command, gently expressing itself in a conciliatory fashion, resorted to such an operationally disadvantageous and even more so, dangerous disposition of the troops.' However, the command of both the 4th Army and the Western District simply had no choice: all the effort was concentrated on building pillboxes and fortifications, not barracks. Moreover, the moving up of all four divisions of the 4th Army was dictated not only by the availability of space for accommodations, but also the desire to cover all 150 kilometers of its sector. Thus, the forces of the 4th Army were positioned in a single line, with no second echelon or any reserves. Nevertheless, units of the fortress were constantly moving out and returning. The rumble of engines of motorized columns and the clopping of hundreds of hooves became a customary sound for the residents of Brest.

The deployment of personnel in the Brest Fortress was as follows:

South Island

Details of the 9th Line and 3rd Reserve border posts of the 17th Red Banner (Brest) Border Guards Detachment's 3rd Kommandatura: their deployment and numerical strength is unknown. It can be assumed that approximately ten Border Guards were combat-ready on South Island. How they were armed is not known – rifles and perhaps also a machine gun.

There was also the regimental school (for non-commissioned officers) of the 84th 'Comintern' Rifle Regiment (commanded by Major S.K. Dorodnykh) on the island, the students and instructors of which on the eve of the invasion had gone to the 4th Army's artillery range south-east of the village of Volynka. A sentry detachment was left behind – probably a platoon (around thirty men), as well as those excused from the field training. In addition to regular-issue weapons for a platoon, they were equipped with three light machine guns. It should be noted that primarily men with a middle or higher education were assigned to this school, which made this unit one of the most combat-capable and steadfast.

The 6th Rifle Division's 95th Medical-Sanitation Battalion was also stationed on South Island: 253 officers and enlisted personnel, who were armed with 135 rifles, including two machine pistols.

Finally, there was the disbanded Brest Military Hospital and the 28th Rifle Corps' newly-created field hospital with 150 beds – there is no information about its staff and weapons. There is also nothing known about the size of the shift on duty in the pillboxes or the number of men working on the field works on South Island.

In sum, there were approximately 180 armed military personnel on the South Island. Approximately forty of them were on duty.

West Island

Details of the 9th Line and 3rd Reserve border posts were also guarding the frontier on West Island: due to the length of the sector of West Island adjacent to the national border (approximately 1 kilometer), they probably numbered ten men.

There was also a transport company (in Point 251?) and a combat engineering platoon of the 17th Border Guards Detachment. Their numerical strength is unknown.

In addition to these units, there were drivers being trained in District driving school for the forces of the Belorussian Border District (Point 242); there were also training camps for light machine-gunners, cavalrymen and sportsmen, as well as a veterinarian clinic.

There were also Border Guardsmen who'd been selected out of the entire Border Guards detachment for athletic teams. On Saturday, 21 June after lunch a number of these soldiers headed back to their border outposts in order to change their underclothing, compose letters or to rest. Only those who were to take part in the forthcoming Sunday competitions – twelve soldiers – remained. In addition to grenades and rifles, there were also two light machine guns available to them. In this same building on West Island there were also Border Guards cavalrymen – approximately fifty men in total under the command of Senior Lieutenant Chikishev.

Lieutenant A.P. Sergeev, the 17th Border Guards Detachment's chief of physical training, who was in charge of the sports' teams, recalls:

> In accordance with the plan of the island's garrison commander Senior Lieutenant A.S. Chernyi, in the event of an alarm I had determined a plan of actions for those remaining participants in the competitions. According to this plan, the athletes were to cover the sector of a wooden bridge that led across the old, dammed branch of the Bug into the fortress. Senior Sergeant Minin had a position that offered a wide, 360° gun.

Speaking about the Border Guardsmen, it is not their number that should be noted so much as their quality – these were effectively select units, the backbone of the troops located in Brest and the surrounding area. Only Red Army men who had passed through a special screening process were chosen to picket the frontier. Of their number, 95 percent had a middle school or higher education. Of course, this doubtlessly made them even more resolute fighters – 72 percent of the newly-arrived Border Guardsmen were Communists or *Komsomol* members.

The border posts of the 17th Brest Border Guards Detachment had a special status, and were more heavily-armed than comparable Red Army units. In addition to rifles, each of the posts had three heavy machine guns and six light machine guns, plus two to three grenade-launchers. Each post had as many as 1,000 RGD-33 combat grenades, and up to 120,000 cartridges. The combat training and morale of the Border Guardsmen were on a high level.

Thus, in total on the West Island there were approximately 300 Border Guardsmen. Of them, a minimum of ten and a maximum of 150 men were in a state of full combat-readiness.

Central Island

From West Island, the Terespol Bridge led through the Terespol Gate into Central Island. As it happened, it was precisely there, at the bridge, that the units best prepared for close combat were positioned: to the right of the bridge in the Ring Barracks were two companies of the 132nd Separate NKVD Military Escort Battalion, while immediately behind the Terespol Gate, which led into the interior grounds of the Citadel, was a building that housed elements of the 17th Border Guards

Detachment (the 9th Line and 3rd Reserve posts), and the 3rd Commandant's Headquarters (*komendatura*). Likely, on the night of 21 June, there were thirty soldiers of the 3rd Reserve Post, approximately forty soldiers of the 9th Line Post, and approximately forty soldiers of the 3rd Commandant's Headquarters. By its authorized strength, a line post had sixty-four men, a reserve post forty-two men, but part of the guardsmen of both Border Guards units were elsewhere on duty. Of the staff of the 3rd Commandant's Headquarters in the building, first and foremost there was the commandant's platoon (in the northern wing of the building). The families of ten Border Guardsmen were also residing in this building. The armament of the reserve posts was analogous to that of the line posts.

The 132nd Separate NKVD Military Escort Battalion was no less a hard nut to crack – the personnel directed into units of the NKVD's internal forces also went through a special screening process. Members had to meet nationality and education requirements and were tested on their attitude toward Soviet power, among other things. The numerical strength of this NKVD Battalion is unknown. The majority of its units on the night of 21 June were serving outside the perimeter of the fortress (some had been posted to guard the bridges across the Muchavec River). On the night of 21 June, approximately 100 men from its roster were in the barracks; of those, approximately thirty were members of the security platoon. In addition, there were also families of the command staff living in this sector: eight families of the commanders of the 333rd Rifle Regiment were residing in the tower above the Terespol Gate.

To the left of the Terespol Gate in the Ring Barracks were the stables, storage facilities and repair shops of the 333rd Rifle Regiment (commanded by Colonel D.I. Matveev). Further on, closer to the Brigidki Gate was the 31st Separate Motorized Transport Battalion. According to its table of organization and equipment, it was supposed to have 255 men (including thirty-two officers). However, since almost all of the officers were absent, one can assume that not more than 200 men were present for duty in the transport battalion. They were armed with 195 rifles and fourteen submachine guns. The motorized pool of the transport battalion (trucks, motorcycles and fueling vehicles) was parked both within the Citadel on its parade ground and on the bank of the right branch of the Muchavec River where it flows into the Bug. The sentry platoon consisted of approximately thirty men.

In the courtyard adjacent to the Terespol Gate, opposite the building holding the elements of the 17th Border Guards Detachment, was an enormous building that housed the 333rd Rifle Regiment. It stretched across practically the entire courtyard, with high, white stone walls on both its northern and southern ends that extended to the Ring Barracks. Sometimes this building is referred to as the 'Headquarters' of the 333rd Rifle Regiment. In reality, practically the entire regiment was billeted in it, including the headquarters, all three battalions and the regimental school.

It is thought that on the night of 21 June, only two battalions and other elements were actually in the building, except for the engineering company which had been withdrawn to the Fortified District, the transport company which was located in

East Fort, the commander's platoon (guarding the headquarters of the 28th Rifle Corps) and the administrative platoon (which was also in East Fort). On that night, the 5th Rifle Company – 178 men – was serving as the regiment's alert unit. The regiment had additional units (batteries of 120mm mortars, 76mm guns and so forth) that numbered around 500 men.

It is possible to assume that approximately 800 men were inside the building of the 333rd Rifle Regiment. It is unknown whether they all had weapons; possibly those who had recently arrived from the Fortified District, those commanders who had just joined their units, men on leave of absence, some of the soldiers of the regiment's headquarters, patients in the medical-sanitation battalion and certain others were not armed.

In addition, some of the posts being manned by soldiers of the alert unit were located outside the 333rd Rifle Regiment's building. The matériel of the 333rd Rifle Regiment's artillery park was positioned across from the Border Guards' building.

On the opposite side of the sector held by the 132nd Separate NKVD Battalion, sections of the 84th Rifle Regiment were in the Ring Barracks on both sides of the Kholm Gate. On the night of 21 June, it had three battalions (750 men) located within the fortress. The 5th Rifle Company (178 men) was serving as the regiment's alert unit. The regimental headquarters and specialized units were also positioned there. However, two platoons of 76mm field artillery guns and a platoon of 120mm mortars had on Saturday departed for the 4th Army's artillery range. The full 1st Rifle Battalion had also moved out to accompany them, as well as the regimental school reinforced with a platoon of 82mm mortars. As a result, there were around 480 men in the regimental units of the 84th Rifle Regiment left within the fortress. In addition, on the second floor of the Ring Barracks almost directly above the Kholm Gate was a dormitory for young commanders; how many of them were there is unknown. Just as in the case of the 333rd Rifle Regiment, there were quite a few soldiers of the 84th Rifle Regiment – for example, Sergeant S.B. Nuridzhanian (an assistant platoon commander in the 84th Rifle Regiment's 5th Rifle Company), who were preparing to take part in a fitness and health parade in Minsk and for this reason had been excused from work in the fortified area. One can assume that the war found a total of 1,200 officers and men in the sector of the 84th Rifle Regiment. The matériel of the 84th Rifle Regiment's artillery park (45mm and 76mm guns, as well as the anti-aircraft vehicles) was parked on the grounds of the Citadel below the windows of the Ring Barracks.

In the courtyard north of the 84th Rifle Regiment's sector were the buildings of the so-called 'Engineering Directorate' and the White Palace. The 6th Rifle Division's 75th Separate Reconnaissance Battalion was billeted in them. The White Palace contained its mess, storage facilities, an officers' club and a guardhouse, while the Engineering Directorate building housed the headquarters and men of the armored car company, and according to some sources, also the armorer's workshop and a gymnasium.

Across the Citadel's grounds opposite the Kholm Gate lies the Trekharoch Gate. On the second floor of this sector of the Ring Barracks (to the east of the

Trekharoch Gate) were the billets of the men of the 75th Separate Reconnaissance Battalion's tank and motorized rifle companies, and off the first stairwell – the headquarters of the 33rd Separate Engineering Regiment, which was subordinate to the District command. Here in the same sector of the Ring Barracks (but on the first floor) were elements of a regiment that had just been formed around a nucleus of the 140th Separate Engineering Battalion in May-June 1941. Later, this sector of the Ring Barracks became known as the 'Officers' House'. At the fork of the Muchavec River, south-east of the White Palace, was the vehicular park of the 75th Separate Reconnaissance Battalion – vehicles and BA-10 armored cars, and beneath the summer canopy of trees, T-38 amphibious scout tanks and new T-40 amphibious light tanks. Perhaps that's why they became a surprise for the 45th Infantry Division – aerial photo reconnaissance didn't spot them! By TO&E, the battalion was supposed to have ten vehicles and sixteen tanks.

On the night of 21 June, the 75th Separate Reconnaissance Battalion had approximately 250 men. The battalion's on-duty officer was Lieutenant Galust'iants. The alert unit isn't known, but was probably one of its platoons – ten to twenty men.

In an addition that had been built on to the White Palace, next to the stables of the 33rd Engineering Regiment, lived the families of its commanders. The strength of the 33rd Engineering Regiment is unknown. However, in any case almost all of the regiment's units were away at work building fortifications – both in Brest and the fortress, as well as on the territory of the Brest-Litovsk and Domachevskii Districts. The regimental school had departed on 5 May for its summer camp in Bul'kovo. I. Dolotov, a platoon commander of a provisional company of the 33rd Engineering Regiment writes that 'on the night of 21 June, approximately half of the regiment was in the fortress. A large team was working a night shift at Fort Berg constructing a pillbox.' The deputy political commander of this same company, A. Nikitin asserts: 'All of the regiment's personnel were away at work sites. Only the unit responsible for guard duty and the administrative platoon plus the clerks remained in the fortress.'

It was this provisional company, commanded by Senior Lieutenant Sorokin, which was performing sentry duties on this final night before the war. It had been formed back on 3 May from residents of Brest Oblast who had arrived in the regiment for re-training, the majority of them being former Polish army military servicemen. It was authorized to flesh out the ranks of combat units with native residents of western Belorussia only when there was insufficient time available to fill the roster with citizens from other areas of the USSR. It was also forbidden to enlist Soviet citizens of Polish nationality for units and military installations, though it seems that this rule was constantly being violated. It should be noted that the provisional company (primarily the enlisted men themselves, because the junior commanders were living in the barracks) was positioned across the Muchavec on North Island, in the Main Wall's gorge barracks (known as Point 145). Three or four canvas tents had been pitched to the left of the Wall for more of its soldiers.

Considering the lack of information, it is difficult to say anything certain either about the numerical strength of the 33rd Engineering Regiment or its alert unit, which was armed and carrying out sentry duties. It can be assumed that there were around 150 armed soldiers, of which approximately 100 would launch an attack against the Church of Saint Nikolai on the morning of 22 June. In addition, some of the soldiers were in the Ring Barracks, covering the attackers with fire, while others had been killed during the artillery barrage as they were emerging from the barracks. Another group of its soldiers remained in the gorge barracks of the Main Wall (Point 145) on North Island.

The 455th Rifle Regiment was occupying the section of the Ring Barracks west of the Trekharoch Gate. In the headquarters on the first floor, the duty officer on the night of 21 June was the 455th Rifle Regiment's chief of chemical services Lieutenant A.A. Vinogradov. He later stated, '. . . of our regiment, the 3rd Battalion, the regimental school and the specialized elements were located within the fortress.' The numerical strength of those of its units remaining in the fortress was comparable to that of the 84th Rifle Regiment, though it is necessary to add the regimental school and take into account the fact that the 455th Regiment's artillery units remained in the fortress. Thus in total we can estimate that the 455th Rifle Regiment had 1,500 men within the Citadel on the night of 21 June. The alert unit is not known.

The 455th Rifle Regiment was one of the most experienced combat units in the Citadel; the majority of its commanders had served in the Winter War with Finland. Its soldiers, however, after those who had participated in the fighting in Karelia had been transferred into the Red Army Reserve, still lacked training. A recent report indicated that the regiment's morale was healthy. However, the 455th Regiment's report for January 1941 noted that the personnel 'had mastered the heavy and light machine gun, but still had a poor grasp of the Tokarev SVT-38 semi-automatic rifle. The best units in the regiment: the regimental school and the 2nd Battalion.' A distinctive feature of the regiment was the fact that 40 percent of its soldiers either had an incomplete understanding of the Russian language or almost no knowledge of it at all. It was these men who hadn't yet mastered their gear or the use of their weapon. The other 60 percent of the men received a good rating. According to the results of the February 1941 tests, the 3rd Battalion was now the best; however, the regiment as a whole was given only an 'average' rating in weapons training. The worst units were the 3rd and 5th Rifle companies.

Next to the 455th Rifle Regiment in the perimeter of the Ring Barracks was the 6th Rifle Division's 37th Separate Signals Battalion. However, prior to 21 June the entire personnel of this signals battalion had moved to a camp several kilometers to the north-east of Brest. Only a designated alert detachment from the 1st Telegraph-Cable Company remained in the Citadel. One can assume that on the night of 21 June, twenty men were carrying out sentry duties.

Beyond the signals battalion in the Ring Barracks were elements of the 44th Rifle Regiment – its regimental school, specialized units (except for a battery of regimental artillery, the anti-tank unit, the 120mm mortars and the transport company – they were billeted in the Main Wall at the Northern Gate), and the regiment headquarters: altogether around 500 men. The 44th Rifle Regiment's alert unit on the night of 21 June was the 1st Rifle Company. It was a training company – over the previous one and a half years it had trained reserve lieutenants, who served a subsequent half-year period of probation with their units, but its posts were at the Northern Gate, in the sector of the 1st Rifle Battalion, and at the storage depots. It isn't known where its watch-house, where the shift could rest, was located. Most likely it was somewhere near the regiment headquarters in the Citadel. Thus, one can assume that approximately 100 men of the alert company were in the Citadel. So in sum the 44th Rifle Regiment had around 600 men on Central Island on the night of 21 June.

Just like the 455th Rifle Regiment, the 44th Rifle Regiment, which was commanded by Major Petr Mikhailovich Gavrilov, was a unit with combat experience in the Winter War. In a report on the results of the combat and political training of the regiment for the period October 1940–March 1941, Gavrilov had noted that the regiment's discipline and combat-readiness were 'satisfactory'; the main disciplinary problem in the regiment was drunkenness.

Summing up the results of these estimates, there were probably around 5,000 soldiers and commanders of the Red Army within the Citadel when the Germans attacked. Of these, approximately 720 were armed, carrying out sentry duties.

North Island

The Central and North Islands were linked by the Trekharoch Bridge, which led to the Citadel's Trekharoch Gate. On North Island, to the east of the bridge, was the Main Wall's gorge barracks (Point 145). As noted above, two of its sections were reduits, and next to them were the three or four canvas tents in which men of the 33rd Engineering Regiment's provisional company were quartered. Adjoining casemates of the Main Wall held supplies, as well as the 6th Rifle Division's 44th Mobile Field Bakery, according to most records. Its active roster should have had around 120 soldiers and non-commissioned officers, armed with one machine pistol and 69 rifles. Its alert detail is not known; nor is it even known whether the 44th Bakery was even responsible for sentry duties. However, in the battle it would become one of the focal points of resistance in the fight for Point 145.

To the east, beyond the gorge barracks and reduits, the so-called 'eastern walls' began to extend to the north. This was the position of the 6th Rifle Division's 98th Separate Gun Artillery Battalion, commanded by Captain N.I. Nikitin. It was supposed to have approximately 200 men and 18 45mm anti-tank guns on its roster, as well as 21 *Komsomolets* T-20 armored tractors. These lightly-armored prime movers (frontal armor – 10mm; side and rear armor – 7mm) were armed with a 7.62mm DT machine gun with 1,260 rounds of ammunition. Subsequently, in messages of the 45th Infantry Division, these prime movers were often referred to as 'tanks'. On the afternoon of 21 June, several of the battalion's artillery tractors had lined up with attached 45mm guns. The drivers and crews had received an order to drive out to the artillery range the next morning for an equipment inspection. The alert unit on this night was the 1st (Training) Battery, approximately fifty men commanded by Junior Lieutenant N.K. Khaver.

To the west of the 'eastern walls' on North Island was the East Fort – as already described, two horse-shoe shaped earthworks, with one concentrically located within the other and higher than the outer work. The distance between them was 25–30 meters. The proper name for the fortification is the 'Eastern Casemate Reduit' (the reduit guarding the rear approach to the Third Bastion), which was built in the years 1864–68 according to the blueprint of E.I. Totleben. Within each of the earthworks, which were covered by a layer of soil, were casemates – 94 in the outer one and 14 double-deck casemates in the inner one. The outer earthwork contained stables for approximately 200 horses and the 333rd Rifle Regiment's ammunition stockpiles. Elements of the 42nd Rifle Division's 393rd Separate Anti-aircraft Artillery Battalion (two batteries and a machine-gun company) were billeted in the casemates of the inner earthwork, as were the 333rd Rifle Regiment's transport company (and probably also its administrative platoon) and the 1st (Training) Battery of the 98th Separate Gun Artillery Battalion. The 393rd Separate Anti-aircraft Artillery Battalion also had its supplies stockpiled here. The separate anti-aircraft artillery battalion was supposed to have two 37mm batteries and one battery of 76mm guns (four crews), but the 393rd Battalion's former deputy supply chief R. Semiunok specifies that the battalion was armed with twelve 76mm guns and one anti-aircraft vehicle mounting a quad-barreled machine gun. Overnight between 20 and 21 June, the 2nd and 3rd batteries of the 393rd Separate Anti-aircraft Artillery Battalion had departed for a tactical field exercise, and only the 1st Battery commanded by Senior Lieutenant S.F. Shramko had been left behind on guard duty. According to other records, one-third of the 393rd Separate Anti-aircraft Artillery Battalion's personnel (the 37mm gun batteries and two crews of 76mm guns with their equipment) had moved to the Brest artillery range for an inspection of the combat equipment and to participate in training drills scheduled for 22 June 1941, which means two crews of the 1st Battery (76mm guns) remained in the East Fort. The duty officer for the unit was the battalion's signals chief Lieutenant A.D. Domienko. In sum there were approximately 180 soldiers and junior commanders in the East Fort.

On the eastern side of the outer earthwork of East Fort, mounted on carriages, stood two of the battalion's 76mm anti-aircraft guns, their barrels pointed in the direction of the buildings housing the senior officers, together with three STZ-NATI artillery tractors for towing them (one tractor was a spare vehicle). On the other side of the outer earthwork stood the equipment of the 44th Rifle Regiment's anti-aircraft company – six GAZ-AA trucks carrying quad-mounted Maksim machine guns. Finally, in front of the East Fort, to the north of it, stood tents that accommodated designated personnel of the 44th Rifle Regiment – residents of Brest Oblast who had been conscripted for a 45-day call-up.

Just to the west of East Fort was a road that ran from the Trekharoch Bridge on the southern end of North Island to the northern end of the island. There it exited the Northern Gate of the Main Wall, and then ran across the Forward Moat into Brest. Elements of the 44th Rifle Regiment's 1st Battalion and the regiment's specialized units were positioned on both sides of the Northern Gate – around

1,100 men, of which seventy were part of the 44th Rifle Regiment's alert unit, the 1st Company. The 44th Rifle Regiment's artillery park was situated on the other side of the Main Wall.

Finally, the position of the 6th Rifle Division's 125th Rifle Regiment extended to the west of the Northern Gate. It was commanded by Colonel F.F. Berkov, who'd been assigned to a different post elsewhere, but hadn't yet departed to assume his new command. In the casemates of the Main Wall at the Northwestern Gate were platoons of mounted and dismounted scouts, a mortar battery, a transport company, a platoon of musicians, and the staff and administrative services. Next to it, in a two-story building, was the regiment headquarters and the signals company. Units of the 2nd Rifle Battalion and the regimental school occupied a neighboring casemate. The barracks of the 1st Rifle Battalion and the regiment's artillery batteries were in the West Fort.

Both Sandalov and Popov testify that two battalions of the 125th Rifle Regiment remained inside the fortress. A private in the regimental band K.G. Gorbatkov recalls somewhat differently:

> On the night of 21 June the regiment's combat battalions moved out to occupy positions in the fortified district. I recall that a portion of the 2nd Rifle Battalion, the administrative platoon, the platoon of musicians, the cook, staff employees and our regimental school remained inside the fortress.

S.S. Smirnov also writes about this:

> On the night the war began, the entire rifle regiment was either in camps or at work sites outside the fortress. Only several sentry platoons, administrative teams, staff workers and part of the regimental school of non-commissioned officers remained in the barracks.

A third (more likely) version is presented in the memoirs of Captain G.A. Landyshev, the former commander of the 125th Rifle Regiment's 1st Battalion – according to Landyshev, he led his battalion out of the fortress only after the battle started on the morning of 22 June. Junior Lieutenant I.V. Isakovich's machine-gun company was at a firing range at the South Training Ground. All three machine-gun companies of the 125th Rifle Regiment had been sent there a week before the start of the war. As concerns the 125th Rifle Regiment's 3rd Rifle Battalion, commanded by Captain M.E. Kolesnikov, it had departed back in May to the Chizhevichi–Vil'iamovichi–Cheleva area (12–15 kilometers east of Brest) in order to build fortifications.

Thus, one can conclude that it was in the north-west section of the Brest Fortress that the strongest unit of those in the fortress was positioned – the 125th Rifle Regiment. Of its roster, 1,600 men (of which 178 comprised the alert unit) of the regimental units, four rifle companies and one rifle battalion were on North Island.

It should not be forgotten that the majority of the command staff's families were residing on the North Island. The street, where the one- and two-story apartment buildings that housed the senior commanders' families stood, ran from the West

Fort to the east, and extended almost to the casemates of the Main Wall at the Kobrin Gate, which were occupied by the 98th Separate Gun Artillery Battalion. The families of approximately 170 commanders and political workers of various military units were living in these apartment complexes. The intersecting road running from the Northern to the Trekharoch Gate split the residential street into western and eastern halves. For example, families of commanders of the 125th Rifle Regiment (including that of the commander of the 125th Regiment's 2nd Battalion Captain Shablovsky) were living in the western section, while those of the 44th Rifle Regiment (including that of the commander of the 44th Regiment Major Gavrilov) were residing in the eastern section. Although many units in which those commanders and political workers who lived in the residences of the senior command staff on North Island served had moved outside of Brest and the fortress by 22 June, on the day off the husbands and fathers had returned to their families.

Thus, altogether on the territory of North Island there were 3,400 military servicemen, of which approximately 300 were carrying out sentry duties as part of alert units.

Summing up, a grand total of approximately 9,000 Red Army officers and soldiers were on the grounds of the Brest Fortress (the Central Bastion) when the Germans attacked. Of these, approximately 1,100 men were part of alert units and thus presumably prepared to meet the German attack. These calculations do not include the alert crews of the 18th Separate Machine-gun–Artillery Battalion in the pillboxes along the Bug River (approximately two men per pillbox), units on the night shift busy with the construction of fortifications in the fortified district in the sector of the 45th Infantry Division's offensive, or the newly-arrived designated personnel located on the grounds of the fortress. One can only guess at the latter's number, but the total numerical strength of the 6th and 42nd Rifle divisions increased by 3,126 men between 1 and 22 June. The majority of them were from the June 1941 draft and had not yet been assigned to units. Those conscripted to build fortifications in the district were excluded, which means there should have been around 2,000 designated personnel on the grounds of the fortress, who were kept separately from the remaining units.

The mood of many of the soldiers and non-commissioned officers, who sensed the menacing atmosphere of June, was unhappy. The chief of the 28th Rifle Corps' operations department Major E.M. Sinkovsky recalled:

> Soon after the TASS announcement, I was in the fortress with the 333rd Rifle Regiment. Together with the regiment commander D.I. Matveev, I spent time among the units. One of the soldiers asked, 'Tell me, Comrade Colonel, when will they pull us out of this mousetrap?' Matveev vaguely answered, referring to the TASS announcement, but it was perceptible that the soldiers weren't satisfied with the response.[1]

V.P. Vavilov (a private and clerk in a machine-gun company of the 44th Rifle Regiment) wrote to his family:

> I'm reporting to you that at the given time I am serving in a new place in the border city of Brest, ever closer to our amicable neighbour Germany. History finds us separated by just several dozen metres. All the same, we'll soon likely have to clash with them . . . (15 April 1941).

Sultan Bauchiev, a clerk of a battery of 45mm guns with the 455th Rifle Regiment, wrote:

> I'm now already convinced that I won't be seeing my native land: it is necessary to thrash someone . . . I have no son! This, however, is a major life blunder! It is important to leave someone behind, who would be proud that his (or her) father died a modest death in a war for his Fatherland . . . (2 May 1941).

V.N Abyzov (deputy political leader, assistant deputy political commander of the 37th Separate Signal Battalion's 1st Telegraph-Cable Company):

> With respect to the international situation, at the given moment it is extremely tense. Indeed it is no accident that we are positioned on the border and that complete combat-readiness is demanded of us, so as to defend our borders at any minute, and if necessary, to smash the foe on his territory. Meanwhile our neighbour is unreliable, despite the fact that we even have an agreement with him.

L.S. Gurchak (a lieutenant and commander of mortar company in the 455th Rifle Regiment): 'I'm now located in the city of Brest, on the very border with our "friend" Germany. The situation so far is good and calm.'

Vano Zedginidze (a private in the 393rd Separate Anti-aircraft Artillery Regiment): 'I'm now closer than anyone to the German border, and you know that it's not so pleasant to have such a neighbour.'

D.P. Kireev (a lieutenant and commander of a machine-gun platoon in the 455th Rifle Regiment's regimental school): 'A threat hangs in the air, and likely the threat will be worse than the Finnish [one]. . . (May 1941).'

N.G. Mishchenko (a soldier in the 333rd Rifle Regiment):

> I'm living well thus far, but within a hair's breadth of something. Meanwhile we have a lot of news, but I won't be writing. The entire country should learn about our news, but to this point nobody knows it. I ask you to write letters more often, while you still have someone to write. If you're interested . . . I ask that you keep your mouth shut. . . (1 June 1941).

The Red Army enlisted men had forebodings, but the country and their commanders were trying to prepare. It is notable that in the program of commanders' lessons for January–May 1941, the subject 'The study of foreign armies' was relabeled as 'The study of the German Army'. In the period January–March 1941, two hours were dedicated to this – each month! For example, in January the subject of study was the organization of a *Wehrmacht* infantry division and its tactics when on the defensive, while in March, the subject was 'Tactics of the German Army in a meeting engagement'. In sum, a total of six hours was spent on studying the *Wehrmacht*. There were no lessons in April or May. However, in contrast much more time was given to Marxist–Leninist training over the period January–May 1941 – six hours a month (thirty hours!).

The study of the German army at that time also had to carry a 'proper world view':

> The extensive saturation of the [German] infantry divisions with weapons and equipment at first glance presents a rather impressive force; however, this still does not explain its high combat capability. People – soldiers – are in control of the equipment and direct it. The German soldiers in their majority consist of workers and peasants, the morale of which is tilted far not in favour of the fascist big-wigs. Widespread incidents of desertion and suicide, which are ever-increasing in the army, speak very eloquently on the morale of the German Army. The soldiers cannot endure the inhumane drills and abuse, upon which the officers build discipline, and many of the soldiers are deserting or ending their lives with suicides. According to reports from the anti-fascist press, 180 German soldiers fled across the Silesian border into Poland, while 300 German soldiers escaped across the East Prussian border. Such is the real situation of the soldier in the German Army.[2]

The amount of time dedicated to the analysis of the remaining disciplines (over the course of study) was respectively: modern aviation and tanks – four hours; cloaked command of the troops – ten hours; communications – four hours. As a result, as the chief of staff of the 4th Army Sandalov recalled, the command staff and headquarters at every level, including the army level as well, didn't know how to direct the troops with the assistance of radio communications, and shunned it because of the difficulty of using radios in comparison with wire communications. The 4th Army headquarters in Kobrin handled its communications with the command of the 28th Rifle Corps and the headquarters of the 6th and 42nd Rifle divisions over civilian telephone lines that had been set aside for this purpose. The 4th Army headquarters had no standing radio communications with higher or lower levels of command, or with neighboring armies. On the whole, the provision of the Western Special Military District with radios was as follows: at the regiment level – 41 percent of the authorized number; at the battalion level – 58 percent; and at the company level – 70 percent.

At the commanders' classes in the 42nd Rifle Division, fourteen hours were dedicated to the study of tactics. At that time, the teaching in the Workers' and Peasants' Red Army was not free of miscalculations – if in the latter half of 1940 questions of preparing and conducting a defense predominated in the themes of the lessons, in 1941 the emphasis switched to attacking. This had an adverse effect on the preparations for a defense, because many of the commanders sent to the Western Special Military District arrived in the divisions at a time when they were focusing only on offensive actions. However, according to the testimony of L.M. Sandalov, in the 4th Army at the time the main attention was given to reaching a correct decision, and the proper formatting and wording of the resulting order. The handling of the forces on the basis of the decision was given little attention. The command staff had almost no experience in directing entire formations, units and elements with all their combat equipment and logistics.

However, even when conducting training, the command sought to take the situation into account – for example, the 42nd Rifle Division's program of commanders' classes for the period of May–September was significantly adjusted. For June, tactics were now to be given six hours of study, while Marxist-Leninist study decreased to four hours. Nevertheless, in May, only a total of two hours of study was devoted to 'Tactics of foreign armies' (the subject had again acquired its original name). The topic was 'The German infantry division and infantry regiment on the attack.' At the same time, in June there were plans to conduct two-hour classes with company commanders as well ('The German battalion and company on the attack'). The lessons most often constituted presentations by commanders, followed by a discussion. For example, Major Gavrilov by 20 April was to present the theses of a report entitled 'The march and meeting battle of a rifle regiment – the vanguard of a rifle division'. The presentation of the report was scheduled to take place on 1 July. Other commanders in the division were preparing other reports on subjects such as 'Preparation of the eastern theatre of war in Germany', 'The organizational structure and armament in the German Army' and 'German artillery in the contemporary war' for the period 15 June–1 July.

In the wake of special agents' messages, worrying reports from the Border Guards began to come in: on 2 June, the movement of all types of forces from Warsaw, primarily at night, had been spotted, and the concentration of pontoons, as well as canvas and inflatable boats, at many points along the border (primarily in front of Brest and L'vov).

On 5 June, the final intelligence summary from the headquarters of the Western Special Military District, which had arrived at the 4th Army's headquarters, noted the arrival of three German artillery regiments (presumably heavy artillery) and five armored trains in Biala Podlaska. There was also mention of fifty vehicles loaded with ammunition that had passed through that town on 13 May on their way from Warsaw to Terespol, and active motorized traffic on the night of 27 May toward Janow-Podlaski and Terespol. The deployment of camouflaged netting and barbed-wire fencing was observed. However, much more alarming was the evidence that approximately 40 German divisions had assembled on the Belorussian border: of these, 24 divisions were on the Brest axis: 15 infantry, 5 panzer, 2 motorized and 2 cavalry divisions. This signified that the assembly of forces for all intents and purposes was already complete, so an invasion might take place on any day. However, nothing had changed in response on the Soviet side of the Bug – there, on one hand they were expecting at least some sort of diplomatic moves from Germany before the start of war, and on the other, they were hoping that the normal routines of the Soviet border units that were plainly visible from the western bank would allow at least some delay to the start of the war.

On 12 June, a special agent's message was passed on to the leadership of the USSR (I.V. Stalin, V.M. Molotov and L.P. Beria), which stated that it was unclear whether or not the Soviet Union would be presented with any preliminary demands, and thus the possibility of a surprise attack could not be excluded. This changed the situation – now it seemed fully possible that Germany would not give the USSR even two or three days to prepare under any sort of diplomatic pretext for aggression. Decisive steps were necessary – so on 12 June, the command of the border military districts, under the guise of training exercises and the relocation of summer camps, initiated a concealed redeployment of the forces of the Districts' second echelon in accordance with plans to defend the national border, moving them up closer to the border. On this same day Timoshenko and Zhukov informed Pavlov that between 17 June and 2 July, the 51st and 63rd Rifle corps would arrive on the territory of the Western Special Military District. Simultaneously there was an inspection in the border districts of the measures worked out in response to an alarm – the soldiers of the 6th and 42nd Rifle divisions in the Brest Fortress were given no sleep between 10 and 15 June, while the majority of the command staff spent the nights together with them in the barracks.

The pace of the movement of forces from the interior of the country into the zone of the western border districts continued to accelerate. Would they be in time? Despite the fact that the forces were now hurriedly being moved to the west, still quite a bit of time was needed – according to a briefing paper of the Red Army's General Staff dated 13 June, another seventeen divisions could be assigned to the border. However, their movement would require 600 trains ...

Time was needed! So on 14 June, the TASS announcement was published, which on one hand was designed to calm the population of the western USSR (there was the danger of its chaotic flight to the east, which might be interpreted by the German intelligence organs as a de-population of the region and trigger an immediate invasion), and on the other, was crafted to explain the movement of the Soviet troops to the Germans:

> ... the summer assemblies of Red Army reserves and forthcoming manoeuvres have no other object than the training of reservists and checking the operation of rail transport. It is well known that this is an annual event, therefore to describe these measures as hostile to Germany is absolutely absurd.

The TASS report, however, lulled only those who wanted to be lulled. Many, understanding that war might begin at any time, began to hoard matches and salt, and lines began to form in Brest for bread and flour. Alarming rumors that exchanges of fire were already taking place in the city circulated among the population. Those who were able to do so sent their families to the east. However, the soldiers and commanders of the units in Brest never read the reports going to Moscow and the headquarters, nor did they communicate with the border outposts on the frontier. Only the sense of danger inherent in every living being caused many of them to become anxious.

To the west of the Bug River, the TASS report was taken with a sense of irony. This quickly became known to Stalin and Molotov, who were tensely waiting for Berlin's reaction. NKVD agents dispelled their hopes: 'All of Germany's military measures in preparation of an armed offensive against the USSR have been fully completed, and an attack can be expected at any time.'

It was now a matter of hours.

Notes

1. On 13 June 1941, Moscow Radio broadcast a TASS announcement, which was widely perceived to be an attempt to receive a public reassurance from Germany about its peaceful intentions. The announcement declared that 'Germany's intentions to tear up the Pact and to undertake an attack on the USSR are without any foundation' and stated that such rumors were 'clumsy propaganda by forces hostile to the USSR and Germany'. Naturally, this announcement has since become notorious in light of the German invasion on 22 June 1941.
2. Gribov, *Germanskaia pekhotnaia diviziia* [*The German infantry division*] (Moscow, 1939).

Chapter 4

'Dortmund'

On 16 June 1941, the invasion order was sent to the German 45th Infantry Division, its neighbors, and the XII Army Corps headquarters. That the situation along the border was more than tense is confirmed by the XII Corps headquarters' order, authorizing the destruction of Russian aircraft that openly crossed the border by anti-aircraft artillery, though to be sure, only those that were overflying German territory (i.e., over German-occupied Polish territory). Incidentally, it was noted by the 45th Infantry Division headquarters that to this point, there had been no such overflights. The headquarters was also notified about the pending arrival on 18 June of the two attached Karl self-propelled 600mm mortars of the 833rd Heavy Artillery Battalion.

Considering that the movement into the jumping-off lines had already begun, the XII Army Corps headquarters was informed that the movement's deadline – 18 June – had been countermanded by the code signal 'Belfort' (the movement would be stopped and the units were to go into bivouac, making sure to remain carefully concealed). If the code signal 'Dortmund' was transmitted on the afternoon of 21 June, then the invasion attack would take place as foreseen, on 22 June. This would simultaneously allow the open transmission of orders. However, if the code word 'Alton' went out, signifying the cancellation of the invasion, all camouflaging of the deployment would be dropped.

In the effort to avoid any leaks of information, the chief of staff of the XII Corps von Waldenburg informed only the commanders of the divisions and of those units directly subordinate to corps headquarters about the date and time of the invasion, while forbidding them to give word of this to anyone else. Accordingly, the subordinate officers and men of the divisions were to be informed of the order as late as possible and only then to the most necessary extent. By 0045 on 22 June, the corps headquarters should expect the code signal 'Kyffhäuser' – the alert to initiate the final movement into the jumping-off positions.

At this moment, the code names established by AOK 4 on 19 April 1941 for all the newly-arriving corps and division headquarters in the army's area since 15 April would lapse. 'King Tiger' would cease its existence in the same way. Code names for the units were preserved, but new ones for them were introduced – for example, 'Reblaus' (Galle's mortar battalion), 'Idealist' (a battery of the 833rd Heavy Artillery Battalion), and 'Realschule' (13/I.R. 133).

The situation at the border was unchanged. Intelligence continued to supply General Schlieper with messages:

(a) Construction has picked up, especially at night ... The construction of field positions has been stepped up. Bushes along the riverbank have been removed to the north and south of the railroad bridge.

Their outposts (and patrols) have not been reinforced. It has been detected that soldiers with black insignia (a technical unit) have replaced the Border Guardsmen on sentry duty ...

Report on the aerial situation: Our own and Russian aircraft are in the border region. Violations of the border have not been observed.

Night-time impressions: No blackout discipline at all. Accelerated construction. Very active transport movement – including trucks with operating headlights on the Brest highway to the barracks' quarter ...

...

(i) New military units: nothing has been established.
(k) Russian preparations for an attack; no indications.
29. Earth and construction works of an unknown type.

* * *

Meanwhile, at the 4th Army headquarters in Kobrin, at the request of General Popov, the commander of the 28th Rifle Corps, 4th Army Chief of Staff Sandalov again suggested to the commander of the 4th Army General Korobkov to send a request to District headquarters about withdrawing the 42nd Rifle Division from Brest and moving it to Zhabinka. However, General Korobkov and Divisional Commissar F.I. Shlykov, a member of the 4th Army's Military Council, immediately rejected this. The latter declared that it was useless to pose this question, because several days before the chief of the 6th Rifle Division's department of political propaganda Colonel Commissar Pimenov had sent a similar letter to the District Military Council, requesting authorization for the division to take up defensive positions, and for the families of the command staff to be evacuated out of Brest to the east. His requests received a categorical rejection.

Discussion began as well about the construction of additional western exits out of the fortress in order to create the possibility of more operational actions in response to an alarm. The 4th Army commander Korobkov also skeptically regarded this proposal: it would be necessary not only to create openings in the thick walls of the Ring Barracks, but also to build new bridges across the canals and fortress moats. Only the combat engineer battalion was capable of such labor-intensive work, but no one would permit it to be withdrawn from its current work constructing fortifications of the Fortified District. There were also no explosives for demolishing the walls ...

* * *

On the morning of 17 June, a conference of the commanders of the regiments and separate battalions of the 45th Infantry Division took place, where Major Dettmer reported on the plan for deploying into the jumping-off positions. The intricate fulfillment of the corresponding order was especially difficult: the battle zone was very cramped, and the possibility of taking up a jumping-off position at Terespol was limited because of the very swampy terrain in the area, which was for the most part under enemy observation. The movement was conducted along the streets of Biala Podlaska and Terespol. According to a XII Army Corps order, marches to the east of Zalesie were allowed only at night. Therefore the moving up of the main forces could be conducted only on the night of the invasion (the shortest night of the year). All of this was necessary to preserve the element of surprise right up to the moment of attack, a point that was stressed by the chief of the general staff. At the conclusion of the meeting, General Schlieper bid farewell to the unit commanders, in case he wouldn't be able to meet with them prior to the invasion.

* * *

The 45th Infantry Division headquarters issued the orders to initiate the movement into the final jumping-off positions within its divisional boundaries on 18 June 1941. Governed by maximum secrecy, during the movement, halts were forbidden in order not to disrupt the precisely-scheduled timetable of marches. It was warned that the commanders would have to reconcile themselves with congestion in the deployment areas and at the same time strive to ensure that the Russians didn't detect anything.

As indicated in the division's attack order, the machine-gun companies of I.R. 133 (which had been attached to the 130th and 135th Infantry regiments) would move up together with I/I.R. 135 and I/I.R. 130. By mid-day on 21 June, a combat engineer platoon of *Oberstleutnant* von Pannwitz's 45th Reconnaissance Battalion would be brought up to join the 45th Panzerjäger Battalion. As had been decided earlier, von Pannwitz's engineers would be assigned to the company of the 45th Panzerjäger Battalion's combat engineers that was to be attached to I.R. 130. However, the composite unit of combat engineers would pass to the control of Helmuth Hipp, the commander of I.R. 130, only at the stroke of midnight on 22 June. Flame-throwers and inflatable rafts, assigned to I.R. 130 and I.R. 135, would already be brought up for them by the 81st Pioneer Battalion. The appearance in place of the combat engineer companies and the assault boats assigned to them, if it had not already taken place, would be overseen by the commander of the 81st Pioneer Battalion. In addition, I.R. 130 was to receive four one-man flame-throwers, while I.R. 135 was to be given eight. It was planned to complete the occupation of the start line before midnight, 22 June, at which point the division headquarters would be informed of the event by 0015 on 22 June with the code word 'Kyffhäuser'. Beginning at 1400 on 21 June, all unit commanders were to be present at their command posts. It was hoped that with the rapid success of the offensive, their subsequent forward command posts as well as the 45th Infantry Division's rear services could soon shift to South Island.

On 18 June General of Infantry Walther Schroth personally got in touch with the commanders of the 130th and 135th Infantry regiments. On this same day, in a report to the headquarters of the XII Army Corps, its command rated the 45th Infantry Division as fully combat-ready and equal to the tasks given it.

That evening there was a message from *Oberstleutnant* Masuch, the commander of the 81st Pioneer Battalion – Red Army men on the grounds of the Brest barracks were stuffing inflatable rafts with straw or hay. Reporting on this on 19 June, the XII Army Corps headquarters stressed that Russian preparations for an attack were not detected in this. Possibly, they were stuffing mattresses ...

* * *

On the Soviet side on this day, anti-aircraft batteries were beginning to take up firing positions in the Grodno–L'vov zone to the Minsk–Novograd–Volynskii line. However, a significant portion of the batteries of the Western Special Military District were at gunnery exercises at Camp Krupki ...

* * *

Finally the XII Army Corps, after searching for both spares and improvised means, decided to allot to the 45th Infantry Division the necessary number of inflatable rafts. Ten assault boats with crews were given to the 34th Infantry Division; in addition, small inflatable boats were distributed to the 214th Pioneer Battalion (twelve such boats) and the 750th Pioneer Battalion (four), while the 81st Pioneer Battalion was given eight large inflatable boats. The 215th and 750th Pioneer battalions also each received four of the latter. Finally, the 215th lent six flame-throwers and crews to Masuch's battalion.

Believing that the 4th Nebelwerfer Regiment was most likely not going to receive all the ammunition promised to it, Major General Friedrich Krischer, the commander of the OKH reserve artillery grouping attached to the 45th Infantry Division (under the headquarters of Arko 27), who was also to coordinate the division's artillery fire during the battle for Brest, appealed to Arko 112 (the command of the 31st Infantry Division's artillery) and 148 (the command of the 34th Infantry Division's artillery), requesting that they alter the fire plan of their *nebelwerfer* battalions for the first five minutes of the artillery barrage. General Krischer wanted two batteries of Arko 112 to target West Island and one battery to target East Fort, and for Arko 148 to focus its fire on the Central Island.

The plan of artillery fire targeting the Central Island that was conceived by Arko 27 and approved by Krischer called for a creeping concentration of artillery fire that would be advanced at five-minute intervals (which was likely determined by the Karl siege mortars' rate of fire). The progressive stages of concentrated artillery fire were given the names of flowers – 'Anemone', 'Narcissus' and 'Tulip'.

The Soviet positions along the Bug River, Soviet troop concentrations, and the exits from the fortress were to be subjected to particularly heavy artillery fire.

* * *

The German observers along the Bug were preparing to wrap up their work. The final information received from them was as follows:

(a) Intensified construction ...
Additionally increased construction of field positions and the removal of tall grass and bushes at the railroad bridge ...

(b) Posts: their strength, as well as that of the patrols, remains the same ...

(c) The nature of the water obstacle: the water [level] is steadily dropping. In general, the flood water has returned to the channel indicated on the map. The ground in places still remains very soft ...

(d) The railroad report: Unchanged ...
The aerial report: Increased aerial activity. At each approach of a German aircraft in the air, Russian fighters immediately take off ...
Night-time impressions: No black-outs. Intense construction work continues, and there is very brisk transport traffic.

(1) Behaviour of the Russians: the Russian [border] posts are noticeably on edge.

On this day, the final units that hadn't yet arrived showed up: a battery of observation balloons and the 1st Company of the 41st Pioneer Battalion from the OKH reserve. The sapper company, however, arrived with only its pontoon and bridging equipment, but without any inflatable rafts or assault boats. Thus the XII Corps headquarters had to readjust the distribution of the available boats. Since the divisions' TO&E provided for only the most necessary engineer equipment, corps headquarters requested support from the Fourth Army headquarters. That evening the request was granted and a message was received stating that five assault boats and twenty-four large inflatable boats would be delivered to the XII Army Corps by air, though no delivery date was given. Later that evening, a train arrived carrying the 600mm siege mortars for the two batteries of the 833rd Heavy Artillery Battalion. Since these were new weapons that hadn't yet been fully tested, the battalion commander *Oberstleutnant* Schmidt didn't manage to bring them into their firing positions: while moving the second heavy mortar into position, the crane broke down (the gear reduction system malfunctioned and a chain snapped). This news was immediately reported to army headquarters.

* * *

In Brest at this time, an expanded plenum of the Communist Party's oblast committee was taking place. Many of the 4th Army's political officers were in attendance. In an address to the plenum, the Oblast First Secretary Tupitsyn emphasized the tensions in the international situation and the growing threat of war. Calling for heightened vigilance, he simultaneously demanded not to talk about this openly and not to take any major measures that the population would notice. To questions of the plenum's participants about evacuating families out of Brest to the east, Tupitsyn responded that this shouldn't be done, so as not to prompt undesirable attitudes.

The high command of the Soviet border districts received a directive to move the armies' headquarters into field command posts by 22–23 June. However, the location of the 4th Army's headquarters didn't change. Whether it even received the directive is unknown.

* * *

In Moscow, an alarming mood was intensifying – ever more unambiguous information was arriving from Belorussia. A special report dated 19 June 1941 from the Belorussian NKGB [People's Commissariat of State Security] to the USSR NKGB about Germany's preparations for war against the USSR stated:

1. The Germans are building bunkers in the woods at a distance of 400 metres from the Koroshchin–Nepli road, and observation posts have been established in front of them at a range of 100 to 200 metres from the road. They are taking readied materials, which had been prepared by peasants for residences, for the construction of the fortifications. Vehicles are standing in Terespol and its environs, loaded with fascines (of sticks bound together by wire), which are intended for passage through the swamps and sandy areas.
2. . . . (On both sides of the border railroad line, bunkers have been built and trenches dug for firing from upright positions).

   . . . The entire population of Warsaw is talking about the pending German entry into a war with the USSR in the next several days. In the small circle of Warsaw professionals, they are insistently saying that Germany's economic situation is desperate and that the population and even the army are going hungry. Germany is seeking a way out by a war with the USSR, justifying it by the slogan 'War for bread'; otherwise, a revolution might break out in Germany in the nearest future.

   (Agent X) on a road towards the border on the Brest axis personally observed a large aggregation of German troops; two infantry divisions that have arrived from Austria are in Terespol.

   [German/Austrian] Soldiers, particularly those that took part in the Spanish Civil War, don't believe the agitation and propaganda being conducted and are expressing anti-war and anti-fascist moods. They are talking about the results of military actions; the frequent bombings of German cities and the death of their family members are the basis of discontent. There are frequent cases of soldier insubordination, malingering and desertion.

The discussion is plainly about the 45th Infantry Division! Of those divisions positioned opposite Brest, only the 45th Infantry Division was formed in Austria. The special report goes on to mention practically all the measures that the 45th Division had implemented.

Influenced by similar reports, the Red Army high command issued an order to the border districts regarding the camouflaging of the districts' airfields, military units and vital sites. The order noted that to this point virtually nothing had been done on this axis to conceal most important military targets. It admonished that the overcrowded and orderly rows of guns and vehicles on the artillery parks and encampments of the motorized-mechanized units, as well as the aircraft lined up on the airfields, made them not only easy to spot, but also enticing targets for air-strikes. The border districts were ordered to camouflage the supply dumps, repair shops, encampments and other military targets, and by 15 July ensure that they were no longer visible from the air.

However, neither the observers of the 45th Infantry Division nor the veterans of the Brest fighting speak of any increased camouflaging activity by the Soviet side in the final days before the war. The artillery parks of the 333rd and 84th Rifle regiments, as well as of other units, continued to stand in the open within a kilometer of the border.

* * *

On the morning of 20 June, the first successfully unloaded Karl siege mortar was emplaced in its firing position. That day the long-awaited news arrived that six assault boats (the table equipment of the 81st Pioneer Battalion's pontoon and bridging park) could be picked up in Legionovo. The *Luftwaffe* was delivering other equipment and supplies. In addition, a still-absent column transporting spin-stabilized rocket projectiles for the *nebelwerfers* arrived that day. The delivery of ammunition continued that night.

Meanwhile, von Krischer continued to give the artillery its tasks, which would regulate the preparatory artillery barrage until the expiration of the fire plan (X + 29 min.) on 22 June. It was decided that one battery of Galle's mortar battalion at X + 30 would open fire on Brest's general post office (Target 632); a second at its radio communications center (Target 633). The expenditure of ammunition: two salvoes of fire, then one round of ammunition per battery each minute.

The third battery would blanket the barracks on the eastern outskirts of the city (that is, at the North Encampment), starting at X + 30. Two salvoes of fire on its main building (Target 636), then one salvo on the barracks complex, followed by a round every two minutes on both targets.

A battery of a battalion of the 99th Artillery Regiment would center a smoke-screen around a white cathedral (Target 613) in Brest in order to block observation to the south. However, since the cathedral held food stores, it was not to be shelled. Therefore the fire would be shifted to the south, for example, in order to concentrate the shelling on the southern outskirts of the town. Both of the other batteries would stand ready first of all to place registration rounds at the call of artillery air spotters and for flash-ranging, as well as for fire missions given to them by the commander of the 99th Artillery Regiment.

Understanding that precise timing was vital, the division headquarters ordered all of the units that were equipped with army radio receivers to stand by at midnight on the day before the invasion for a signal that would give the accurate time, and for the compulsory transmission of that time to the remaining units by telephone. After this, all of the watches would be coordinated to show the identical time as given by the signal.

Two days remained until the invasion.

* * *

On 20 June in Bialystok, the headquarters of the NKVD's Border Forces of the Belorussian District issued an order for heightened security: leaves were cancelled until 30 June 1941. Everyone was to be at their assigned posts on the border between the hours of 2300 and 0500, except for those returning from duty details at 2300 and the sentries at the frontier posts. Border detachments were ordered to take position no closer than 300 meters from the border.

* * *

On the morning of 21 June, the command group of the 45th Infantry Division's headquarters moved into a command post (an old casemate in the Terespol Cemetery). The headquarters of Arko 27, the 65th Signals Battalion (with the radio communications center and the telephone exchanges), and I.R. 135 were also located here.

The commander of a machine-gun squad with the 12th [Machine-gun] Company of I.R. 133 Leo Lozert started his combat diary, thinking back to this day:

> Saturday. The summer solstice. In the morning we set up camp in our final bivouac. Several days ago our commander drew up the plan of our positions on the Bug. However, neither I nor anyone else was informed of the situation. Being in an infantry company, though, I had the opportunity to study aerial reconnaissance photographs and a map of the fortress, which later proved quite valuable for me. In the afternoon, Leutnant Schultz took me to the position of our platoon on the Bug.
>
> This was very important, because as a result of this on the following night I was able to instruct not only our company, but also a different company at their positions. Later this was very useful in order to extend the position of my squad on the night of the invasion, since in the darkness I would not have been able to recognize its advantages and shortcomings.
>
> Thus, I could act against targets not only in front of me, as directed, but also from a point 1,000 metres to one side of the citadel. Having done my analysis, as a result of a daytime inspection of the position, I ordered

> the construction of a one-and-a-half-metre-thick wall of compacted earth to shelter two heavy machine guns and further reinforced it with a sufficient number of ammunition cases.

The division's forward headquarters – those officers not part of the command group – was also moving up to the area of the start line. The quartermaster department was inspecting a command post in some woods to the south-west of Wolka Dobrinska. Its commander, the Ib [chief supply officer] Major Karl-Heinz Wirsing, was visiting the rear units: he was temporarily given a field reserve battalion of the division (minus those elements already committed to Galle's mortar battalion, the 81st Pioneer Battalion, or that were cordoning off Terespol).

* * *

1430, 21 June: The schedule of reporting was now on a wartime footing. The first 'daily' reports were arriving: Galle's mortar battalion was ready to open fire from a position 1 kilometer to the north of Kobylian. He had been at his command post since 0700, having set up the telephone and radio communications. Batteries of the 45th Panzerjäger Battalion were beginning to come up. I.R. 135 was implementing its final measures – III/I.R. 135 was setting up two additional groups of squad-sized sentries on the main highway directly to the north of where the Bug River enters Brest from the south. They would be relieved fifteen minutes after daybreak. An assault platoon was deployed east of a building on the main highway, as a reserve for immediate intervention, if necessary, during the seizure of the bridges.

At 1400, the command posts of individual combat units were occupied. The 45th Division's Ic [chief intelligence officer] *Oberleutnant* von Rühling issued the *Führer* Order to the soldiers on the Eastern Front. At 1500, *Leutnant* Meyer received the code word from the XII Army Corps headquarters: 'Dortmund'! That meant the invasion was on for the next day ... That evening, the chief of operations Major Dettmer signaled the code word to the division's units.

* * *

It was on 21 June, the last day before the war, that the headquarters of the Western Special Military District in Minsk, pursuant to a directive of USSR People's Commissariat of Defence and the Red Army General Staff 'in order to increase combat-readiness', ordered the 44th and 47th Rifle corps, and the 17th, 50th, 121st and 161st Rifle divisions to move to camps in the areas that had been designated for them by the covering plan. The General Staff directed that the movement be completed by 1 July. Accordingly, the Western Special Military District headquarters ordered the movement to begin on 23 June. People's Commissar of Defence Timoshenko and Chief of the General Staff Zhukov ordered the border divisions to remain in place, and to move into their defensive areas on the border only upon receipt of a special order. The 47th Rifle Corps was ready to begin moving toward the 4th Army's sector (toward Baranovichi) from Bobruisk and Gomel'.

Around 1800, a 28th Rifle Corps command staff exercise on the subject 'A rifle corps offensive involving the overcoming of a river obstacle', which was being conducted by 4th Army headquarters at the corps' training ground and involved the headquarters of the 6th, 42nd and 75th Rifle divisions, was wrapping up at the command post of the 28th Rifle Corps headquarters in some woods 2 kilometers to the south-east of Zhabinki. The corps headquarters was ordered to remain at its command post until receipt of a special order, while the divisional headquarters were to return to their current locations. Korobkov also set out back to his headquarters from the training ground. In his discussion with the commanders of the divisions and units, he hadn't noticed any enthusiasm for the upcoming field exercise (and inspection of combat equipment) scheduled for 22 June. Having returned to army headquarters in Kobrin, he told Sandalov:

> It isn't hard to understand them – they're worn out. One or two battalions of each rifle regiment are working in the border zone. All week long they've been spending nights in dugouts and tents, and now in addition on Sunday we'll be engaged in training and all sorts of meetings. A stop must be put to this ... The commanders of the units positioned in the fortress pointed out several new observation towers built by the Germans on the other side of the river. They are saying that the sounds of motors are audible at night. Today again several aircraft overflew our territory ...

Sandalov had his own problems – a telegram had arrived at the army headquarters from the headquarters of the Western Special Military District regarding the immediate evacuation of the reserve supplies of the 6th and 42nd Rifle divisions, the stocks of which were located in the Brest Fortress, to a point no less than 30 kilometers to the east of Brest. Leaving them with 1.5 standard combat loads of ammunition, they were ordered to move out thirty-four train car loads of ammunition from the 6th Rifle Division and nine train car loads from the 42nd Rifle Division. This, even though this excess ammunition had been virtually imposed upon their 4th Army by the District's artillery supply organs a short time before against the protests of its headquarters! Such an amount of ammunition couldn't be evacuated in the course of just several hours, but it seems nonetheless that having obtained some rail cars, they managed to begin the loading process.

Around 1900, General Korobkov in a telephone conversation with Klimovsky, the chief of staff of the Western Special Military District, requested permission to move at least the divisions of the Brest garrison out of their billets in the fortress and into their combat sectors. His request was denied: he was only permitted to postpone the field exercise that had been scheduled for 22 June until Monday or Tuesday. Trying to get their minds off their work, Sandalov and Korobkov went to see a performance of the operetta *The Gypsy Baron* at a Belorussian theater. At the same time, Shlykov and the head of the Department of Political Propaganda drove into Brest to attend a concert being put on by a troupe of performing artists from Moscow. In the concert hall there were a lot of men in uniform dress coats.

However, many of them were feeling anxious, uneasy or melancholy. Korobkov was particularly nervous. He had absolutely no interest in the plot unfolding on the stage of the House of the Red Army. Now and again, turning toward Sandalov, he would ask in a whisper, 'Shouldn't we go back to headquarters?' Eventually, without staying for the operetta to finish, they returned to army headquarters.

* * *

Corps commander Popov and his chief of staff G.S. Lukin were on their way to Brest, having left the 28th Rifle Corps' command post. The corps' chief of operations Major E.M. Sinkovsky remained as the senior-in-command at the command post. The mood at the command post was one of bewilderment – many of the officers were wondering why they had been ordered to remain at their posts and had not been given leave in order to go into Brest to spend Sunday with their families.

* * *

Back on 10 June, there had been a graduation ceremony for the new platoon commanders at the Kalinkovichsky Infantry School. Among those who received the rank of lieutenant was Aleksandr Makhnach. On 15 June, their full platoon (minus two individuals) of new lieutenants was assigned to the 42nd Rifle Division in the town of Bereza-Kartuzskaia. However, having arrived at the 4th Army headquarters in Kobrin on the following day, the young lieutenants found out that the 42nd Rifle Division was now in Brest. They arrived there on the evening of 16 June and were received at the headquarters of the 455th Rifle Regiment. Many of them were in fact assigned to serve in this regiment. Makhnach recalls:

> The chief of staff, a senior lieutenant, received us ... [he] informed us that we had to carry on the glorious traditions of the division, which had taken part in the Finnish campaign, and that there were many in the division who'd been awarded medals, including the commander of my future battalion Senior Lieutenant Pankratov. He'd been decorated with the Order of the Red Banner and the 'For Courage' medal. I also found out from the chief of staff that there was one Hero of the Soviet Union in our division.

* * *

On 19 June Lieutenant Makhnach at last took command of a platoon in the 7th Company of the 455th Rifle Regiment's 3rd Battalion and received his side-arm – a pistol. Makhnach's platoon, like the rest of the 3rd Battalion, spent Friday 20 June engaged in tactical exercises outside the city; the subject was 'The Company on Defence'. As always before a weekend, the exercises ended a bit early – before dispersing, the commanders were given an order to appear at the training ground by 0800 on Sunday for the inspection of combat equipment. Saturday, however, the commanders of the units in Brest were given the day off. Toward evening,

Makhnach met with another platoon commander in his company, Junior Lieutenant Smagin, and together they headed off to see a former classmate of Makhnach's at the infantry school, Nikolai Damaratsky, who now commanded a machine-gun platoon in the 84th Rifle Regiment. He had some of Makhnach's things. Damaratsky, who was housed on the second floor of the Ring Barracks, was envious of his friends, because he was getting ready to go to the training ground the following morning. Having stopped by to pick up Smagin's girlfriend, the three friends walked the streets of the city and visited the House of the Red Army. Their route ended at a park in the city center, either the KIM Park or the 1st of May Park. On this day an especially large number of young commanders had gathered there, probably having spotted other familiar faces among the recent graduates. Lectures were delivered, and then a band began to play music, while the lieutenants and their new girlfriends gaily danced the foxtrot.

Sergeant Vladimir Osaulenko, an assistant platoon commander in the 1st Battery of the 18th Separate Machine-gun–Artillery Battalion, was acting as the battery's sentry. As always, so it seemed, its commander had dropped by just an hour before, somewhat upset: 'Why are you here? Get the guys ready, as it should be. Give notice that everyone should come back together. On Monday we'll begin stocking the pillboxes with ammunition and rations . . .' There was still time before Monday, so Osaulenko's soldiers, among them those recently called up from the Ukraine and Samarkand, one after another were heading toward the dance hall. That was the main place for meeting the young ladies of Brest: Poles, Jews and Belorussians were dancing with Ukrainians and Uzbeks, Siberians and Georgians. One of the dancers, the young soldier Reshetilo, the No. 2 man for a Maksim machine gun in one of the pillboxes of the 18th Special Machine-gun–Artillery Battalion's 1st Company, spoiled the mood of his girlfriend: 'A soldier won't be good for you tomorrow . . . war will start.' 'What war?' she replied.

* * *

In these hours, units of the 45th Infantry Division were beginning to form up in their jumping-off areas. The *Führer*'s order was read out to the troops. It dispelled all the remaining doubts – oddly, right up to the final moment, many of the soldiers had believed that there would be no war with the USSR.

Walther Loos, an officer in I/I.R. 130:

> On the evening of 21 June we received an order: with the onset of darkness, we were to begin moving into our carefully reconnoitred and laid out jumping-off areas, and to complete the process by midnight. When the companies stood ready to move into their positions, which they took up in response to an alarm [the positions for the Berta alternative], the *Führer* order was read aloud by the commanders to their men, about the struggle with Bolshevism, which was threatening our empire, leading right up to the enemy's complete destruction. Now no more doubts remained! This meant war against the Soviet Union.

Joseph Wimmer, a signaler with 4/I.R. 130: 'We were stunned – everyone believed that here we were only waiting permission from the Russian leadership for passage rights to Egypt.'

What to say about the soldiers and officers, though, if at the division headquarters, the situation struck everyone differently, sometimes from a rather fantastic angle. Rudolph Gschöpf, a 45th Infantry Division chaplain, writes:

> If you will, there were no longer any doubts that the presence in Poland meant action against Russia. However, these were only conjectures expressed on the basis of circulating rumours. The most widespread among them concerned a pending anti-Communist revolution in Russia, to which supposedly Germany was showing intense interest, supporting the revolutionaries. Moreover, as an expression of gratitude for the support, Germany would receive from the military dictatorship that would be established in Russia a long-term lease of an urgently needed granary (the Ukraine). After which the German armies would cross the Black Sea and further, the Caucasus, to the south towards the Suez Canal. Having seized this, the most vital route in the Middle East, they would force the Western powers to come to terms.

The soldiers and officers of the 45th Infantry Division had no doubt in the success of the upcoming operation. *Leutnant* Michael Wechtler, the commander of 5/I.R. 133, which had been placed in reserve, estimated that it would be 'easy', noting that the line to be reached by the end of the first day was 5 kilometers to the east of Brest. By this time, those who had viewed the fortifications from a distance held the common opinion that 'they were more like ordinary barracks than a fortress.' This optimism was reflected in the fact that only two of the nine infantry battalions, or 22 percent of the infantry strength, would be committed in the initial assault. Three others, in the meantime, would still be deploying, while the remaining four battalions would be held back in the reserve. However, the assignment of such significant strength to the reserve more likely suggests the German command's lack of confidence and its wish to hold reserves ready to overcome any surprises. The first wave would thus be more like a reconnaissance-in-force.

Likely, not everyone shared the optimism of Wechtler and his comrades. The *panzerjäger* Hermann Wild of 14/I.R. 130, while exchanging opinions regarding the upcoming operation with his close friend Müller, who was a member of *Leutnant* Kremers' group, was struck by Müller's premonition that he would die in the assault. It isn't known whether Müller volunteered for the assault boat teams, but the approach of the attack's start time was seriously troubling him.

It isn't known what the division and corps command were experiencing. Subsequently, in July and later, a lot would be said regarding the fact that the difficulties had been anticipated, but that there had been no other option. But now, in these final hours? They had received enough boats and flame-throwers, the heavy artillery – including that of their neighbors – were in their firing positions, and they had the Karl heavy mortars, which were capable of destroying any target in the barrage zone. Possibly, some sense of the unknown was troubling them – the Russian side of the river seemed almost too quiet.

However, the events were now inexorably in motion and could no longer be changed. The units were now making their final preparations for the invasion. Assault groups were being formed and ammunition was being issued. The assault group of the 1st Platoon of 10/I.R. 135, which was formed by *Leutnant* Wieltsch only after the order about the invasion was read out to the troops, assembled around a sand table and began working out the details of the looming assault. With the aim of preserving secrecy, the units' assault groups were organized and given their objectives only several hours before the attack. This adversely affected the effectiveness of their actions.

It was getting dark ... With the setting of the sun, the first wave of the attacking units, striving to keep as silent as possible, moved into their jumping-off lines, which in some places were right on the western bank of the Bug River. The activated movement began quietly and under the strictest discipline.

Leo Lozert writes:

> At 2100 we set off towards the Bug in order to take up our positions. The entire company of heavy machine guns, as well as the heavy weapons of the 133rd Regiment had been activated. Everyone was hauling the mass of ammunition cases and became terribly sweaty.

The colossal Karl heavy mortars were also moving into position. Lozert continues:

> In complete darkness of the night, I saw the wonder-gun 'Thor' [the No. 3 mortar 'Odin' and No. 4 mortar 'Thor' were both in the 2nd Battery] move into its heavily-guarded position. When I wanted to examine this tall marvel, a private stopped me at gunpoint, despite the fact that I was a Feldwebel.

I.R. 130 was also in motion toward the Bug – the first echelon of I/I.R. 130 under the command of *Oberstleutnant* Erich Naber. The war correspondent Gerd Habedanck was moving up with them:

> The battalion commander gives us instructions. Lightly, very quietly we creep right up to the Bug. So that the nails of our boots didn't make any sound, sand had been strewn over the highway. In silent columns, the formed assault groups were moving up along the side of the road. The inflatable rafts they were carrying stood out against the backdrop of the dimly glowing northern sky. A wonder was silently approaching: a heavy anti-aircraft gun being dragged by hand.
>
> The battalion headquarters is located in a solidly-constructed casemate of the old fortress. However, at a distance of only 100 metres, a Soviet-Russian soldier is sitting in a bunker on the opposite side of the Bug from where our destructive fire will begin. What is visible to him is unknown,

> but here we can distinctly hear when they are speaking, and the sounds of a radio in the distance.
>
> Now we know the road. We are returning. On the swaying bridges, we are advancing over the moats of the fortress which are half overgrown with reeds. The dimly gleaming contours of a willow tree stand out above the undergrowth: the preparations are coming to an end.

The time of moving up into the jumping-off positions – from the onset of darkness to midnight (which was the deadline for completing the movement) – was filled with uncertainty. Would the Russian campaign collide with an active defense? A pre-emptive artillery barrage by the Russians prior to midnight would have fallen upon the exposed main forces of the German units and might have prematurely ignited the rocket-launchers, as well as destroyed the units together with their readied crossing equipment. After midnight (according to the order), active measures by the Russians would have provoked the German invasion. As a consequence of the fact that on this night the Germans continued to work on trenches and engaged in other activities that didn't differ from the recent routine on their side, they succeeded in not prompting any suspicions on the Russian side.

In actual fact, though, the movement of the German troops into the start line had been detected (see, for example, the Western Special Military District's final intelligence summary). However, in the sector of the 45th Infantry Division, the final night did in fact pass quietly. The 45th Division's Ic *Oberleutnant* Baron von Rühling indicated that the '... maintenance of secrecy on the German side, conducted in model fashion, averted anticipatory interference by the foe.'

The final hours of the 45th Infantry Division's intelligence department before the start of the invasion were filled with work on documents about Russia, especially the evaluation of the results of observation that had arrived that evening, which noted no substantial changes in the behavior of the opposing side whatsoever. Nevertheless, the night was very tense, because right before the start of the invasion, the Russians, having found out about the German preparations, might pre-empt it with their own attack.

* * *

22.00. The dances in the park were in full swing, but some of the attendees were already leaving – some arm-in-arm with a young woman, others to return to the fortress, hoping to get a little sleep before heading out to the training grounds the next morning ... Makhnach was in no hurry to leave, not now, when in the gathering darkness things were becoming particularly romantic in the park.

Captain Ivan Nikolaevich Zubachev, the assistant commander for supplies of Major Gavrilov's 44th Rifle Regiment, was heading home, as always after it was already dark. Getting a carafe of beer, he had told his wife, 'Shura, spread the table, let's sit down together for a bit this evening.' His sons, the adolescents Iura and Tolia returned home from the movie theater a bit late. Captain Zubachev, embracing them, asked them not to upset their mother 'if anything happens'. They went to sleep late.

Regimental Commissar Efim Moiseevich Fomin, the deputy political commander of the 84th Rifle Regiment – compact, freshly-shaven and ruddy – was holding a short discussion with soldiers of the regiment before a viewing of the film *4-i pereskop* [*The 4th Periscope*]. The session was being held in the 84th Rifle Regiment's club – the former garrison Church of Saint Nikolai. Portraits of Lenin, Stalin and Timoshenko were on the walls, while the film projector was up in the choir balcony. The evening was quiet – one could hear that the film projectors in the various units of the Citadel had already started to show other films like *Chapaev*, *Tsirka* [*The Circus*] and *Ruslan i Liudmila*, as well as documentaries – *Vetra s vostoka* [*Wind from the East*] and *Voennaia prisiaga* [*The Military Oath*]. Some of the viewers were out of sorts for some reason, while the rest reacted with outbursts of laughter to the white-teethed film heroes being shown on the plain white screens. From the club Efim Fomin went to the train station; he had to travel to Daugavpils, where his family still resided at his former place of service. Now Fomin wanted to bring them back to Brest with him. Three days ago, on 19 June, his wife Avgustina in a phone conversation had told him that certain commanders were sending their families to the east. What should she, the wife of a commissar, do? Fomin hesitated in giving an answer. Just recently he had been the deputy political commander not of a regiment, but of a division, the 23rd Rifle Division. Simultaneously, he'd been the chief of its headquarters' Department of Political Propaganda. In March he had been removed from this post and sent to Brest. 'Do whatever the others are doing,' he finally said to Avgustina. But later he had added that the best thing to do would be for him to come and pick them up, and bring them back to Brest. He was 32 years old.

The regiment's duty sentry walked up to the commander of the 44th Rifle Regiment Major Gavrilov. He reported, 'Comrade Major! You are urgently being summoned to division headquarters.'

* * *

It was now 2255: the German regiments were behind schedule in moving into their jumping-off position. The available space was congested and cramped. Nevertheless, despite the logistical problems, the delivery of ammunition for the rocket-launchers had been completed.

Finally, in these hours the 81st Pioneer Battalion obtained the five motorized assault boats at the Biala Podlaska airfield. Surveillance of the Russians across the Bug River was being maintained, but now an order had been given to cease it at the start of the attack. The elements that had previously been activated for this purpose were returning to their units and being given their new assignments. It was stressed that their vehicles and observation equipment (stereoscopes, etc.) had to be returned to headquarters by 0100 on 22 June.

* * *

Around 2300 at the 4th Army headquarters in Kobrin, General Korobkov was summoned to the telephone to receive the call of General Klimovsky, the Western Special Military District's chief of staff, who was passing along Pavlov's order to remain at the headquarters and stand by for further directions. No special instructions were given to bring the troops up to combat-readiness. The sleepless atmosphere reigning at the District headquarters is perceptible in a prepared intelligence summary which was in fact not immediately distributed (the document bears a note: 'Sent 22.06.1941 at 15 hrs 20 min'):

> The large movement of groups of troops in the Terespol area has been systematically noted by observers ... primarily in an eastward direction, as well as trench work on the western bank of the Bug River. Forty trains carrying bridging equipment (wood trusses, iron pontoons) and ammunition have arrived in Biala Podlaska.
>
> Conclusion:
>
> (1) According to available evidence, which is being verified, the bulk of the German army in the sector opposite the Western Special Military District has occupied a jumping-off line.
>
> (2) On every axis, the movement of units and means of reinforcement towards the border is being noted.

Korobkov was restricted by Klimovsky's instructions to summoning senior officers of the army command to headquarters.

* * *

In Brest at the headquarters of the 42nd Rifle Division: meanwhile, for more than an hour, Major Gavrilov and the other unit commanders who had gathered there had been waiting for the division's commander Lazarenko to show up. Where was he? At army headquarters? So in fact they stopped waiting – just before midnight the Regimental Commissar I.N. Bogatikov, having reminded everyone about their need to be present at the inspection the next morning, to increase their vigilance and so forth, dismissed the group of assembled officers.

* * *

Midnight, 22 June 1941. In Bialystok, at the headquarters of the Belorussian NKVD Border Forces, a sleepless night was also expected – the commander of the Brest Border Detachment had reported that a deserter had crossed the river into the USSR west of Volchin, bringing information that Germany was preparing to invade. On the basis of this, the headquarters of the Belorussian NKVD Border Forces issued an order to keep up to 75 percent of the personnel armed, to bring all the border outposts up to full combat-readiness and to repel any possible provocation. But the order still had to be delivered to the outposts... Even so, there is evidence that the border outposts had been put on combat alert already on 21 June. In general, questions regarding the actions taken by the units, Border Forces and the

Red Army (including its air force) immediately prior to the German invasion remain largely unanswered. Who, when, why and what orders were given are not easy to clarify for a variety of reasons.

In Kobrin, at the 4th Army headquarters: at his own responsibility, General Korobkov ordered the printed 'red packets' containing instructions about the steps to be taken in response to a combat alarm (according to the RP-4 covering plan) to be distributed to all the divisions and separate units. The packets were kept at army headquarters, so the District command hadn't yet confirmed his decision.

* * *

0030 (165 minutes prior to the start of the attack): at the 45th Division headquarters in Terespol, there was a sense of relief – prior to 0030, all the subordinate regiments had transmitted the code word 'Kyffhäuser', indicating that they were now assembled in their jumping-off positions. However, *Oberstleutnant* Zahn's *panzerjägers* were still stuck somewhere in the swamps.

0045 (150 minutes prior to the start of the attack): despite Zahn's unknown whereabouts, the completion of the 45th Infantry Division's assembly on its jumping-off line was reported to XII Army Corps headquarters. *Hauptmann* Ressel, the officer responsible for the sector's border security, reported that all the measures had been implemented to prevent the local population from fleeing. Everything was quiet on the Russian side: only the usual sounds of work on fortifications and the maneuvering of the steam engines at the Brest train station were audible.

* * *

Having returned to his quarters on the second floor of one of the pump station's buildings in front of East Fort, Major Gavrilov laid down to sleep, having set his alarm clock for 5 o'clock in the morning.

Staff officers of the 84th Rifle Regiment were still awake. Many were reading books or writing letters home. Commissar Fomin dropped by. According to the recollections of the headquarters' clerk:

> He came by to find out why no one was sleeping. To our question, 'Why haven't you departed?' he replied, 'Something a bit strange ... even unexpected – all the tickets were sold out.' Then he joked a bit and left to sleep. We also headed to bed.

The rustle of dozens of pairs of feet didn't reach the fortress from Brest. There, in the darkness, people were moving from every direction toward the train station. People were beginning to flee the city ...

* * *

0100 (135 minutes before the start of the attack): every hour on the hour, the 4th Army command was contacting the headquarters of the Brest Border Detachment and the subordinate divisions. They were all reporting that German forces had moved up to the line of the Bug. However, the headquarters of the Western

Special Military District didn't issue any orders whatsoever in response to this information. Korobkov, as army commander, had the authority to raise one division on combat alert. However, now genuinely alarmed, before alerting the 42nd Rifle Division, he nevertheless decided first to seek Pavlov's approval of this decision. Pavlov overruled him . . .

Reports were coming in from Brest that the lights were out in several areas of the city, and the water supply system had stopped working. Electric cooking appliances were cooling down in the barracks of the northern compound, and the cooks were swearing up and down, not understanding what had happened. A break in the power lines? An accident at the power station in Kobrin? The loss of electricity occurred only in several areas of the city (for example, at corps headquarters on Levinovsky Street) and at the railroad station. In Brest there were several autonomous sources of electricity, which didn't depend on the Kobrin power station.

At the headquarters of the 17th Border Detachment in Brest: the chief of the detachment, A.P. Kuznetsov, after taking occasional calls from army headquarters, would immediately contact the commandants' offices, or else even get directly in touch with the border posts. At seventeen of the twenty border posts the situation was quiet, but at two of the posts, both south of Brest, the Border Guardsmen were continuing to be concerned by the sound of tank and vehicle engines, and the movement of horse-drawn columns. But such sounds had been heard before at these posts . . . However, there was no response at all from the third post, in the Volchin sector, where the deserter (perhaps sent by the Germans as a provocateur?) had shown up. Kuznetsov, increasingly worried, several times contacted District headquarters, but always received the same reply: 'Stand by for instructions.'

'Finally!' – having received the order from Bialystok, Kuznetsov directed the border posts to go to a condition of combat-readiness, and in the 13th Sector – to prepare the bridge on the Bug River for demolition. The order to go on combat alert began to be transmitted to the commandants' offices.

* * *

0110 (125 minutes before the start of the attack) at the command post of the 45th Infantry Division in Terespol: Zahn turned up on the eastern outskirts of Wolka Dobrinska, his vehicles having overcome the swamps and sand. He reported that he was now ready. Everything else was going according to plan. The units stood motionless in shelters, behind the embankment, in trenches, and in the stands of willows.

Walther Loos of I.R. 130 later wrote:

> The movement into the jumping-off position passed without incidents. The Bug, at only a moderate water level, was flowing lazily by, the moonlight reflecting off its dark waves. The hands on the clock were moving slowly. The assault groups were lying very densely on the bank, ready to spring forward with their inflatable rafts. Behind them were the assault companies, closely packed together in the trenches that had been dug over the

> preceding weeks, right up to the day before, by specially selected groups of workers. Interspersed among them, sometimes in direct physical contact, were command posts, the firing positions of the heavy infantry weapons, reserves, more command posts and reserves, and the firing positions of the artillery and the rocket-launchers, which were much more primitive in design than today. Behind these were jumping-off areas of the panzers and the airfields of various Luftwaffe fighter squadrons – extending for many kilometres into the deep German rear, everything was ready to lunge at the foe at the designated time. The individual senses a special and hard-to-describe feeling among such a highly compressed but precisely designed mechanism.

0125 (110 minutes before the start of the attack): from the headquarters of the Western Special Military District in Minsk, the commanders of the 3rd, 4th and 10th armies were beginning to transmit the directive of the District command, based on the People's Commissar of Defence's Directive No. 1 regarding a possible surprise invasion by the *Wehrmacht* in the course of 22–23 June 1941:

> 1. A surprise attack by the Germans ... is possible during the course of 22–23 June 1941.
> 2. The mission of our forces is to avoid provocative actions of any kind, which might cause major complications ... At the same time ... forces are to be at full combat-readiness to meet a surprise blow by the Germans or their allies.
> 3. I order:
>   (a) Secretly man the firing points of the fortified regions on the state borders during the night of 22 June 1941.

The orders began to go out to the army headquarters. There was no contact with the 4th Army. Communications between its headquarters in Kobrin and both the Western District headquarters and its subordinate forces had just suddenly been broken.

* * *

0130 (105 minutes before the start of the attack), at the Imenin airfield of the 123rd IAP [Fighter Aviation Regiment], which was tasked with covering Brest: back at the beginning of nightfall on all the airfields of Colonel Belov's aviation division, the aircraft had been dispersed and camouflaged beside the airfield. The pilots were sent into shelters. This didn't include the flights of the duty squadron – its pilots were already seated in the cockpits of their aircraft, ready to take off into the night sky at any minute. The commander of the 123rd IAP Major Surin was sleeping in his headquarters, still fully dressed, when a new order came in – to raise the regiment to full combat-readiness. One after the other on the airfields of Imenin, Brest and Loshitsy, the engines on the I-153 fighters, fully loaded with ammunition for their ShKAS machine guns, were started up.

Only no one approached the twenty brand-new Yak-1 fighters, which had arrived at Imenin only the day before. There was no fuel, ammunition or pilots for them.

0200 (75 minutes before the start of the attack): the 45th Infantry Division signaler Rudolph Gschöpf is surveying the ground over which the division is to attack. From the window, he can see the flat field that extends to the railroad bridge that leads across the border. At that moment, a train is crossing it, carrying goods from the USSR to Germany in accordance with the German–Russian economic agreement signed in 1939.

Almost immediately next to his building, the primitive frameworks of the loaded rocket-launchers were standing in their firing positions:

> 'On the other side,' he would later write, 'in the citadel, inside the houses, the barrack objectives and casemates, all appeared to be sleeping unconcerned. The waters of the Bug lapped peacefully while a tepid night lay over territory where, in a few blinks of an eye, death and destruction would break out. The nearer H-hour approached, the more terribly the minutes dragged.'

In Brest, the park closed. The last couples were drifting away. Makhnach was walking along the nighttime streets toward the fortress, together with other young commanders who had received a leave until 0200. Among them was Senior Sergeant Ivan Dolotov, a platoon commander in the 33rd Engineer Regiment, who had been at the city theater before going for a stroll. Now heading back to the fortress, he encountered a young citizen Znoska, who 'worked part-time in the repair shop and searched for apartments for the command staff.' According to his memoirs:

> Znoska walked quietly along the road to the fortress for a while, but then suddenly stopped me and advised me not to go to the fortress. I was very surprised by this sudden turn of events and noted that he obviously had never served in the military and that he didn't know what a liberty pass or military discipline were, or that being five minutes late already meant a duty detail or some reprimand. He declared that this was all just a trifle, that he knew what service meant, but there was ample evidence that war was about to begin. As confirmation he alluded to the nearly instantaneous disappearance of salt, matches and other products in the shops and at the market: 'Ours know that this is war, as it was in 1939 when the Germans attacked Poland.' I, of course, laughed at such not very compelling arguments and we said our goodbyes. I entered the fortress, while he turned off down one of the city's streets.

On the German side at this time, the final decisions were being made. Men with watches had a special status. At the unit command posts, the subordinate commanders were coordinating their watches. Leo Lozert: 'All the commanders of the heavy machine-gun companies, including ours, were ordered to return.' The unflappable Gerd Habedanck had managed to take a nap: 'The alarm clock rattles in the vehicle. Time to rise! The great day has started. In the east, the sky is already glistening like silver. Noiselessly we walk along the familiar road to the command post.'

* * *

0230 (45 minutes before the start of the attack), at the headquarters of the 4th Army in Kobrin: communications had been re-established. In Zaprudy and Zhabinka, signalers discovered that dozens of meters of line had been cut out in a number of places. Immediately, the District commander summoned the 4th Army commander to the Boudot device – Korobkov and Sandalov quickly descended the staircase into the cellar, where the army's communications center was located. Here, under the light of kerosene lamps, almost all the important staff officers of the 4th Army headquarters had gathered. They were exchanging uneasy glances – a directive to bring all the units to combat-readiness was being transmitted by the Western Special Military District headquarters! Next, Pavlov gave Korobkov specific instructions, but he was still being cautious:

> Your assignment is to capture German troops that have penetrated. Do not cross the state border ... Quickly and quietly move the 42nd Rifle Division out of the fortress 'in batches' in order to move into the prepared positions. You are stealthily to occupy the pillboxes of the Brest Fortified District with units.

... Entering the fortress, Dolotov felt disturbed by Znoska's strange premonitions, though around him everything was quiet. Returning to his company, he was immediately reporting to the duty sentry, just as a messenger from headquarters approached and ordered an armed signaler to be sent to Brest immediately. Within five minutes a signaler had ridden up on a horse, but he was now waiting for ammunition to be issued. Suddenly, though, it turned out that there were no cartridges in the company – all 600 rounds had been given to the guard detail of the duty company. They had to rouse the sergeant major of a neighboring unit who was on duty, listen to all his grumbling, and borrow three rifle cartridge clips. After this, Dolotov hit the sack and instantly fell asleep.

However, not everyone was sleeping – in some places they were playing chess, in others men were whiling away both time and shifts in numerous alert detachments (totaling about a battalion at full combat-readiness), and kitchen details were cooking food for the morning. Having returned to the fortress, Lieutenant Makhnach decided to drop by the company's position before going to sleep to check whether the soldiers had folded their uniforms and cleaned their weapons.

* * *

0245 (30 minutes before the start of the attack): having finished receiving Pavlov's message, Korobkov immediately contacted the 42nd Rifle Division's chief of staff Major V.L. Shcherbakov. Shcherbakov began to assemble the unit commanders in order to give them their orders, and tried to locate the division commander.

* * *

0300 (15 minutes before the start of the attack). Gschöpf writes:

> Soon after 0300 we were dismissed and stood about waiting on the dissipating twilight. There was not the slightest evidence of the presence of the assault groups and companies directly on the Bug. They were well-camouflaged. One could well imagine the taut nerves that were reigning among men, who, in a few minutes, would be face to face with an unknown enemy.

Likely, this is purely artistic license – Gschöpf, it seems, was in the sector of I/I.R. 135 – and there the soldiers were lying prone behind a berm. Most likely, in the entire divisional sector, only the machine-gunners of *Oberstleutnant* Loertzer's 12/I.R. 133 were directly on the riverbank, and they were crouching in trenches. However, this inspiring image (soldiers of the *Wehrmacht* directly on the bank of the Bug River, in front of Brest) became one of the most widely-circulated.

* * *

Having checked his sleeping platoon, Makhnach decided not to return to his quarters, but to stretch out right there, on a couch in the office of the company commander: a 3 × 4 meter room in the corner of the barracks, walled off by boards from the soldiers' portion of the space. However, the orderly was already occupying the couch. The young lieutenant, deciding not to disturb the sleeping orderly, lay down on a love seat in the neighboring company's headquarters, and immediately fell sound asleep.

* * *

0310 (5 minutes before the start of the attack), the command post of Panzer Group 2 in a lookout tower to the south of Bohukaly, 15 kilometers north-west of Brest-Litovsk. It was still dark. Panzer Group commander Heinz Guderian arrived:

> Detailed study of the behaviour of the Russians convinced me that they knew nothing of our intentions. We had observations of the courtyard of the Brest-Litovsk citadel and could see them drilling by platoons to the music of a military band. The strongpoints along their bank of the Bug were unoccupied. They had made scarcely any noticeable progress in strengthening their fortified positions during the past few weeks. So the prospects of our attack achieving surprise were good and the question arose whether the one-hour artillery preparation which had been planned was now necessary after all. I finally decided not to cancel it; this was simply a precaution lest unexpected Russian counter-measures cause us unavoidable casualties.

0314 (one minute before the start of the attack): the commanders of the 14th Mechanized Corps and the 10th Composite Aviation Division, who had been summoned by Korobkov, arrived at the 4th Army headquarters in Kobrin. At that moment, an urgent message began to come in from the Western District's commander-in-chief, now that communications with the 4th Army headquarters had been restored. The telegraph began to tap out the text of People's Commissar of Defence Timoshenko's Directive No. 1, instructing Korobkov to put his divisions on combat alert and to counter any German surprise attack, but at the same time not to succumb to German provocations and not to take any other measures without special orders.

... Brest, Levanovsky Street, the headquarters of the 28th Rifle Corps: Colonel Krivosheev arrived with a written order for corps commander Popov, which spelled out the corps' tasks in the event that a combat alert was declared. There was still no electricity at the headquarters. The corps commander began to read the order under the light of a kerosene lamp.

... The 42nd Rifle Division headquarters: regiment and battalion commanders were gathering in the office of its chief of staff. Division commander Lazarenko had not yet been located. For some reason, the commander of the 44th Rifle Regiment Major Gavrilov was also absent ...

... The border posts at Brest had still not received the order about going to full combat-readiness. However, everyone understood that it seemed something out of the ordinary was occurring – it was strangely silent, and for some reason the dogs of the German Border Guards were also silent.

... At the Terespol railroad bridge: the next shift of German sentries had arrived. One of them checked his watch. All the other 'sentries' for some reason at this moment were standing particularly close to the Russian post.

Gerd Habedanck in Terespol, at the command post of the 45th Infantry Division's III/I.R. 135: 'A profusion of shoving, steel helmets, rifles, the constant shrill sound of telephones, and the quiet voice of the Oberstleutnant drowning everything else out, rising above it all: "Gentlemen, it is 0314 hours, still one minute to go."'

Part II

The Assault

Chapter 5

Like a Knife through Butter

0315: 'Anemone'

It started! The earth shook ... Along the entire front, the German artillery opened fire. The 10th Company and the command post of III/I.R. 135, which were situated in old fortress shelters about 30 meters from the Bug, were not far from the wall of explosions on West Island (though only the infantry guns of I.R. 133 and two batteries of II/A.R. [Artillery Regiment] 98 were targeting this area). *Gefreiter* Hans Teuschler, a squad leader in the 10th Company's 1st Platoon, confessed after the war that he never experienced such a powerful artillery barrage elsewhere during the entire Second World War: 'The sky was filled with bursting shells of every calibre. It was an awful roaring, exploding, crackling and howling as if hell was actually about to come on earth.' He and his comrades were gripped by an 'uncanny feeling' ...

The opening of the artillery barrage was no less stunning to Gerd Habedanck, who was located in a neighboring bunker:

> We had barely heard it when the earth shook, boomed and rolled. Strong drafts of air blew into our faces. It was the artillery strike! The Oberstleutnant was correct when he told me yesterday, 'It will be like nothing you have experienced before.' ... An infernal whistling, droning and crackle of explosions filled the air. Young willows were bent over as if in a storm.

However, the machine-gunners of Loertzer's 12/I.R. 133 were even closer to the Bug. The unflappable Lozert wrote: 'The fireworks began on the dot. Long minutes. It was very fine. We had no casualties.'

A little bit to the south, among the soldiers of I/I.R. 130, was Walther Loos:

> It seemed that a curtain over the terrors of the underworld rose above our heads. At first we were still hearing the discharges, the thunder and howling of wailing shells passing overhead, streaking in death-dealing trajectories towards the opposite bank from hundreds of barrels ranging from the smallest to the largest calibre. Involuntarily ducking our heads, we were almost forgetting to breathe. However, a second later the artillery fire of a different heavy gun gathered such a deafening and breath-taking strength like I never experienced later. Even those participants in the First

> World War among us later acknowledged that at that time, they had never experienced fire of such concentrated power. The sky turned red, and even though it was night, it became as light as day. Large trees fringing the Bug swayed wildly and were torn to pieces as if from an invisible force by the atmospheric pressure of the passing shells. Over four minutes of time, 60,000 rocket shells, which were being used for the first time in combat with electrical ignition, fell on the Russian-held bank. They launched sheaves of 6–12 rockets with fiery tails like comets, and their howling muffled the storming of our own artillery.

Incidentally, according to Loos the artillery preparation started around 0300 and swelled to its maximum strength by 0311. Moreover, he wildly exaggerated the number of shells launched by the *nebelwefers* during the preparation. Indeed, what could have startled the soldier so? After all, the *nebelwerfers* and the Karl siege mortars were not given targets on the western sides of the South and West Islands (in order to avoid striking their own forces), so only 13/I.R. 133 was working over the ground in front of I.R. 130. Possibly it was the thunder of the launching of the rockets that spooked them (at that time the weapon was still relatively rare, and moreover, rocket-launchers of that caliber were being used for the first time) – as well as the excessively wide scattering of the rocket shells.

Just as in I.R. 135's sector, in the sector of I.R. 130's forced crossing, in the wake of the artillery's rapid series of volleys, the heavy machine guns opened up, striving to keep their fire at a height of approximately 1 meter above the Russian-held bank. Somewhat to the north, 11/I.R. 135 rushed forward on bicycles: dinghies were already waiting for them in bushes along the riverbank. *Leutnant* Engelhardt's anti-aircraft gunners, which had been assigned to target two pillboxes on the southern tip of West Island opposite the positions of the 10th Company from point-blank range, opened fire from their 88mm anti-aircraft guns. However, the anti-aircraft gunners could only place their first several shots on target before everything became blanketed by smoke. Swinging their guns back and forth, they continued to fire in the direction of the fires that were now raging on the entire island.

At the railroad bridge, Rudolph Gschöpf watched as the shells from the Karl heavy mortars raised enormous geysers of black smoke on West Island. The earth shook, debris went flying into the air, and smoke covered the horizon. Ashes, carried by the wind, began to fall from the sky. Deafened by the heavy artillery, he almost couldn't hear as the machine guns opened up at the railroad bridge. There, the assault team had barely had time to pull their knives from the bodies of the Russian sentries – one of them, already dying, nevertheless managed to fire a shot. From behind the berm, infantrymen and combat engineers of *Leutnant* Zumpe's assault group (3/I.R. 135), riding bicycles, were already hurrying toward the bridge. The guns and machine guns attached to Zumpe's company, destroying the huts of the bridge's security outposts in a matter of moments, continued to fire at any aperture from which a machine-gun burst might come. Every second counted. Zumpe's group pedaled furiously as their bicycles sped across the bridge's wood decking.

Sappers of 1/81st Pioneer Battalion and of the 1st Railroad Engineer Battalion were dashing forward on foot. They were trying to stick close to the iron girders of the bridge, hoping that the Russians wouldn't have time to blow it up before they reached the detonation cord. They were meters away from it when a machine gun opened up from a Russian emplacement. However, *Gefreiter* Holtzer's machine gun immediately suppressed the hostile machine gun. Leaping from their bicycles, the combat engineers rushed the bunker and finished it off. A white flare soared into the sky and Holtzer ceased fire. Now the main task was to locate and disarm the demolition charges.

* * *

In Terespol at the command post of the 45th Division, its command staff was exchanging their impressions of the first minutes. The concentrated fire on the Brest Citadel in the division's sector was clearly visible. According to the messages coming in from everywhere, the sequential salvoes of the lined-up *nebelwerfer* rocket-launchers, which were being used for the first time, made the strongest impression in the first moments. However, in distinction from Gschöpf, the units were noting that the discharges and shell impacts from the 600mm mortars were being lost amidst the tempest of the artillery fire. Several tall columns of fire on the enemy territory indicated the destruction of fuel or ammunition dumps; enemy resistance was nil. Only far in the distance, many kilometers beyond Brest to the east, the tracers of anti-aircraft fire were rising into the sky, apparently defending against a low-altitude *Luftwaffe* attack.

* * *

It was now 0319. The tracers visible from the 45th Division's command post were from the Imenin airfield's anti-aircraft defenses at Kobrin, which in accordance with Soviet standards required five to ten minutes to open fire. Most likely, the anti-aircraft units were firing at He-111 squadrons that were barely visible against the sky, which was only beginning to lighten.

Over these four minutes since the artillery barrage had begun, the Citadel had turned into a sea of fire. There, wherever the 600mm shells from the Karl mortars struck, there were no surviving eyewitnesses. Or more accurately, at the 45th Division's command post to the west of the Bug River, it seemed that had to be the case. Along the western bank of West Island, the listening posts had been wiped out, and several buildings were in flames. The north-west of West Island particularly suffered – the *nebelwerfers* and the Karl siege mortars were both working over that part of the island. The latter were striking at the pillboxes, next to which in a casemated redoubt was the District school for Border Guards' drivers. However, the explosions of the *nebelwerfer* and Karl shells, which seemed so picturesque to the German observers, weren't having the anticipated effect. There was no one in the pillboxes or in the fieldworks. Those Border Guards who were not manning listening posts were either in the Citadel or in the rear casemates under a thick layer of earth. Neither the *nebelwerfers* nor the guns of the 98th Artillery Regiment were able to penetrate the massive walls of the Citadel. Two Karl shells (it was their explosions that indeed Gschöpf had witnessed) dropped with a thunderous crash, but of course, only those who were close to the point of impact were struck down.

The main victims of the first minutes of the war were the Border Guardsmen who had gathered for the cavalry and sports' courses – their building collapsed, burying many of those who were inside it beneath the ruins. Fire became the main problem for those who survived the collapse – the heat and smoke didn't allow them to breathe.

Nevertheless, the Border Guardsmen, the soldiers of the transport company and the cadets of the District's driving school, having instantly dressed and grabbed a weapon, emerged at a run out of the burning buildings to take up a defense or to attempt to take cover from the incoming fire in the unfinished pillboxes and the multi-entranced casemated redoubt to the right of the road running from the Terespol Gate to the Bug, which held stockpiles of captured Polish weapons. Several student drivers spotted someone moving in the ruins of the barracks occupied by the cavalrymen and sportsmen, and managed to dig two of them out. More soldiers not cut down by the incoming fire took shelter in the casemates of the Ring Wall. Their commanding officers, who were billeted on West Island, were already running to join their troops. The entire northern side of the island was enveloped in smoke – indeed, it seemed that the 45th Division, when planning the assault, believed that none of the defenders there would survive the artillery barrage. Consequently, it was precisely because of this conviction that the northern end of West Island remained untouched by an infantry assault. The smoke, which blotted out half the sky, obstructed observation and targeted fire, and which prevented an accurate assessment of the situation became the first problem confronting Engelhardt's 88mm anti-aircraft gunners and the German command post in Terespol.

Targeting South Island, two 150mm guns of the 130th Artillery Regiment were pounding the riverbank; the guns of I/A.R. 98 were shelling the area of the Southern Gate, while two batteries of Galle's mortar battalion focused their fire on the hospital. *Nebelwerfers* were also rocketing the hospital, but because of their unpredictable trajectories, the shells landed across the entire island. However, it was in fact the rocket shells that inflicted the most terrible damage – the hospital erupted in flames. Patients and medical personnel that escaped the building took cover in underground casemates and cellars. But many of the approximately eighty patients in the surgery ward were bedridden. Having woken up from the thunder of the artillery and the sharp sound of shell fragments striking the walls of their ward, in terror they soon caught the smell of smoke …

There were practically no troops on South Island, and likely the Border Guardsmen manning the listening posts were all killed during the artillery barrage on the sector of the riverbank. The most potent combat force on South Island was soldiers of the 95th Medical-Sanitation Battalion and the men enrolled in the 84th Rifle Regiment's regimental school that was located between the hospital and the Ring Wall. They were reliable soldiers, but they had a serious problem – a shortage of ammunition and weapons. At the start of the artillery barrage, the men of the regimental school thought to dash to Central Island – but they saw they would have to cross beaten, exposed ground. As a result they took cover in the Ring Wall at the Southern Gate, with the intention to wait for the 'main forces' to come up. A few of the surviving Border Guardsmen also fell back to the same place.

On North Island, the first minutes of the war were filled with the explosions of heavy artillery shells and rocket shells. The *nebelwerfers* were firing a mixture of high-explosive and incendiary shells at its western side, blocking the path to any force that might attempt a counter-attack against the railroad bridge that had just been captured; the 2nd Battery of the 31st Division's Nebelwerfer Battalion was targeting West Fort, while the 1st Battery pounded the East Fort. Elements of the 125th Rifle Regiment were billeted on the western side of North Island. The rocket-launchers' blow fell on its semi-empty barracks. As happened everywhere else their shells landed, the strong walls withstood the attack, but the incendiary shells ignited fires. The majority of the soldiers in the area were in the barracks; there were few casualties, though outside 'shells were landing on every square meter'.

Unfortunately, there is no information about what happened at the West Fort during the German preparatory barrage. But at the East Fort, where the stables and the 333rd Rifle Regiment's ammo dump were located in the outer wall, and the transportation company and the 1st Battery of 76mm anti-aircraft guns of the 393rd Separate Anti-aircraft Artillery Battalion were in the inner wall, the response to 'Anemone' was rather calm. When the first shells struck the earthen walls, the casemates within them hardly quivered. Awakened, the soldiers didn't understand what had happened: 'Some shouted that it was thunder, others thought it was an earthquake; someone even thought to yell that Germany was invading Hungary.' The thickness of the earthwork and the casemate walls protected the Red Army men; only the sentry guarding the ammunition stores was killed. Dressing, the soldiers began to run outside.

The thunderous explosions of the first shells also roused the residents of the apartment complexes located in front of the East and West Forts, where the commanders of the units stationed in Brest lived together with their families. The majority of them instantly realized what was happening. Leaping out of bed, M.P. Kropel'nitskaia threw on only a coat, grabbed and dressed her child, and descended the staircase to the first floor, where she already found her neighbors, the Kolesnikovs (his wife, two children and elderly mother). Captain Gonchar (the 3rd Company commander in the 333rd Rifle Regiment), who lived on the first floor, was at home at this moment. Mrs Kropel'nitskaia recalls,

> He gathered his family and all of us, and we ran towards the streams that were located near the embankment of the storage depot. Several soldiers were already there. Gonchar shoved us towards them and then set off at a run towards his unit's location.

The commander of the 37th Separate Signal Battalion's 2nd Telegraph Cable Company, Junior Lieutenant Aleksandr Bobkov, directed his wife to wrap their 3-year-old daughter in a blanket and to dress their 6-year-old son. In a matter of minutes, having dashed outside, he ran toward a magazine, which had been converted into a storage room. Dar'ia Prokhorenko (the wife of Junior Lieutenant I.V. Prokhorenko, who commanded the 333rd Rifle Regiment's 2nd Machine-gun Company) and her three young children in these minutes found shelter at the East Fort in a stable of the 333rd Rifle Regiment:

> There was a loud explosion, which blew out a window in our room. Half asleep, I thought it was a clap of thunder. But just then bullets (actually, these were shell fragments from the barrage of the 34th Infantry Division's nebelwerfers, which were striking Target 608, West Fort) began to buzz past, embedding in the wall next to our bed. I took cover with the children behind the stove, not knowing what was happening or what I should do next. But then my husband told me to follow him in a crawl, making sure not to stand up. He said that the enemy had crossed the frontier. He told me, 'I'll lead you and the children into the cellar, and then I'll head to my unit.' He took us into the cellar and then left.

Junior Lieutenant Prokhorenko would go missing in action during the break-out attempt from the East Fort at 2200 on 24 June. According to P.M. Gavrilov's recollections, Prokhorenko was leading one of the break-out groups …

This first wave of North Island refugees, who fled their homes virtually within a moment after the start of the barrage, often only in night robes and having had the time only to grab their children, was the 'luckiest', suffering the fewest losses. They found shelter primarily in the casemates along the embankment of the Muchavec River, and in the former magazines and rear security barracks of the East and West Forts and of the Main Wall – just as did E.I. Kostiakova, the wife of the deputy political commander of the 98th Separate Anti-tank Artillery Battalion, A.A. Kostiakov:

> I woke up from a terrible rumble and crashing. My husband was already on his feet and dressed, and was fastening the clasp of his watch on his arm. He told me, 'Don't be afraid. It is the exploding shells of the anti-aircraft gunners.' I listened to him for a moment, before leaping out of bed and saying to him, 'This is war.' He replied, 'Yes, but don't be afraid, they'll evacuate all you women straight away; run to headquarters.'

Kostiakova, together with six to eight other women and ten children, having run to the Main Wall, took cover in the repair shops on both sides of the Eastern Gate. Soon, several wounded artillerymen of the 98th Separate Anti-tank Artillery Battalion came running into the same places.

However, many families, having descended to the first floor of their apartment buildings, had nowhere to go, or they lingered to pack up their valuables, hoping that the German shells would spare the living quarters. Moreover, to run anywhere across the grounds, which were blanketed with shell explosions, was just as dangerous as remaining at home. One such family was that of the commander of the 125th Rifle Regiment's 2nd Rifle Battalion, Captain Vladimir Shablovsky: his wife Galina and their four daughters, the oldest of which was 8, and the youngest, just 8 months. On the night of 21 June, the majority of Shablovsky's companies had moved out to work on building fortifications of the Fortified District. Only the regiment's alert unit, the 2nd Rifle Battalion's 4th Company, remained inside the fortress. On days off Shablovsky himself remained at home, in Building No. 5 of the officers' residential complex. Stocky, compact and with a powerful physique, Shablovsky had exceptional physical strength. In the regiment Shablovsky had the reputation of being a capable, demanding and strong-willed commander. Woken up by the explosions that were shaking the fortress, Shablovsky and his wife, having grabbed their daughters, went down to the first floor – there, under the staircase, the frightened wives and children of other officers that lived in this building were milling in confusion. Shablovsky was first and foremost a battalion commander – leaving his family, in only his underwear he took off at a run toward the regiment's position, where his battalion's 4th Company was located. Other commanders, who lived in the residences of the command staff, having quickly dressed, were running beside him toward the same place.

It was precisely the Citadel which received most of the *nebelwerfers*' fire. The rocket shells were unable to penetrate the walls, but those buildings with windows that faced the south-west were set aflame by the incendiary shells. The entire roof of the Ring Barracks began to burn, as did the vehicles of the 31st Motorized Transport Battalion and the billets of the 333rd Rifle Regiment, the windows of which faced the church. After the rocket-launchers' strike, there was virtually no one left alive in the Citadel's interior courtyard, though in the wee morning hours of this Sunday, there were not many people there; only sentries and those men of the designated personnel in several of their tents. No one survived to talk about the effects of these large-caliber rocket shells or their own experiences under their barrage. The only eyewitnesses left to talk about the *nebelwerfer* attack and its effects were the Germans employing them. Helmuth Böttcher, an assault group sapper, recalled their effect on the enemy:

> We used rockets . . . They didn't fly far, but their effect was horrifying. I believe that then there was nothing worse . . . Everyone within a perimeter of approximately 3.5 meters of the explosion perished, killed by the resulting vacuum that destroyed the lungs of both people and animals. It was terrible. In general everyone saw people simply sitting there, motionless, frozen like puppets. Ja! Many had wounds, but some were just sitting there on chairs and benches. Death was guaranteed and came very quickly . . . It was terrible!

Ivan Dolotov woke up from the thunder of explosions – fire was raging on the second floor in the sector of the 84th Rifle Regiment, the third floor was also burning, as was the watchtower of the White Palace. Sheds, hay in the stables and piles of firewood in the courtyard were all ablaze. In these minutes, it was precisely the barracks of the 84th Rifle Regiment, the White Palace and the large building holding the Engineering Directorate that the 1st and 2nd batteries of the 34th

Infantry Division's Nebelwerfer Battalion were targeting. The 1st Battery was firing on the north-west portion of the Citadel, at the boundary between the 44th and 455th Rifle regiments. The resounding explosions of thirty-six 210mm shells only shook the garrison – those who didn't immediately run outside feverishly began to get dressed after the first explosions, to search for their weapons and to take shelter in the cellars. Those who had darted out into the yard were killed under the heavy artillery's barrage.

0319–0325: 'Vinca'

Having fired off most of their ammunition, the *nebelwerfers* in their firing positions were beginning to fall silent. Enormous clouds of smoke were blanketing the sky above West Island across from the positions of III/I.R. 135. It still hadn't grown light: cinders, columns of smoke and ashes were blocking the early morning sun's rays. The barrage on the zone of the riverbank had ceased, but 13/I.R. 133 was continuing to pound the island's interior; now it was up to the infantry. Leaping from their bunkers, in several bounds the 10th Company's first wave reached the bank of the Bug and slid their dinghies down into the water. Officers of the III Battalion command post linked up with them there, as well as did war correspondent Habedanck. Immediately, the machine-gunners of Loertzer's company opened fire at previously revealed targets. Habedanck describes the scene: 'One boat after another slid into the water. There were excited cries, splashing and howling of assault boat engines. Not a shot from the other bank as blood-red flames dance in the water. We jump on shore and press forward.' The same picture was repeated up and down XII Army Corps' sector.

The first echelon of I.R. 130's battalions moved out – on the left were companies of *Oberstleutnant* Naber's I Battalion, while Major Hartnack's II Battalion advanced on the right. Major Ulrich's III Battalion followed in the regiment's second echelon. The organized assault groups leaped from their shelters, crossed the several meters to the Bug in several rapid bounds, dragging their small inflatable rafts to the water, and began paddling toward the opposite bank with all their might.

Finally, I/I.R. 135 also received the go-ahead: the bridge had been cleared of mines – Forward! The boots of the soldiers of Major Oeltze's battalion began clattering across the bridge. At 0325, other companies of I.R. 135's I Battalion went into motion.

The crossing of the Bug was being conducted in two sectors. Men of 3/I.R. 130 were also dragging their assault boats to the Bug. *Leutnant* Kremers' assault group consisted of volunteers: they faced the most dangerous task – at top speed they were to paddle between the Russian-held West and South Islands, and having reached the Muchavec between the Kholm and Terespol Gates, they were to turn to the right. There they were to paddle quickly up the Muchavec along the Russian-held Central Island and seize bridges that were undoubtedly well-guarded and already prepared for defense. Kremers' soldiers had already labored to drag their assault boats to the Bug... Suddenly, there were explosions in the very midst of them, resulting in the deaths of the first men of the 45th Infantry Division to be killed in the battle and the cries of the wounded. The Russians?! Kremers was stunned ... four of the nine boats had been destroyed, and twenty soldiers of the 3rd Company were either dead or wounded.

Half the group had been lost before even crossing the border! How had this happened? Had the Russian artillery opened up? No, this was the work of their own *nebelwerfers*. There was a reason why all the German troops crouched in their jumping-off positions had been apprehensive, observing the rockets' wild flights.

Hermann Wild described the events somewhat differently. According to him, the rocket salvo struck Kremers' group after it had launched. Among the killed was his friend Müller, who five hours before had been downcast by a premonition of his own death ...

Josef Gusenbauer of I.R. 133's platoon of combat engineers recalled:

> I, like the majority of other 'comrades', was designated to be a navigator of a large inflatable boat. Our mission was to transport soldiers of I.R. 130 across the Bug five minutes after the war began. The rounds of some of the German guns were falling short, jeopardizing several of the assault boats. We had just reached the arm of the river in our fully loaded inflatable boat, when to the left, right and behind our assault boats, enormous geysers of water rose from dropping shells. I (as the navigator) was sitting on the rear section of our inflatable boat, when suddenly I fell backward into the water. A large shell fragment had torn the rear inflatable chamber directly under my butt. This incident failed to shake the calm of the infantrymen now swimming with me. They were paddling, trying to reach the opposite bank as quickly as possible, and there to clear it, having gone on the attack. Meanwhile I, up to my chest in the water, was moving the damaged boat back toward the friendly bank.

The 11th Company crossed without any particular problems. To the north, from behind the berm, the fresh soldiers of Oeltze's I Battalion were already dashing across the railroad bridge that had been seized by Zumpe's assault group.

0326–0335: 'Crocus' and 'Lily'

On West Island, two more shells from the Karl siege mortars dropped in the same locations. Border Guardsmen and the drivers being trained in the District's driving school were continuing to hunker down in the walls. They couldn't emerge – the contents of the *nebelwerfers*' incendiary shells continued to burn. In addition to the Karls, the mortars of one of Galle's batteries were pounding the northern portion of the island. Shellfire was subsiding in the center of the island – there, where the 11th Company's boats were heading toward the bank.

On South Island, the Red Army men were still in no position to resist; German heavy artillery was ranging over it and the buildings of the hospital were burning. There, in the smoke the bedridden patients in the surgery ward were waiting for their own agonizing deaths.

Nurse Praskov'ia Tkacheva was not on duty that night. However, as soon as the rocket salvoes had ceased and it seemed that the German barrage had lessened, she overcame her fears and ran to the hospital. Quickly climbing the stairs to the surgery ward on the second floor, she plunged into the smoke-enveloped room and grabbed the first patient she came across. To the cries of the other patients and the resumed thunder of exploding shells outside, she hauled the patient to shelter. There was little time …

On North Island, soldiers of the units in the East Fort were leaving its shelter at a run. Fragments of the exploding shells fired by the 34th Infantry Division's Nebelwerfer Battalion wounded many of them. Nevertheless, the men kept heading to their guns. The alert battery was to open fire within five minutes of the declaration of an alarm, and the combat alert in their barracks was announced when the first German shells began exploding on the island.

Mortars of the 31st Infantry Division were firing on the West Fort. Its walls were shaking, but the shells were failing to penetrate them. However, several shells dropped directly on the homes of the command staff located in front of the fort. Those commanders and their wives who had still not fled were feverishly getting dressed, and taking their children into their arms, they were trying to grab whatever was of most value in their meager possessions. In a room on the second floor of Building No. 9 lived the family of Ivan Pochernikov, who was a senior *politruk* (political leader) and the acting secretary of the 333rd Rifle Regiment's Party bureau: his wife Aleksandra (a kindergarten teacher) and their 5-year-old son Alik and 6-year-old daughter Nina. Across the street, in Building No. 8, also on the second floor, was the Dzhindzhishvili family – he was the chief of the 333rd Rifle Regiment's regimental school. His wife Tamara Dzhindzhishvili recalls:

> We were close friends with the Pochernikovs. The residential buildings began to be shelled simultaneously with the barracks. Undressed, we went out into the corridor. Opposite, through a window, one could see Shura [affectionate name for Aleksandra] bustling about the children's beds as her husband Vania [affectionate name for Ivan] was handing her items for the children to wear. At that moment, a shell struck the building, which sheaved off the exterior wall and part of the structure like an axe. When the dust settled, I could see only Vania and Shura. There were no children; they and their beds were buried under rubble from the wall. I began to shout, but they didn't hear me. Shura received a leg wound from the shell's explosion. Vania was wounded in the face by shell fragments, and blood was flowing down his face. Transfixed, I pulled Tamazi closer to myself and looked at them. They were standing in the corridor. Ivan was holding his daughter's slippers; Shura for some reason rushed back into the room, returned with a photo album and one of her son's pants, and suddenly sank down onto a step of the staircase. Vania also took a seat on the next lower step …

At 0320, having fired off their final shells designated for the support of the 45th Infantry Division, the neighboring *nebelwerfer* battalions began to fire in support of their own divisions, which were attacking on the left and right of the fortress. During 'Vinca', the Citadel had been left untouched. Now within several minutes, it would catch the brunt of the artillery fire under 'Crocus'. In the XII Army Corps' entire sector, approximately 200 inflatable boats were now approaching the Russian-held bank – and not a single shot was being fired at them.

In Brest, the high-frequency line in the office of the oblast committee's 1st Secretary, Tupitsyn, was still working – but having just heard the voice of the responding duty clerk of the Belorussian Central Committee, he had barely had time to give his name when there was a tremendous crash and a strong blow hurled Tupitsyn into a corner of his office. Through the settling dust, he could see a hole in the wall – a direct hit. The next shell exploded next to the oblast committee building's garage. Tossing aside the now useless telephone receiver, Tupitsyn shoved the oblast committee seal into his pocket and ran down into the cellar …

In Minsk, urgent messages were arriving at the headquarters of the Western Special Military District one after another from the armies about artillery barrages and air-raids. From the 10th Army came a report that a group of saboteurs had crossed the border, of which '2 had been killed, 2 wounded, 3 taken prisoner, and one escaped.' What was this – war? A provocation? Now without any reflection, it was urgently necessary to notify Moscow! Combat Report No. 001/op, signed by the chief of staff Major General V.E. Klimovsky, went out from the headquarters of the Western Special Military District to the Red Army's Chief of the General Staff. It contained little information on the situation in the Brest area: '4th Army – at 0420 [Moscow time], a bombing of Brest began. The number of aircraft involved isn't clear … Along the entire border there is an exchange of artillery fire according to the information from the aerial observation posts.'

In the sector of 10/I.R. 135's crossing, Lozert's platoon ceased fire. The artillery fire also fell silent – the Russian bank, shrouded in smoke, was still quiet. However, a tremendous din was coming from the Central Island – two of Galle's mortar batteries were firing on it, while one-third of the artillery regiment continued to pound the zone a little to the east of the hospital on South Island.

At 0327, the first of the 45th Infantry's boats, ferrying the 10th and 11th Companies of I.R. 135, reached the Russian-held bank, and then immediately turned around to pick up the second wave. The assault groups, leaping from the boats onto Soviet soil, spread out to defend the small beachhead. The machine-gunners resumed firing at the island's interior. At this moment it was decided that Lozert's platoon would remain in position, but the 2nd Machine-gun Platoon commanded by *Leutnant* Schultz would attack together with the assault groups, led by the platoon commander himself. Schultz's men lugged their machine guns and ammunition toward the waiting boats.

* * *

Leutnant Zumpe had just disarmed a demolition charge on the railroad bridge's center support; other charges weren't found. He flashed a green light toward the waiting German troops – the way was clear! At 0327, a report from I.R. 135 arrived at the 45th Division headquarters that the bridge had been seized intact. An incredulous Schlieper mentioned the need for a thorough check of the bridge for possible demolition charges and ordered a second search to be conducted. He immediately reported to XII Army Corps headquarters that his division possessed the bridge and simultaneously informed the 31st Division, his neighbor on the left. Only at 0330 did the XII Corps headquarters now confidently record: '... the intact railroad bridge is in our hands.'

* * *

The primary objective of the 'Crocus' fire mission was to strike two targets on Central Island: the area of the Terespol Gate, where the 333rd Rifle Regiment and 9th Border Detachment were located, and east of the Kholm Gate, where the 84th Rifle Regiment was positioned together with the 75th Separate Reconnaissance Battalion.

The third shell fired by one of the Karl siege mortars shook the Border Guards' building, landing directly on the wing where their families were living. Two batteries of Galle's mortar battalion were firing without stop – with a crash, the second, north wing collapsed, which held the commandant's platoon, the course of observers and the reserve frontier post. Junior Sergeant Sergei Bobrenok ran out into the courtyard of the Border Guards' wrecked building. Later he wrote:

> ... Woodpiles, sheds, posts and trees were burning fiercely all over the grounds. A gun from the 333rd Regiment's artillery park was hurled over a stone wall into the yard of the commandant's office. With a crash, it fell into a burning woodpile. Women and children came running out of the building's central entrance, above which apartments of the command staff were located. Some were running to the right towards the reserve frontier post's building, others to the left towards the commandant's office.

However, many of them were blown to pieces by the Karl mortars' shells, or were wounded by fragments. The scale of the destruction was stunning – but shells continued to rain down ... Those who were flattened on the ground were now telling each other about some 'barrels of petroleum falling from the sky'. The broad conflagration raging squarely in the center of the courtyard, sending an enormous column of dense, black smoke into the sky, seemed to verify their words. What could burn there, the ground itself? No one yet knew of the spreading contents of the rocket-launchers' incendiary shells. The Border Guards' Alsatian dogs were howling despairingly in their enclosures.

The infantry guns of the attacking regiments were still silent, awaiting orders from Hipp and John. Infantry Regiment 133's 13th Company continued to place fire on the eastern outskirts of West Island, walking the shells back toward the center of the island. The 98th and 99th Artillery regiments began to lay down smoke-screens, alternating the smoke shells with high-explosive fragmentation shells. This swept the road clear for I/I.R. 135, half of which was still waiting for the second inspection of the bridge to be completed. Meanwhile, II/A.R. 98 was pounding the northern end of West Island while the III Battalion concentrated its fire on the rifle range on the Bug River's bank. The sector of the Main Wall, where I/I.R. 135 was to break into the Central Fortress, was being covered by I/A.R. 99. Then finally, the culminating 'argument' – the third shell fired by the second Karl mortar exploded on the north-western part of North Island, smashing the old fortifications on the eastern bank of the Bug. To the south, I/A.R. 98 was dropping a smoke-screen, also mixing the smoke shells with high-explosive fragmentation shells, on II/I.R. 130's line of attack, 200 meters east of the center of South Island.

By that time, the motors of the assault boats of Group Kremers, which had lost almost half its strength in the first minutes, were howling: hastily providing for the wounded, he had decided to proceed with his mission. Several minutes later, the assault boats were surging toward the Muchavec where it entered the Bug between the Kholm and Terespol Gates, and having decelerated in their turn up the Muchavec, they steered toward the Kholm Gate. Junior Lieutenant F.E. Zabriko, who was located in the Ring Barracks at the Kholm Gate, witnessed the assault boats' appearance: 'From the west, a motor boat appeared on the Muchavec. There were five or six German officers sitting in it, wearing forage caps and black oilers.' The 'oilers' were the sappers' rubber-coated jumpers. Closer to Kremers' boats, in the bushes lining the bank of the Muchavec, Border Guards Sergeant N.M. Morozov was concealed: 'Suddenly I saw a motor boat coming toward me, on the deck of which a group of German officers was standing ... As the motor boat was passing me, I rose and tossed my grenade.' Why were the Germans standing upright, subjecting themselves to the risk of gunfire or of toppling into the water at a sudden stop or sharp turn? The loss of the four boats forced the overcrowding of the five remaining boats with passengers, forcing some to stand upright in order to squeeze onto the boat!

However, it wasn't Morozov's single grenade that managed to stop Kremers' boats. They were already preparing to tack between the supports of the Kholm Bridge, when suddenly the bottoms of the boats' hulls began to grind against sand – a sandbar! It is impossible to think of anything worse that could have happened. They had stopped directly in front of the Ring Barracks, where armed men of the 84th Rifle Regiment, fully recovered from the barrage, were now alert and in position. Their surprise at seeing the Germans' appearance lasted only for a moment – there ensued such heavy rifle fire that the water around the boats started to seethe from the bullets. The men of Group Kremers leaped into the water, taking cover behind the boats, and tried to drag them off the sandbar. If the Red Army soldiers had possessed a couple of machine guns at that time, then the epopee of Group Kremers would have ended here. However, this was only the first minutes of the war – the Russians didn't have combat experience. Their grenades couldn't reach the boats, and because the second floor of the Ring Barracks in their sector was burning, they were forced to shoot from the ground floor, where the smoke that was drifting over the river's surface hindered their aim.

Finally, Kremers' men freed the boats. Hardly believing that they were still alive, they climbed back into the boats again. Now where? Onward!! Water was coming into the boats from the numerous bullet holes in them ... within a couple of minutes, still not having reached the fork in the Muchavec River, two of the boats were sinking. Now in the water, their crews swam to the bank – clambering out onto the dry land of Central Island, these Germans became the first to set foot on it. The remaining three boats, having turned to the left, were now speeding along the upper branch of the Muchavec.

At 0328, the inflatable boats of I and II battalions of the 45th Infantry Division's 130th Regiment grounded close to the opposite bank. The squads immediately disembarked and rushed forward. Josef Gusenbauer:

> Under the command of the lieutenant that crossed with us, the infantrymen rushed towards the riverbank, beyond which lay the Citadel. In the process a lieutenant of our machine-gunners was so severely wounded that he died almost immediately – falling right at my feet. We loaded the body in the following boat, took the damaged inflatable boat in tow, and headed back across the river to pick up the next batch of soldiers. Thus I saw my first corpse – this quickly served to turn an inexperienced youth into a man.

In the sector of 10/I.R. 135's crossing, the boats that had deposited the first wave had already returned to the western bank – the 10th Company's second wave was climbing into them, including *Leutnant* Wieltsch's platoon. At this time, the first wave was already attacking – since there was still no incoming fire, they were striving to make maximal use of the element of surprise. The direction of attack was along the Bug River toward the eastern side of West Island. Gerd Habedanck was with them:

> We jump on shore and press forward. Verdant dykes between swampy ditches, barbed-wire fences, and the lower casemates. The body of a dead Soviet-Russian soldier, and the carcasses of dead horses in an enclosure. Onward, onward! Machine-gun fire!! It's barking over there, on the first floors between the foliage of the tall cottonwood trees. There? It's just a false alarm – crackle and snapping, a wooden stable is burning, and the ammunition aboard a blazing vehicle continues to cook off in bursts of gunfire. Trembling, individual groups of 'Soviet Russians' approach us with upraised hands. Others are leaping between trees, fleeing with rifles in their hands. Again and again, bursts of our machine gun. They [the Russians] are tumbling, dashing into shelters, and surrendering.

The first wave was trying to reach the Terespol Bridge as quickly as possible – it was necessary to seize this key point before the Russians came to their senses.

It wasn't their task to sweep West Island – either follow-on forces would do that job, or the Russians themselves would surrender.

* * *

The second wave of I.R. 130 was also jumping into boats; part of this wave consisted of the *panzerjägers* of the 14th Company, among them Hermann Wild. However, things were much more difficult for the crews of the 37mm guns (which weighed 450 kilograms each) than for the infantrymen. The 14th Company strained to man-handle their guns across the swampy riverbank onto the boats. The heavy-duty rubber dinghies were threatening to buckle under the weight of the 37mm anti-tank guns. The engineers cautiously paddled. Meanwhile the forward elements of III Battalion had already crossed the river. Walther Loos jumped ashore. Here came the first Russians – clustered in groups, stunned by the horror of the artillery barrage, or hiding one by one. They had faces pale with fear; many, it seemed, had lost the ability to speak and were surrendering in a daze. Incidentally, the main thing to notice is that III/I.R. 130's river crossing went without a single shot being fired from the eastern bank.

At 0335, the second wave of 10/I.R. 135 was scrambling ashore. Now fully assembled on the opposite bank, they clambered up the steep slope, removed the sparse barbed wire, and moved forward. Encountering no resistance, Wieltsch's platoon searched through a garden and several stables lying in front of it.

Oberstleutnant Naber's I/I.R. 130 was attacking toward the Muchavec bridges. *Leutnant* Lohr's 2nd Company led the way. To the right, Major Hans Hartnack's II/I.R. 130 was making its way through swamps. The swamps, which were unexpectedly wide and difficult to negotiate, were badly delaying the progress of the II Battalion – would it manage to reach the bridges in time?

Hipp's second echelon, Major Ulrich's III/I.R. 130, which included Walther Loos (later Loos' company would go the length of Brest) was attacking along one of the fortress's forward moats toward South Island, alongside Panzer Rollbahn No. 1. Its objective was a bridge across the moat. So far, just like with Oeltze's advance, it was like a knife through butter. It had been harder in France!

The second wave of Hartnack's battalion was just coming ashore on the eastern bank. The gun crews of the 14th Company were beginning to haul their 37mm guns out of the boats. They hadn't yet rested from their toils in the swamps of the western bank, but now it seemed that things were much worse on the eastern bank. The first adversaries of Colonel Hipp's *panzerjägers* in Russia proved to be the sludge in the drainage ditches and the mire of the swamps. Wild wrote, 'In places the anti-tank guns sank up to their axles in mud. We were pushed extremely hard to keep the momentum of the advance going.' Dragging their guns through the swamps, the crews encountered Russians too – however, so far they were only prisoners, half-dressed and stunned by the pre-dawn invasion.

On the North Island's north-western quarter, where within several minutes Oeltze's battalion was to push across, 'Odin's' fourth shell shook the ground. At the same time, I/A.R. 99 was working over the Main Wall for I Battalion, while Galle's mortar battalion continued to batter the East and West Forts, as well as the housing complex of the command staff. I.R. 133's 13th Company was targeting the south-eastern section of the Main Wall on North Island, where the 98th Separate Anti-tank Battalion was positioned. Having heard the thundering explosions of 'Anemone', the artillerymen of the 98th Separate Anti-tank Artillery Battalion rushed to their equipment and started up the tractors and vehicles, and hitched up the guns, while others dashed to spigots in order to fill flasks with water before moving out, but there was no water. Where, though, were they to go? There were no commanders to be seen. The shells of 13/I.R. 133 exploding around them forced the men to take cover again. From there they could only watch as the explosions set one after another of the tractors ablaze and sent their guns somersaulting through the air. Those who remained inside the barracks, where it had suddenly become light from the red glare over the border, were collecting rifles, greatcoats and gas masks. But there were no cartridges – the orderly was flatly refusing to distribute them without orders.

The Red Army soldiers running across the Trekharoch Bridge didn't know that the fourth shell from 'Thor' was designated for them. Its intended target was just to the left of the bridge's access ramp on North Island. If it had been fired, the shell would have caused extensive damage and casualties in a wide circle around the impact point. However, the brass band around the fourth shell was too thick, poorly finished or warped, and the shell jammed in the breach. Now the numerous crew-men were bustling around 'Thor', turning the air blue with their curses: attempts to extract the shell were unsuccessful. But then the crew of 'Odin' also began working frantically around their heavy mortar, which was prepared to fire on West Fort: they faced the very same problem – a shell stuck in the breech. They were trying to remove the shell through their own efforts, hoping to resume firing. However, the problem put both siege mortars out of action for the next several hours.

The 98th Artillery Regiment was walking its fire eastward; I Battalion was targeting the area south-east of South Island (where there were no Red Army troops to speak of), the III Battalion was dropping shells along the railroads to the north-west of North Island, where elements of I.R. 135 would be advancing in order to cut the fortress off from the city, and II Battalion was pounding the north-eastern section of the Citadel's Ring Barracks, where the 455th Rifle Regiment and the 33rd Separate Engineering Regiment were positioned.

At the same time, at 0335 the first *Luftwaffe* ground-attack aircraft were crossing the Bug River at low altitude.

0336–0340: 'Narcissus'

At 0337, meeting no enemy opposition, the first wave of the 34th Infantry Division was crossing the Bug. At 0340, XII Army Corps headquarters sent a report to Fourth Army command on the current situation, informing it that its neighbor on the left was meeting no resistance whatsoever. Arko 27 was shifting its artillery barrage further to the east. All the islands except North Island were now excluded from the barrage zone – the mortar battalion was firing on the West and East Forts and the area between them, where people were now running, trying to escape through the Northern Gate. However, most of them were still in shelters, waiting out the barrage.

In the first moments, Lieutenant Bobkov's family darted out of their home, one of the apartment buildings of the command staff in front of West Fort. They ran to a former powder magazine, where they hoped to find safe shelter within it. A heavy lock on the door dispelled their hopes. Several families with children had already gathered here, in a small alcove beneath the entrance's concrete overhang, unsuccessfully trying to break the lock. Those families situated much closer to the East and West Forts would have to flee across open ground – and the tempest of artillery fire raging over the forts, which on North Island were the main targets of the heavy artillery, was visible to those below the concrete overhang. Soon a shell exploded almost right next to the people gathered around the entrance, followed quickly by two more . . .

The guns of 13/I.R. 133 were shelling the road leading from the Eastern Gate, blocking an escape route for the tractors of the 98th Separate Anti-tank Battalion, which was then under bombardment from I/A.R. 98. This artillery regiment's II and III battalions had already shifted their barrage beyond the fortress itself – II/A.R. 98 was working over the fork of the railroads at the bridge across the Muchavec; III/A.R. 98 was targeting a highway overcrossing north-west of the fortress. The walls of the bastion west of the Northern Gate were being shelled by I/A.R. 99. Thus, the effort to reduce the Main Wall was coming to an end – virtually its entire extent had been struck by the barrage. Everything there – the barbed-wire entanglements and machine-gun nests – should by now have been destroyed, so the Main Wall, as the Germans believed, was ready to be assaulted. The difficulties of 1939, which had showed the significance of the Main Wall, were not to be repeated.

* * *

The artillerymen of the 98th Separate Anti-tank Battalion were now experiencing the full fury of the artillery barrage – out of fear many of them were trembling as if in a fever. One of its men later wrote, 'In order to calm ourselves, we pressed ourselves against a wall, but it was also quaking. In the pandemonium and tumult, we looked at each other in the eyes and asked, "What's going on? Why wasn't the alarm sounded?" '

* * *

On West Island, the German assault groups were now inexorably advancing toward Central Island. At that time, Soviet soldiers of the Border Guards detachments were concentrated in the southern portion of West Island. The men of 11/I.R. 135, having quickly advanced along the central road, had split the island in two and had cleared its midsection of enemy resistance. However, in the southern and northern sections of the island, approximately eighty Red Army soldiers had clustered in the Main Wall's gorge barracks and the casemated redoubts (Points 242 and 247).

Shots were ringing out from the barracks of the District's driving school. It was surrounded by twelve to fifteen soldiers of 11/I.R. 135. The first exchange of fire erupted ... Legends also circulate around this Red Army unit. Its odd location, right on the border and on an island that had no motor vehicle testing course, provide the basis for rumors that the District's driving school was actually a subterfuge concealing a secret Soviet special service unit. In addition to all the rest, the stubborn defense put up by the 'drivers' lends support to this speculation.

At this same time, in the center of West Island, other squads of 11/I.R. 135 were rushing past the location of the 17th Border Guards Detachment's transport company. Its commander, Senior Lieutenant A.S. Chernyi, had managed to join his subordinate soldiers already in the first minutes of the barrage (he was billeted on West Island next to the barracks of the transport company). There he found approximately thirty of his men; the rest had already been killed, wounded, or had fled across the bridge into the Citadel. Chernyi decided that his first order of business was to evacuate the vehicles, so leaving behind a couple of soldiers in the present position, he and the rest of the men ran to the garages, which were located to the left of the barracks of the District's driving school. En route they bumped into its commander Senior Lieutenant Mel'nikov, who was quartered in the same building as Chernyi.

Now Border Guardsmen were running toward the border, over the same route that the attacking troops of 11/I.R. 135 had rushed just several minutes before, only in the opposite direction. Having reached a point near the driving school's barracks, the Border Guardsmen noticed that it was encircled by Germans. Taking cover in the shrubs surrounding the school, Chernyi's group opened fire from two of its machine guns. Now the attacking Germans of the 11th Company were themselves encircled! However, the majority of the Border Guardsmen who had been in the path of 11/I.R. 135's advance across the center of the island fell back to its northern portion. Lieutenant A.P. Zhdanov, who was also billeted on West Island and was one of the officers of the District's driving school, took command of this group. Most of Zhdanov's group was located in the school building itself, while fifteen men were on the northern outskirts of West Island; all were armed.

The Citadel in these minutes, between the end of the preparatory artillery barrage and the encroachment of the German assault groups, was like a disturbed ant hill. The majority of the inhabitants were trying to escape through the Trekharoch Gate; however, the continuing heavy barrage on its eastern end frightened many of them. Therefore, hoping to wait it out, troops were taking shelter in the eastern portion of the Ring Barracks, where the 455th and 33rd Engineering regiments were quartered, and in the fortress's gorge barracks, which subsequently became famous under its designation as Point 145. However, most of the men had nowhere to run – terrified by the barrage, their commanders absent, receiving no orders of any kind, and lacking weapons which were now burning somewhere in the Ring Barracks, they were crowded in cellars or in any seemingly secure shelter they could find. Many panic-stricken men were simply rushing around the Citadel's courtyard in terror, among the flames, smoke and corpses.

It mustn't be forgotten that over the preceding month, the numerical strength of the Red Army formations in the Citadel had risen sharply through the arrival of fresh recruits and designated personnel. These men were not veterans of the war with Finland, but inexperienced young soldiers, who had spent the greater portion of their first month of military service working on the construction of border fortifications. What could a Red Army soldier do without a commander? Perhaps only get dressed and grab a rifle standing nearby. But then what? Head out to the positions indicated in the covering plan? However, the sergeants, who in the best case might have been close at hand at the start of the barrage, could hardly have been expected to know the assembly area backwards and forwards – and anyway, these areas were now being plastered by German artillery fire, or had *Wehrmacht* assault groups cautiously advancing across them. Moreover, how were the men to reach them? Motorized transport was burning and fatally-wounded horses were neighing in terror. Flee to the east? However, the majority of the units in the Citadel were specialized (i.e., transport, artillery). Flee, leaving behind their equipment? In the Red Army, that was impermissible! Flee, without orders? That was also inexcusable in the Red Army. What about the alert forces and the posts? Moreover, there'd been no declaration of war and no alarm had sounded (the alert forces were supposed to have triggered the latter), and as of yet, there were no enemy soldiers around. What was going on? Artillery fire and aircraft in the smoke-filled sky – these were not yet sufficient cause to abandon everything and flee to the east without weapons and boots.

Meanwhile the commanders, whom everyone was waiting upon, in the first minutes were either on their way to join their units, having hastily bid farewell to their families, or were waiting out the barrage that was raining down on the eastern portion of North Island. The chief of staff of the 98th Separate Anti-tank Artillery Battalion, Ivan Akimochkin, who'd left behind a wife and two children in his apartment, managed to reach his unit's headquarters, still carrying his belt and forage cap which he hadn't had time to don. Running into the headquarters, he saw the soldiers gathered around the orderly, and immediately ordered the latter to issue cartridges to the men.

0340–0345: 'Tulip'

At 0340, a white signal rocket was spotted rising into the sky 900 meters to the east of the bridge. Who was over there – one of Oeltze's forward groups (one of *Hauptmann* Kaehne's companies advancing to the north of the Citadel)? If that was the case, they were taking a big risk – within moments von Krischer's artillery was to begin shelling that area. The bulk of I/I.R. 135 was already on the eastern bank; some of the companies were sweeping through the barracks of the 131st Artillery Regiment, others were moving in the direction of the Main Wall 'like a knife through butter'. Here *Oberst* John had set up his command post. There were a lot of Russians still around, but they were all in a state of shock. The first prisoners were already running across the bridge ...

At 0342, the third wave of I.R. 135 began crossing the Bug. The main forces of I.R. 130 were already across the river and pushing across South Island. By 0343 there was still no enemy artillery fire whatsoever, and resistance was negligible. Fort V was being reduced to ruins by the fire of the mortar battalion using flash-ranging. The fire of Arko 27 was shifting further to the east. Now von Krischer was concentrating on supporting the infantry of Major Oeltze's I/I.R. 135, which was enveloping the fortress from the north, and Major Ulrich's III/I.R. 130, which was bypassing it to the south-east, seizing the bridges on the Muchavec. Supporting Ulrich, I/A.R. 98 was firing on an area 500 meters to the south-east of South Island, while II/A.R. 98 continued to bombard the railroad fork, where a mortar battery was also concentrating its fire. Galle's remaining mortars were firing on the fortress's eastern walls. After the barrage from the 210mm mortars, there was supposed to be nothing left there to hinder movement along Panzer Rollbahn No. 1. The third battalion of A.R. 98 was shelling the ground between the Main Wall and the railroad, and I/A.R. 99 was firing on the Main Wall west of the Northern Gate.

The main success during these minutes was the emergence of Naber's I/I.R. 130 on the banks of the Muchavec – at 0345 *Leutnant* Lohr's group took Bridge 'Hipp' and the Kholm railroad bridge, which according to plan had been Group Kremers' mission. But where Kremers was at this moment wasn't known.

Leutnant Kremers' group was at this time suffering another loss – now the third boat that had been riddled by the bullets of the 84th Rifle Regiment was sinking at the fork of the Muchavec. Its passengers were leaping into the water directly below the barracks of the 33rd Engineering Regiment, in plain view of dozens of Russians that were running across the bridge. All the Germans of this boat could do was to seek cover underneath it. The remaining two boats hurried onward ...

Several minutes before the seizure of the bridges on the Muchavec by *Leutnant* Lohr, elements of Ulrich's battalion had entered South Island across the bridge spanning the forward moat. Having rushed into the walls on either side of the Southern Gate and set up machine guns there, they provided fire cover to the assault groups pushing forward onto the island through the Southern Gate, striving to reach the hospital.

At this time the groups of trainees of the 84th Rifle Regiment's regimental school, soldiers of the 95th Medical-Sanitation Battalion and the few surviving Border Guardsmen that had gathered just to the left of the Southern Gate were taking no actions at all – the situation was still murky. Flames had now spread throughout the hospital's surgery department, but Nurse Praskov'ia Tkacheva was continuing to rescue patients. Together with Nurse Nina Kosenkova, who had joined her by now, she carried more than twenty patients out of the flames. She could hear those whom she hadn't been able to save calling for her out of the smoke. The roof was collapsing, and the last desperate cries for help intermingled with the roar of the flames ...

Major Oeltze, the commander of I/I.R. 135 that was attacking from the north, sighed with relief – his companies, meeting no resistance, had entered the Northwestern Gate and seized a large section of the Main Wall! With the seizure of this most important defensive line, September 1939 wouldn't be repeated! Now onward, rounding up bewildered Russians and tossing grenades into the numerous buildings and underground barracks, wasting no time to mop them up. The objective was the road spanning North Island from north to south. The sector of Oeltze's advance included the barracks of the 125th Rifle Regiment, the residences of the command staff, and the West Fort.

Sergeant V.I. Fursov, the commander of a mortar crew of a mortar battery in the 125th Rifle Regiment, recalls:

> The soldiers of our battery grabbed rifles (it turned out there were only twelve of them, some of them training rifles, and only several dozen cartridges), and dashed out into the street. At this moment, Lieutenant Poltorakov (the commander of a reconnaissance platoon), came running up to us from regiment headquarters, brandishing a sabre, shouting, 'Comrades, after me, Germans are in the area of the stables!' – having in mind the stables of the reconnaissance cavalry platoon in the Main Wall.

Having dashed to the Main Wall, the Red Army men began to exchange fire with Oeltze's soldiers who had seized that portion of it.

The final phases of the 45th Infantry Division's artillery barrage focused precisely on the north-western area of North Island. Captain Shablovsky was trying to make his way to his regiment's sector there, hoping to withdraw the 4th Company, but the artillery fire prevented him from reaching it. The captain and other commanders of the 125th Rifle Regiment (among them were the regiment's artillery chief, P.D. Voitenko; Battalion Commissar S.V. Derbenev, the regiment's deputy political commander; the military doctor Gavrilkin; Junior Lieutenant Kravchenko, political instructor Sinichkin; and ten to twelve others), armed only with pistols, were waiting out the German barrage in a stone building that was holding supplies of some unit's signalers, which was located between Building No. 2 and Building No. 3 of the command staff's residences. Here they caught their breath – just a short distance behind them, on the same short path they'd followed, lay two dead lieutenants. Several women, trying to reach the road, were running from building to building toward them in short dashes. When the barrage subsided, Shablovsky and his group were just about to emerge from the building when the first German machine-gun burst struck some Red Army troops that were rushing past it. The commanders, headed by Shablovsky, dashed toward Building No. 3, but before they could reach it, machine guns of Oeltze's battalion, firing from the right, opened up from the stables. Shablovsky and part of his group fell back to Building No. 5. They had almost covered the distance when they could see trainees of the regimental school leaping out of the windows on the second floor of the 125th Rifle Regiment's barracks, having first tossed mattresses down in the effort to break their falls – the staircase between the first and second floors had been smashed by a shell.

The fact that the barracks of the 125th Rifle Regiment stood directly across from the Northwestern Gate became a problem for I/I.R. 135. Fire from these barracks forced I Battalion to bypass the barracks, and having split up into groups, to break into North Island from different directions. Things went most successfully for those groups that followed the Muchavec – along this side of the wall there were primarily storerooms, in which families of the command staff were waiting out the barrage. From here the soldiers of I Battalion set out for the West Fort, which was the main objective, after the Main Wall, on the west side of North Island. In their path lay the western residential complex of the command staff. In a wing of Building No. 9 (or more accurately, its ruins), Ivan and Aleksandra Pochernikov were sitting, having just lost their children.

Tamara Dzhindzhishvili resumes her story:

> At dawn, German submachine-gunners burst into our residence (Building No. 8). Pushing aside women and children, the Germans rushed down the corridor and through the rooms, opening closets and tossing aside beds, plainly searching for our husbands. Having finished their searches of our apartment and the Ivanovs' apartment, they began running over to the Pochernikovs. We began to shout to Vania. He jumped up with a pistol in his hand. The very first German, a big fellow with a turned-up collar, was shot and fell onto his back. A second German broke into a run, but Vania shot him as well. There followed two more shots ... Vania had pointed his pistol at Shura. Having shot her, he put the pistol to his head and shot himself.

In Building No. 5 of the residential complex, residents spotted the Germans approaching from a long way off, and decided to hide in the attic. There, in addition to Shablovsky and the aforementioned Voitenko, there were other commanders as well, who hadn't managed to get through to their units. There, in Building No. 5, N.I. Nozdrina had also found shelter: 'In the apartment building where we stopped, there were women and military men. The military men were in the attic ... Senior among them was Shablovsky; they all knew him and listened to him. They were armed with pistols.' In addition to the commanders, several soldiers of the 125th Rifle Regiment were also located in Building No. 5. Striving not to betray their presence (they couldn't expect to put up much resistance armed only with pistols), they waited for an opportunity to escape – but Germans were already surrounding them.

Tamara Dzhindzhishvili, as were all the residents of Building No. 8, was lucky, since as a rule, the only alternative to being searched was a German M-24 grenade, which were flying into any premise that presented possible danger. The harsh principle of street-fighting 'Your grenade always precedes you' became fatal in these minutes for many members of the command staff's families ... Catching the sound of non-Russian speech, women (among them M.P. Kropel'nitskaia as well) who were hiding in the storerooms within the walls along the Muchavec, at the advice of Captain Gonchar, crawled under the bunk beds, hiding their children in the same places. However, the Germans that were dashing past them didn't even bother with a search – a grenade flew into the door, fatally wounding a Red Army soldier who was also hiding there. Several fragments also wounded two of the women and Kropel'nitskaia's 2-year-old son. The Germans ran on – several dozen meters still remained to reach the road leading to the Trekharoch Bridge, the attack's initial objective.

On the Central Island, not everyone succumbed to panic. The 84th Rifle Regiment's 3rd Battalion was flushed with a sense of victory after shooting up *Leutnant* Kremers' boats. Commissar Efim Fomin was attempting to restore order, helped by *Komsomol* organizer Samvel Matevosian. Approximately seventeen men of the 9th Border Post remained alive after the ending of the German artillery barrage, including its commander Lieutenant Kizhevatov. Shag tobacco was the first remedy against the heavy nervous stress. The ringleader Alekseev had some. So as the first order of business, they had a smoke. Then they began to clean and ready their weapons. The Border Guardsmen of the 3rd Border Post, who were also half-dressed and were located in the opposite wing of the same building, were trying to dig out their rifles from under the rubble of the walls. Documents were being destroyed. In the twilight of the cellar of the 333rd Rifle Regiment's barracks were more than 100 men, among them ten junior commanders and five lieutenants. Lieutenants Sanin and Potapov were gathering familiar soldiers around themselves. So there was no unified leadership in the cellar of the 333rd Rifle Regiment. Judging from the available evidence, the most active soldiers were grouped around those commanders that were most familiar to them from their pre-war service.

Meanwhile on Central Island, which had lost virtually all the motorized transport (it was in fact the smoke from the burning trucks of the 31st Motorized Transport Battalion that was covering half the sky), chaos was at its peak. Junior Sergeant K.I. Zharmedov of the 75th Separate Reconnaissance Battalion relates:

> As we with great difficulty began to approach our tanks, suddenly we were hit with bursts of machine-gun fire from our own tanks. So those who remained alive, and there proved to be few of them, fell back to the barracks. There were no commanders among us.

Red Army troops were continuing to flee across the Trekharoch Bridge in groups or in ones and twos, using the last remaining possibility to escape the conflagration in the fortress. However, at the same time many men were dashing across the bridge in the opposite direction: finally the commanders were arriving, and among them were those who in the next few hours would take command of the fortress's defense. Senior Lieutenant V.I. Bytko, the chief of the 44th Rifle Regiment's regimental school (which was located in the northern sector of the Ring Barracks), who was billeted in a residence of the command staff, was one of the first to make the dash across the Trekharoch Bridge onto Central Island. Having assembled a group of trainees and wasting no time to search for the others, he led it back across the Trekharoch Bridge to the Northern Gate: beyond it was the location of the regiment trains, where the regiment was to assemble in the event of a combat alarm.

From there, all the elements of the 44th Rifle Regiment were to move to its designated assembly area – an old firing range to the north of Brest.

On the heels of all the other commanders making their way into the Citadel was the commander of the 44th Rifle Regiment Major Gavrilov, who was hoping to withdraw the regimental school and to bring out secret documents together with the regimental banner, both of which were located in his headquarters. However, he was unsuccessful: the headquarters were burning, and Gavrilov encountered no more than twenty soldiers of his regiment. The others had already made their way to the Main Wall themselves, without waiting for commanders, or were taking shelter in cellars, and Gavrilov had no time to round them up. Just several minutes later, the commander of the 44th Rifle Regiment ran back to the Northern Gate, where the most intact of his units remaining in the fortress was located – his 1st Battalion, which was positioned to the left of the Gate.

The 333rd Rifle Regiment was retiring in intact units being led by their commanders (the on-call company, the most combat-capable of them in these minutes, was moving toward the Trekharoch Bridge with almost all its personnel and officers), and in groups. Clerks of the 333rd Rifle Regiment, awakened by the artillery barrage, were running out into the corridor with the intention to head up to the headquarters on the second floor; one of them was wounded in the leg by a shell fragment that flew in through a window. The guardhouse located nearby was already empty; the clerks could hear the cries and groans of wounded men from up above on the second floor. The staircase landings were piled with debris ... The corridor was gradually filling with smoke – somewhere a fire had started. The clerks, lacking weapons, instead set off at a run toward the Trekharoch Bridge.

At the same time, but on North Island, Senior Lieutenant Mamchik, commander of the 333rd Rifle Regiment's 2nd Battalion, was also heading quickly toward the bridge. He was one of the most experienced commanders, who'd passed through the war with Finland. There, at the Trekharoch Bridge, he encountered one of his subordinate companies, which had just managed to dash across the bridge. An experienced battalion commander and a fully-armed company had now linked up – thus one of Brest's first strong combat groups was formed. They gathered together at Point 145, concealed by the smoke. Here, atop the wall, even the grass was burning – likely, one of the incendiary *nebelwerfer* shells had exploded here.

On South Island, several soaked Border Guardsmen, who had retreated from West Island, had assembled among the buildings of the hospital – Kukushkin's and Rusakov's groups. They took cover in the casemate into which Nurse Tkacheva and Kosenkova were carrying the patients. Several employees of the hospital also joined up with them there – a total of twenty-eight men. While bandaging one of the wounded men, a rifleman of the 3rd Reserve Border Post, they learned that the wounded Kukushkin was lying in the bushes out in front of them, and the 19-year-old nurse Vera Khoretskaia rushed out to bandage him. Everyone in the casemate was expecting friendlies, Red Army field units, to appear at any moment.

At 0345, the dust of the final explosions around the eastern walls was settling. The 45th Infantry Division's artillery had fulfilled their task. The roads on South

Island were densely strewn with branches and leaves that had been torn from the trees by shell explosions; here and there among them were dead horses and the bodies of dead Russians, some clad only in their underwear or only half-dressed. There was almost no one left alive – and thus very quickly the first soldiers of Major Ulrich's III/I.R. 130 were appearing among the burning buildings of the hospital. By this moment, the majority of the patients had already been placed in underground casemates for shelter. Understandably, neither the patients nor the majority of the medical personnel had any weapons or ammunition. Nevertheless, according to its table of equipment, the 95th Medical-Sanitation Battalion had 5 self-loading rifles, 2 machine pistols, 33 pistols, and 99 rifles and carbines. As concerns Brest's military and corps hospitals, at the very least their leadership had a personal sidearm. In the Brest military hospital, its chief was Military Doctor 2nd Rank Maslov, and his political deputy was Battalion Commissar N.S. Bogateev. During the German artillery barrage, they both organized the evacuation of the wounded. When the Germans appeared, Maslov had time to take cover in an underground room, but Battalion Commissar Bogateev, who'd been destroying the classified documents in his office, didn't. Drawing his pistol, he dashed out to meet Ulrich's soldiers just as they reached the hospital – and was instantly killed by shots from several carbines. In these same minutes, the chief of the 28th Rifle Corps' hospital Military Doctor 2nd Rank S.S. Babkin was mortally wounded. Nurse Vera Khoretskaia was in the process of bandaging Kukushkin when suddenly two German soldiers showed up. 'Stop! There are wounded here!' the young woman shouted as she attempted to cover Kukushkin with her own body – but both of them were killed. Within minutes Germans were already approaching the casemate where Nurse Tkacheva was located – immediately shots began echoing under the casemate's vaulted ceiling. Then Ulrich's soldiers departed ...

Meanwhile, elements of III/I.R. 130 were seizing the hospital. More shots rang out here and there, but the Germans didn't manage to sweep the entire hospital, nor moreover could they approach the banks of the Muchavec because of fire from the Ring Barracks (from the sector at the Kholm Gate, where soldiers of the 84th Rifle Regiment's 3rd Battalion had now fully recovered from the opening barrage). Nevertheless, Ulrich, having taken South Island, had carried out his assignment.

0400

The soldiers of the first waves of the 9th, 10th and 11th companies were advancing quickly toward Central Island. They all heard the chatter of machine-gun fire and several shots coming from the Terespol Gate. They could also hear, despite the firing on the South and North Islands, the cries of the wounded and dying.

Ivan Dolotov recalled: 'There was heavy rifle fire mixed with automatic weapons fire coming from the direction of the Kholm and especially the Terespol Gates.' Germans were in their rear? In the barracks of the 84th Rifle Regiment, a couple of machine guns were moved up to windows that overlooked the Citadel's interior. Several dozen soldiers equipped with rifles took position at other windows facing the same direction.

Several half-naked surviving Border Guardsmen and Kizhevatov's family were clustered in a pigeonhole beneath the staircase in the building of the 9th Border Post. Kizhevatov himself had already gotten dressed. There was a burst of automatic weapons fire at the nearby Trekharoch Gate – and a minute later, men in a foreign uniform went running past the windows of the building in the direction of the Trekharoch Gate. Kizhevatov, instantly assessing the situation, gave an order: 'Eremeev, dig out the machine gun!' Two machine-gunners rushed to the pile of rubble and began to clear away bricks with their hands.

* * *

At 0403 in the headquarters of the 45th Infantry Division, the Ia Major Dettmer was sending a preliminary report to XII Army Corps – the attack was going as planned and the main forces of the attacking units had crossed successfully and had breached the Citadel. The attacking elements of *Hauptmann* Praxa's battalion (III/I.R. 135) had split into three groups. The first group was quickly advancing toward the Kholm Gate; the second toward a church standing in the middle of the Citadel's grounds; and the third was moving toward the Trekharoch Gate. In addition, several soldiers of the 10th Company were now clearing rooms of the Ring Barracks at the Terespol Gate.

Running past the demolished and burning Border Guards' building, an assault group of the Soviet 333rd Rifle Regiment quickly reached the Trekharoch Gate and the bridge. Commanders were continuing to filter across the bridge to join their units.

The assistant chief of staff of the 44th Rifle Regiment Lieutenant N.A. Egorov bumped into Germans in the right-hand passageway of the Trekharoch Gate. Egorov managed to fire three shots before darting into a door on his right, which led into the kitchen of the 455th Rifle Regiment. Most of the men inside were busy at the cooking stove. Leaping over the stove, Egorov dropped to the floor behind it – and immediately a grenade exploded in the middle of the kitchen. The stove protected Egorov. Waiting a bit, he then entered an adjacent room, and catching the sound of muffled voices, he dropped through a hatch that led into the cellar. His pursuers ran on ahead, but a few of them ran into the officers' mess of the 33rd Engineering Regiment in the Ring Barracks adjacent to the Trekharoch Gate, where there was no one other than cooks and an on-duty detachment. The rest of the Germans ran out onto the bridge, where they unexpectedly met 'comrades' who were rushing toward them. These were the crews and passengers of two of Kremers' sunken boats. (By this time, at 0355 Kremers had come alongside Bridge 'Hipp' with his two remaining boats and after a brief discussion with *Leutnant* Lohr, he had moved on ahead.)

There was a brief exchange of greetings, and the 'boatmen' headed on into the Citadel, while the soldiers of III/I.R. 135 continued across the bridge onto North Island. They were spotted from an ammunition dump of the 44th Rifle Regiment at the Northern Gate by N.M. Isplatov: 'The Nazis were near the Trekharoch Gate, moving toward the [Northern] bridge across the Muchavec. They were advancing slowly, freezing now and then like dogs on the point ...' The plan of attack for I.R. 135 anticipated first the seizure of the Central Bridge leading into Brest, and only after that was accomplished did it seem possible to reach the grounds of the Central Train Station by crossing over the Northern Bridge. However, it is likely that it seemed to Praxa's soldiers, intoxicated by their initial success, that the situation was such that the orders could be changed. After all, the Russians were putting up no resistance!

Seeing that the Germans were already on the Central Island, the flow of people streaming across the Muchavec doubled. Wasting no time, the soldiers of Praxa's battalion that had made a lodgment in the 33rd Engineering Regiment's officers' mess began firing at the Trekharoch Bridge and part of the Citadel's courtyard – they were firing at almost point-blank range at Red Army men that had no weapon and didn't know where the fire was coming from. Among those trying to make it across the Trekharoch Bridge was the commander of a platoon of designated personnel of the 33rd Engineering Regiment, Senior Sergeant Ivan Dolotov (his platoon was located in the walls near the Trekharoch Bridge). Having grabbed a Degtiarev light machine gun from its mount and a box with drums of ammunition, Dolotov jumped out of a window on the eastern bank of the Muchavec and rushed toward the bridge, hoping to reach the North Island. He recalls,

> Men were running towards the bridge from every direction, but those who stepped onto the bridge were dropping dead. In this smoke-filled, early morning mist it was impossible to determine the source of this hurricane of fire ... There was no way across the bridge.

Red Army soldiers and commanders, among them Ivan Cherniaev, abandoned the attempt to cross over the bridge and dove into the river to swim across.

Bytko and his trainees were just a bit too late – met at the Trekharoch Gate by German fire, he led his men toward the large gap in the eastern side of the Ring Barracks, toward which now dozens of half-dressed men were running. Dolotov also ran up to the riverbank of the Muchavec, but realized he couldn't swim across the river while holding the machine gun. Behind him, a rumble of engines started up – glancing back, Ivan saw three T-38 tanks of the 75th Separate Reconnaissance Battalion entering the river through the gap in the Ring Barracks outside the White Palace, each with one or two Red Army soldiers clinging to the back of them. Dolotov ran over to the 75th Separate Reconnaissance Battalion's position, hoping to grab a ride on one of the tanks. However, there were no more operational T-38 tanks; four of them were left abandoned at the White Palace, apparently because of malfunctions or damage received during the artillery barrage. The T-38s that had driven into the Muchavec, having clambered up the opposite bank, skirted the wall and disappeared in the direction of the Kobrin Gate. Vasilii Bytko also headed for the same place, together with the trainees that had swum across the river. Next Bytko performed an action that stood out for its courage – he decided to return to the Citadel for the remaining trainees and to retrieve the regimental banner. Secretary of the 44th Rifle Regiment's Party bureau V.Z. Maksimov wrote:

> We met him around 6 o'clock in the morning on 22 June, when he was returning to the fortress. Bytko said that it was his duty at whatever the cost to make it through to the headquarters to arrange for the retrieval of the regiment's banner.

At this time, the assault group of III/I.R. 135, having crossed onto North Island, turned to the right and headed along the Main Wall there. Dolotov was one of the first to see them:

> A group of four or five men were running in my direction. We drew up alongside each other in front of a bakery that was located in an earthwork. They were not far away, and I was struck by their uniforms. I instantly dropped to the ground, and through the foliage of the willow shrubs growing along the riverbank came bursts of automatic weapons fire. I lay there for some time without moving, sheltered behind a small knoll. 'There they are – Germans!' I had to load my Degtiarev. I almost let out a howl of chagrin, when I discovered that the drums were empty. Of course, why hadn't I noticed this before? After all, loaded, they would have been much heavier, but I didn't notice this in the heat of the action. So it turned out that I was unarmed, and only then did I recall that we didn't have any cartridges at all. At least there weren't any in my platoon.

Having sprayed Dolotov's position with bullets, the German assault group pushed on, advancing past Point 145 in the Main Wall, in the casemates of which was deputy political instructor A.M. Nikitin, the deputy political leader of a company of the 33rd Engineering Regiment's designated personnel. Hearing the gunfire, Nikitin and several other soldiers who had survived the artillery barrage by taking shelter here grabbed the rifles that had been standing in a pyramid next to the casemate's entrance. They found ammunition in a box that was sitting next to the rifles (Nikitin had come across two containers of ammunition). They fashioned a breastwork out of the mattresses and desks, then dropped down behind it. The Germans, having split into groups, were running past their little defensive position, toward the stockroom, where at the entrance of which under the concrete overhang were the surviving members of the commanders' families and the dying Lieutenant Bobkov, whose legs had been torn off by an exploding shell. Spotting the women and children in the alcove, the Germans ordered them to come out and to stand by the entrance – probably with the intention to clear it out later with grenades. However, soon these Germans disappeared somewhere, and not knowing where to go, the people immediately took shelter in the alcove again. Three more Germans later came running up to the stockroom, and without wasting time to check it, one of the Germans tossed a grenade into the alcove. The blast tore the lock from the doors and blew the doors open. Bleeding, the survivors of the grenade attack crawled into the darkness of the underground casemate.

Here in fact the heady advance of 12/I.R. 135's assault group came to an end – beyond were the eastern walls, where now after the twenty minutes had passed since the end of the opening artillery barrage, the majority of the Red Army soldiers had recovered from the shock. The soldiers of III/I.R. 135 encountered such heavy fire that it left no doubt that they could not advance any further. Moreover, gunfire was flaring up all across the entire fortress. They fell back quickly to the bridge, following the same route past the point where Nikitin's little group was now waiting for them:

> We were waiting tensely. A group of seven or eight fascist soldiers appeared. They were running in a crouch along the bank of the Muchavec [in the direction of the bridge] and didn't notice us. Letting them approach to within 10–15 metres, we simultaneously opened fire. Two fascists dropped and lay motionless. The remaining Germans crawled down the riverbank to the Muchavec. Bursts of automatic gunfire rang out in response to our firing ... We reloaded our weapons from the second, final container.

However, Nikitin's casemate wasn't adapted for defense against attacks from the rear, from the direction of the Muchavec. Thus the stand-off ended quickly – a couple of German infantrymen dashed to the wall, where the unarmed men of the designated personnel group who'd been billeted in the tents were hiding in the bushes. Having climbed atop the wall, the Germans were outside the zone of fire from the casemates. Next, they ran along the top of the wall to a point above the casemate sheltering Nikitin and his small group, before dropping down right in front of the entrance. Before the surprised defenders could react, they tossed in a couple of grenades and took cover. Nikitin recalls, 'I didn't even have time to raise my rifle. There was an explosion. I could hear moans in the smoke: two men were killed and the others wounded. The plank beds and mattresses began to burn. The casemate became filled with smoke.' Grabbing clothing, Nikitin and his desperate soldiers put out the fire after about five minutes.

The Germans were falling back further, toward the Trekharoch Bridge. Here they were covered by fire from the windows of the 33rd Engineering Regiment's officers' mess – however, it was now already dangerous to dash across the bridge to reach it. The sound of gunfire now coming from every direction indicated that a serious battle had begun. Possibly, the soldiers of 12/I.R. 135 were now regretting that their headlong advance had taken them too far. However, it was now too late – taking up a defense in the wall at the Trekharoch Bridge, with only limited ammunition supplies and with enemy now virtually surrounding them, they could only hope that help would soon arrive.

The second assault group of III/I.R. 135, which had headed toward the Church of Saint Nikolai, reached it without any particular problems – they'd only come across Russians that had become crazed by the artillery fire. Detaining them and driving the Russians in front of them, the Germans broke into the church, which had been converted into a Red Army club. Kremers' stranded 'boatmen' ran out from the Trekharoch Gate to join them. The rapidly-intensifying gunfire put an end to scurrying about inside the fortress – some of Kremers' men ran on to the church, while the rest took cover in the officers' mess adjacent to the Trekharoch Gate.

However, those Germans of III/I.R. 135 who had headed toward the Kholm Gate or had remained behind at the Terespol Gate to cover them were genuinely unlucky. The machine-gunners and riflemen of the 84th Rifle Regiment's 3rd Battalion were lying in wait for the attackers in the Ring Barracks at the Kholm Gate, with their weapons aimed in the direction of the Citadel's keep. When the quickly-advancing assault group of III/I.R. 135 drew level with the loopholes of Matevosian's casemate, he waited until most of it had entered the kill zone before giving the command to open fire. The machine guns began to chatter almost at point-blank range, and the rifle shots easily found their targets. Those Germans that tried to return fire were instantly killed. The remaining scattered – some back to the church, some forward along the walls outside the Engineering Directorate's building (where they practically had no chance to survive), and some went rolling back toward the Terespol Gate. A few of them, having fallen back some distance, attempted to take cover behind trees and to open fire. But the doors of the casemate flew open and dozens of soldiers of the 84th Rifle Regiment spilled out of them, intending to finish the job with bayonets and point-blank shots.

S. Matevosian recalls:

> When I shouted, 'Follow me! For Stalin!' many of the men ran past me. Literally at the exit I nearly collided with a German officer – a tall, stout fellow. I was lucky that he was also armed only with a pistol. In a flash, we fired simultaneously, and his bullet grazed my right temple. I bandaged the wound, assisted by our medic.

Matevosian grabbed the dead German officer's pistol and field pack (inside of which there was only a plan of the fortress). A quick search of the body yielded nothing but an identification tag. While Matevosian was bandaging his head, the Germans running along the wall outside the Engineering Directorate were being picked off, some as they ran along the road, others when they tried to escape by swimming across the Muchavec. Some of the Germans raised their hands in surrender – an officer among them. They were prodded into the Ring Barracks (according to some sources, eleven Germans were taken prisoner). Those who had fled back toward the church were more fortunate – the park's trees hindered aimed fire from the machine guns, while the pursuing Red Army men were cut off by the forty to fifty of Praxa's soldiers who had remained at the Terespol Gate. Hearing the gunfire from the direction of the Kholm Gate, within a matter of seconds they saw their comrades fleeing in their direction. Just minutes before, they'd been chasing the Russians across West Island; they couldn't believe their eyes that now those Russians had assumed the role of pursuers. Some of them were wearing only their nightshirts, but they had rifles. Hiding behind the wood stables that were standing perpendicular to the Ring Barracks, the Germans opened fire from their carbines. The remnants of the assault group that had fled back to the church now felt a sense of relative safety. They couldn't guess that this was only the start of their ordeals.

By this time, Eremeev and the two machine-gunners had dug a Maksim machine gun, several rifles and some ammunition out of the rubble. Returning with the weapons back to the group, Eremeev was immediately given a new assignment from Kizhevatov, who was observing the battle from the Kholm Gate – to destroy the Germans lurking around the woodpile on the rear side of the Border Guard post's building. Apparently, diverted by firing at the soldiers of the 84th Rifle Regiment, the Germans had failed to mop up the seemingly abandoned Border Guards' building! Moving stealthily into the first floor of the building and setting up a machine gun at an exit leading out into the grounds, Eremeev opened fire. Dolotov, who was located in his barracks of the 33rd Engineering Regiment, could distinctly hear the machine guns when they opened up – '... the fire was continuous and heavy.' The firing continued for eight to ten minutes. From such close range it was difficult to miss – the bursts of machine-gun fire cut down many soldiers of III/I.R. 135. Only ones and twos managed to get away.

Fighting was now going on at the Terespol Gate – but the 33rd Engineering Regiment was still silent: Dolotov didn't know to whom to report – of the mid-ranked commanders, there was only the unit's on-duty officer Junior Lieutenant Korotkov. It was plain that he still hadn't grasped the situation. The attempts that had been immediately undertaken to send one or two runners at a time to the residences of the command staff (there, regiment commander Major I.N. Smirnov, as well as Junior Lieutenants Piataev, Terekhov and Peshkov all resided in the four-story buildings in front of East Fort) had all failed – the runners had been killed, even before reaching the Trekharoch Bridge, which was being peppered with fire from every direction. However, in the building of the 33rd Engineering Regiment, order was being restored.

Of the Red Army men who had lined up in the corridor, those still undressed or half-dressed were quickly pulled out of the line and sent back to their quarters to make themselves presentable. The junior commanders of the *Komsomol* members were taking charge of the situation. The formation was in a clamor. The Red Army men present were split into groups, which took up defensive positions at the windows on the first floor. They were armed only with rifles with attached bayonets, but had no cartridges. However, thus far only the Germans were firing from the walls – the pinned-down assault groups of 12/I.R. 135 in the heat of battle fired several bursts at the large windows of the 33rd Engineering Regiment's building – several wounded and dead men were already lying on the floor.

The sector of the Terespol Gate was the Germans' last hold-out on Central Island, not considering those few men now isolated in the officers' mess of the 33rd Engineering Regiment and the Church of Saint Nikolai. 'Well, let's settle with them as well' – Eremeev and Alekseev hauled the Maksim up onto a table in Kizhevatov's office and aimed it at the passage of the Terespol Gate. The curtains that had remained intact by some miracle allowed them to remain unseen for some time. The sniper Golubtsov took a prone position on the roof of the Border Post's building. However, thus far things were still quiet at the Terespol Gate.

Thus, the pendulum was now swinging toward the opposite direction. Near the Bug River on West Island, the Chernyi–Mel'nikov group had destroyed in close combat the group of German soldiers of 11 Company that was holding out in the barracks of the District's driving school – it had outnumbered the defenders by almost three to one. What next? Evacuate the vehicles? However, the sound of fighting was coming from the direction of the Terespol Bridge, the only connection that West Island had with the Citadel to its east and to points beyond. Chernyi, believing that everything that was happening was something temporary, decided to remain here, at the garages. Mel'nikov, having gathered the trainees, headed toward the Terespol Gate, but was only able to reach the building of the 17th Border Guard Detachment's transport company. Apparently, the second wave of attackers from *Hauptmann* Praxa's battalion stopped Mel'nikov's group.

No one at the headquarters of the German regiment, much less at that of the 45th Division, yet knew what was happening on Central Island. The headquarters didn't even know that the commander of III/I.R. 135 himself, *Hauptmann* Praxa, was leading the second wave! His decision to lead the attack in person was dictated not only by his desire to inspire the troops by his personal example or the bravery that was inherent in Praxa – in the *Wehrmacht*, the battalion commander was obliged to be among the forward elements when penetrating a defense. His task was to bring up a heavy weapon in a timely manner, point out targets for it, and at the decisive moment, motivate the attackers by his personal example. This was especially necessary during the second wave's attack – the key moment of the battle. Brought up to the forward line, it would be committed wherever the attack was developing most successfully, and by its commitment, bring about the decisive turning-point. By this process, the battalion commander was personally to introduce his reserves into the fighting. Just like now – Praxa was full of determination to change the situation.

0415

At the command post of the 45th Infantry Division, there was the belief that the advance was going well – the assault guns of the neighboring division were crossing the railroad bridge. The command posts of the attacking infantry regiments, of A.R. 98 and of the 81st Pioneer Battalion were being moved across the Bug. This conviction was summed up in a report to XII Corps headquarters: 'Thus far, still no resistance.'

On South Island, the situation was unchanged. Ulrich's battalion was exchanging fire with Russians in the Ring Barracks, and would likely soon begin mopping up the island – in its patches of woods, it seems, there were still more than a few Red Army soldiers. However, on North Island, the situation was serious. Although Oeltze's soldiers had without difficulty breached the Main Wall, which had been mangled by the artillery, and had advanced deep into the island, bypassing the barracks of the 125th Rifle Regiment, defensive fire had forced a halt to the advance.

Initially in the smoke, all that could be seen were dozens of Red Army men dead or fleeing in panic. Now, though, the enemy was even trying to counter-attack! The fighting had become confused. The German attack had broken down into several local firefights. Most nasty for the attackers was the fact that Red Army men, who had been left behind by the rapid German advance of the assault groups, had opened targeted fire at German officers. The battalion was now engaged in a serious battle.

Groups that had moved along the bank of the Bug–Muchavec and along the walls on the perimeter of North Island had made the most progress. But soon even they had been stopped – the closer they neared the Trekharoch Bridge, the more Red Army soldiers they encountered, which in the end stopped the attack.

Corpses of dead German soldiers were lying at the Kholm Gate; those Germans who had by some miracle escaped being overrun at the woodpile behind the building of the Border Guards' post were still rallying; those pinned down at the wall were preparing for further combat; and the second wave of III/I.R. 135 was approaching the Terespol Gate. Meanwhile, the main thing had already been accomplished – the outer defenses had been overrun and the Citadel itself had been breached. No, it is impossible to call the assault a failure. However, in these minutes, something occurred that in the Russian language is expressed elliptically, but concisely – 'The scythe struck a stone'. Berlin time was 0417.

Chapter 6

Like a Scythe around a Stone

At 0430, the Commander-in-Chief of the Western Special Military District Pavlov issued his first combat order to the District's army commanders: 'In view of the widespread military actions on the Germans' side, I order: to alert the troops and to go on a war-time footing.' The words 'military actions' were written in pencil in place of the stricken 'border violations'. The 4th Army headquarters, which had been experiencing actual combat in its sector since 0315, received the order only at 0500.

* * *

The chaotic gunfire on North Island was continuing; Red Army troops in groups or ones and twos were continuing to stream through the Northern Gate in retreat, many unarmed and out of uniform. Within the Citadel, in the final minutes of lull before the Germans' second attack, fires had blazed up that split the north-western segment of the Ring Barracks in two. The soldiers of the headquarters' companies of the 44th and 455th Rifle regiments, which were located there, still hadn't joined the fighting; they could only hear the sounds of fierce fighting from the directions of the Kholm and Terespol Gate, and on North Island. The unique feature of the Ring Barracks was the fact that there were no passageways linking all its sectors, so the units in each individual casemate, blocked from exiting the casemate because of the flying shell fragments, were cut off from each other. Thus in these minutes, having recovered from the heavy shelling, without any prior arrangement, the soldiers began to break through the walls between the casemates, striving to link up with each other.

The platoon commander of the 455th Rifle Regiment Lieutenant Makhnach, emerging out from under the bunk bed where he had taken shelter at the start of the barrage, shouted, 'This is Lieutenant Makhnach! Listen to my order – to arms!!' His narrative continues:

> Gradually, soldiers began to respond. Not more than twenty men (including junior commanders) of the company answered the call. Since there was no possibility to return the enemy's fire (they were firing from the opposite side [of the Citadel], and there was a lot of intervening dust and smoke), in the meanwhile we began to prepare a defence: we punched holes through the walls of the building that were dividing the companies, built

> up a reserve of the cartridges for the security guards, which each company kept in zinc cases, and collected the wounded.

On the opposite end of the north-western sector of the Ring Barracks, soldiers of the headquarters' elements and of the 44th Rifle Regiment's regimental school also began to break down the interior walls. They were using anything at hand – iron rails from bunks, bayonets, and pieces from the burned-out wreckage of the 31st Motorized Transport Battalion out in front of their barracks. Many of the vehicles were still burning.

Immediately after the clash within the Citadel at the Kholm Gate, Samvel Matevosian began to interrogate the captured German officer taken in the hand-to-hand combat. The Red Army men standing around began calling him 'The Artist' – the prisoner looked strange, wearing an old-style Kaiser's spiked helmet and a multitude of medals on his chest. The interrogation was heated – Matevosian was waving his pistol and swearing in his native Armenian tongue. The prisoner was insolently silent, refusing to answer any of the questions – thus 'without any excess formalities or foot-dragging', Matevosian shot him in the mouth. Even after the war, when recalling this incident, Samvel Matevosian still believed that he couldn't have acted in any other way: 'It was a combat situation – we couldn't send him to the rear, since we ourselves were encircled. Such impulsive actions in the initial phase of the war, when both panic and confusion were widespread, also played a role.' The remaining prisoners taken by the 84th Rifle Regiment in its counter-attack (according to various sources, there were between three and eleven of them) were also shot. Matevosian continued:

> We took three German submachine-gunners that had been captured to Commissar Fomin. Under interrogation, they revealed that divisions of the XII Army Corps were opposite us. The frightened Fritzes were only able to babble these words, and then – 'kaput'. The combat situation didn't allow their lives to be spared.

The interrogation abruptly over, Matevosian received an order from Commissar Fomin to break out of the encirclement into Brest in order to learn more about the situation, and to bring back the battalion's command staff, who were quartered in Brest.

Despite the heavy mortar barrage, 'Crocus' left three BA-10 armored cars of the 75th Separate Reconnaissance Battalion that were parked in front of the White Palace intact (of the thirteen BA-10s on the battalion's table of equipment). The six-wheeled BA-10 was armed with one 45mm gun and two 7.62mm machine guns, and had 10mm of armor protecting it. It had a crew of four men, and could carry 49 shells and 2,079 cartridges. Matevosian decided to use these three armored cars to break through to Brest. By this moment he had donned the combat blouse of a regimental commissar, which would indicate the presence of a commander among the defenders. The armored cars were loaded with shells from the ammunition depot, the roof of which was burning. Having been loaded with ammunition, the three armored cars set off toward the Trekharoch Gate at Makhnach's order.

Around fifteen to twenty minutes passed as Makhnach's soldiers worked to breach the interior walls. Having created passages through several of them, they linked up with adjacent companies. Up to this point, Makhnach had been the sole officer among them, but just then, a short, black-haired lieutenant without a forage cap burst through a casemate entrance – 'Sashka the Pistol', whom Makhnach knew from their days together back at the specialist school. Makhnach recalls:

> He immediately addressed me (we had recognized each other right away; it was Lieutenant Naganov). However, we conducted ourselves according to the book. He immediately answered my questions, once I recognized him and had asked, 'Where are you going? What's over there?' He replied, 'Give me a couple of men with light machine guns. I need to go that way . . . over there is the regimental school . . . All of our commanders are there, probably . . . But I'm . . .' He added that it was necessary to take the left-hand route, through a building that had been demolished during the Polish campaign, in order to reach his company.

Makhnach gave him soldiers with machine guns, and Naganov, promising to send back a runner, left, saying upon parting: 'Just let Moscow know that the fortress is encircled, and not even dust of the foe will be left.' In the autumn of 1949, while clearing out the ruins, Naganov's remains were found together with those of fifteen other soldiers; he was recognized by a *Komsomol* card found among the bones and fragments of a decayed combat blouse. Three bullets were found in the clip of his Tokarev TT pistol, and a fourth lodged in its barrel. Rusted through, 'Sashka the Pistol's' TT is now preserved in the collection of the Battle Museum.

The second wave of III/I.R. 135 by now had reached the Terespol Gate. It mostly consisted of soldiers of the 10th Company, including *Leutnant* Wieltsch's platoon; one of its assault teams was led by *Gefreiter* Hans Teuschler. Up to this point Wieltsch's platoon hadn't encountered any significant resistance – it had been attacking along the Bug, advancing through the barracks of the 17th Border Guard Detachment's transport company. Most of the latter's surviving soldiers had departed together with their commander Lieutenant Chernyi in order to evacuate their vehicles from the garages. Mel'nikov's group, which had remained in the barracks of the transport company after Chernyi's group left, had subsequently decided to head into the Citadel and was still en route toward the Terespol Gate. As a result, only two soldiers were left at the barracks to keep an eye on the wounded. Of course, they couldn't offer any serious resistance to the German 10th Company.

Dashing toward the Terespol Gate, the second wave of III/I.R. 135 could already hear the sounds of fierce fighting and understood that the 'promenade' was over. Having reached the gate, they gathered in front of the Ring Barracks, while the officers discussed the plan of attack, which battalion commander *Hauptmann* Praxa was to lead personally. As the officers talked, several men of the remnants of the first wave, who had been ensconced in the sector of the Terespol Gate, came out to meet them. The purpose of the follow-up attack wasn't clear: having learned of the destruction of the first wave, it might have been best for them to report the situation to the regiment commander, who likely believed that the Central Island had been taken and was continuing the attack on North Island. The other thing that Praxa might have done was to link up with the battalion's men in the Church of Saint Nikolai and in other encircled pockets, in order to extract them. This was still possible. But Praxa underestimated the Russian resistance, possibly believing that it wasn't the Germans that were encircled, but the Russians.

* * *

Having taken position on the northern bank of South Island at the bridge leading to the Kholm Gate by 0430, some elements of Ulrich's III/I.R. 130 began to search the buildings of the hospital. Their groups uncovered the Border Guardsmen that were lodged in the casemate of the Main Wall together with the surgery patients and the nurses: altogether, twenty-eight people. Combat erupted, and at the soldiers' request, Nurse Tkacheva quickly jotted down their family names on her trade union card, hoping that she would survive and be able to inform their families about the fate of their husbands, fathers or sons. There was no longer even a scrap of paper in the casemate – nor any water: Tkacheva wiped the lips of the wounded men with a damp rag.

The fight was brief: shots from the casemate, grenadiers near the entrance, and MG-34 machine guns shredding bodies. Staccato bursts of gunfire, cries, chaotic firing, moans – and then everything fell silent. Within minutes, several Germans entered the casemate, which was heaped with corpses, and having checked several of the bodies, they left. Among the four that were only feigning death was Nurse Tkacheva: they all ran to the adjacent casemate.

The search continued – just as everywhere else, it was accompanied by bursts of MG-34 machine-gun fire at the more suspicious locations. The hollow thumps of grenade explosions and the sounds of German speech drew nearer to the next casemate in the Main Wall, in which more hospital patients had taken shelter.

By this time, this casemate had been converted into a miniature infirmary – wounded men had sought it out during the artillery barrage. There were practically no bandages or medicines, but the hospital chief Maslov, his doctors and nurses worked to save whomever they could. A shout rang out: 'Germans are coming!' Maslov could have opened fire from his pistol, but he chose a different course of action – having donned a fresh, white surgery gown, he climbed out of the underground casemate. Going to meet Ulrich's soldiers, he racked his brains to recall his half-forgotten German and shouted that there were wounded men there, below ground. '*Verwundet*!? *Dort*?' ['Wounded!? There?'] Several German soldiers, holding grenades at the ready, approached the casemate, cautiously glanced inside, and then left.

It was impossible to evacuate the wounded – bullets were whistling all over the island. Maslov stayed with the patients and medical personnel. Those four who had feigned death and had survived the slaughter in the adjacent casemate heard Maslov's voice – and Maslov took in Nurse Tkacheva and her three associates.

Moving along the Main Wall as they further attempted to mop up South Island, Major Ulrich's soldiers were forced to hit the dirt – isolated enemy groups, apparently having overcome the initial shock, were now beginning to offer resistance. Trainees of the 84th Rifle Regiment's regimental school and men of the 95th Medical-Sanitation Battalion managed to consolidate in casemates of the Main Wall under the leadership of Lieutenant M.E. Piskarev.

Matevosian's three BA-10s were unable to break through to the city of Brest – they found the Eastern Gate obstructed by the 98th Separate Anti-tank Battalion's burned-out tractors. They moved on to the Northern Gate, along the way firing on 12/I.R. 135, which was continuing to hold out there, but there too found burning trucks blocking the passageway of the Northern Gate. They hurried on to the Northwestern Gate, but having reached the housing complex of the command staff on North Island, they learned from their defenders that the Germans were holding this Gate. They turned around and headed back to the Trekharoch Gate, passing to the left of the church. However, at this time the German assault groups of the second wave were crossing the Citadel's grounds, approaching the Trekharoch Gate at a run. Eremeev's machine gun opened fire, but was quickly suppressed. *Gefreiter* Teuschler, who was among the attackers, recalls:

> Just as we were running past the next gate, two Russian tanks began to rumble directly towards us. I barely had time to shout, 'Armour-piercing bullets – Fire!', when we were already coming under their fire. Nevertheless, after a short battle the tanks were forced to turn around and retreat. It was still those times when it was possible to turn back enemy tanks (of course, only light tanks) by such means.

However, most likely these weren't tanks (T-38s), but Samvel Matevosian's BA-10 armored cars, which were on their way back to the 84th Rifle Regiment when they spotted the Germans and turned to attack them. Matevosian took the armor-piercing bullets for armor-piercing shells – possibly that is why Teuschler's group was able to send the armored cars packing. Nevertheless, the armor-piercing bullets did mortally wound a main gunner on one of the cars.

Sergeant Major A.I. Durasov, the commander of the 84th Rifle Regiment's ammunition platoon, which was occupying a position in a garden near the White Palace, witnessed Matevosian's return to the sector of the 84th Rifle Regiment:

> Suddenly an armoured car came rolling into the garden grounds, and having pivoted, it stopped on the line of defence that we were holding. The wounded driver, staggering, climbed out of the vehicle, and behind him there appeared Matevosian in a combat blouse with the insignia of a regimental commissar.

Meanwhile Teuschler's group pushed on to the Trekharoch Gate, where other groups of the battalion that had attacked to the right of the church were now gathering. Here there occurred a hitch in the attack as the Germans paused in front of the Trekharoch Bridge, and the Russians immediately opened fire at the Germans that were clustered at the Gate, inflicting more casualties. *Gefreiter* Teuschler, having shouted 'Will anyone follow me voluntarily?' crossed the Trekharoch Bridge with six privates, who were carrying two MG-34s. The rest of the Germans followed in their wake, and they all arrived just in time to support the troops of the 12th Company that were pinned down here and exchanging fire with Russian anti-tank guns. Teuschler's impetuous advance continued. Passing to the left of Point 145 of the Main Wall and the large tent camp lying in front of it at the double quick, they surged forward toward an anti-aircraft firing position that the Russians had abandoned. Reaching it at a run, Teuschler's group suddenly and unexpectedly emerged on the flank of a Russian anti-tank gun, which allowed them to pick off some of the crew. Several of the artillerymen were able to run away. Thus, Hans Teuschler was probably the first of the 45th Infantry Division to wind up next to the East Fort, somewhere at an intersection among the buildings of the officers' housing complex. Several moments later, *Hauptmann* Praxa and his men arrived next to him. From this vantage point, they could easily see Oeltze's soldiers, moving by bounds as they worked toward the East Fort from the west.

Observing the advance of Oeltze's battalion against evidently light enemy resistance, and expecting that his soldiers at any moment would be arriving at the East Fort, Hans Teuschler didn't know that around this time (0438), the commander of I.R. 135 Friedrich John, who was watching the battle from the opposite direction, reported to the division command post that it was necessary to halt the offensive at the railroad fork to the east of North Island. First it was necessary to reorganize the attacking units and to mop up the North Island. Located with I Battalion, *Oberst* John didn't know about the fate of III Battalion. However, 'reorganizing the units' meant nothing other than a withdrawal, even if only for 100 meters or so. Halting the offensive at the railroad forks – this was an attempt to bring back part of the German force that was there, because on North Island their absence was becoming increasingly felt. Thus, Praxa and his groups, which had broken through to the East Fort, could no longer expect any assistance from Oeltze. Moreover, the lessening of Oeltze's pressure meant that the Russians could now fall upon Praxa's men with redoubled strength. This in fact is exactly what happened.

Suddenly, three men appeared atop the casemates of a Main Wall's gorge barracks, which were lying approximately 300 meters in front of Teuschler. The *gefreiter* at first couldn't clearly establish whether these men were friends or foe, but every split second counted in battle, and the law of the assault groups – 'If you're not sure, fire!' – forced him to open fire from his group's machine guns. However, Praxa, who was expecting Oeltze's men from that direction, ordered the firing to stop, assuming that they were Germans. Soon he and his command group (together with some of the survivors of the first wave) fell back to the Trekharoch Bridge, where they became heavily engaged by a Red Army group that was attacking toward

Point 145. This group, led by Mamchik, consisted largely of commanders who hadn't been able to break through to the Citadel (Ivan Cherniaev among them). It had already been exchanging fire with 12/I.R. 135 for quite some time. However, the German machine-gun fire hadn't given Mamchik's group a possibility to close with them. At that moment, a T-38 tank appeared from behind the East Fort: one of those that hadn't been able to leave the fortress. Small and maneuverable, it began to fire on the bridge while on the move. Under the cover of its fire, Mamchik's group went on the attack.

A heavy machine-gun crew had been left behind at Teuschler's position, where they immediately went to work setting it up on its tripod on the forward edge of the anti-aircraft position. However, they didn't succeed in doing even this. It immediately turned out that the three men atop the casemate were not only Russians, but also rather experienced snipers. Lying prone on the edge of the casemate (which is to say, they were atop the inner wall of East Fort), where picking them off would require an incredible stroke of luck, they opened accurate fire. Standing in the anti-aircraft firing position, Teuschler was observing the fire of his group at the Russian snipers, using every weapon at its disposal, through an optical sight. A light machine-gun crew was lying prone next to Teuschler, firing furiously and cursing the 'damned snipers'. Suddenly, the No. 2 of the crew shouted at Teuschler, 'Get down!' The first bullet flew just over the head of *Gefreiter* Teuschler, but a second struck him in the chest. The blow was so powerful that Hans spun around twice before falling. He was certain that he was dying.

The presence of the battalion commander didn't save the situation at the Trekharoch Bridge – the remnants of 12/I.R. 135 fell back across the bridge, covered by fire from the 33rd Engineering Regiment's officers' mess. Some of the men in fact sought refuge in the officers' mess, but the remainder continued to retreat toward the Terespol Gate. At 0445, a bullet fired by a Red Army soldier struck one of those retreating across the Citadel's grounds – it was the commander of III/I.R. 135 *Hauptmann* Praxa. His death became known at the 45th Division command post at 0745.

Only a few Germans managed to reach the Terespol Gate – a few others decided to take cover in the seemingly abandoned building of the 333rd Rifle Regiment, but they were spotted. Mamchik's group seized the Trekharoch Bridge and Point 145. But this was only the beginning of the 'epopee of Point 145'!

By 0447, the impression was forming in the 45th Infantry Division command post in Terespol that because of the complete surprise, only those enemy units that hadn't come under the actual and psychological effects of the opening artillery barrage were offering resistance. Reports from the neighboring divisions, which were encountering hardly any resistance, didn't give any cause to suppose that the enemy was preparing even a half-hearted defense. A signals officer with XII Army Corps headquarters reported that the prevailing point of view of the command staff was that the corps had struck empty space. The commander of the Fourth Army, General Field Marshal von Kluge, arrived at the division command post. Having received a briefing on the situation, von Kluge immediately contacted the commander of I.R. 135 Friedrich John by telephone. Then he advised the command staff of the 45th Infantry Division on the situation. From his comments one can draw the conclusion that surprise had been complete in every sector of Fourth Army's offensive. This seemed to be confirmed, for example, by the interception of a Russian message that had been sent in the clear by a Russian aviation division, asking what it should be doing now. This message made a strong impression on the commands of the 45th Infantry Division, the XII Army Corps and the Fourth Army!

Despite the fact that fighting on South Island was gradually increasing, I.R. 130 was occupying a defense in the area of both bridges across the Muchavec (directly to the east of South Island) with elements of I Battalion. The regiment's II Battalion, attacking in the direction of the next bridges to the north, crossed over the railroad embankment.

Ulrich had already been engaged in fierce fighting for the last half hour on South Island – but since this was considered a mopping-up operation, and not a battle, he believed that two of his companies (the 9th and 12th) would be more than sufficient. Leo Lozert's detachment of heavy machine guns at this time was guarding the Terespol railroad bridge against possible enemy air attack. There were no such attacks against the bridge, but Lozert and Gschöpf, who was located nearby, were both in position to observe aerial combats, which had started around 0500. Russian aircraft in large groups were heading toward the border zone; however, the German fighters had already achieved almost complete superiority in the air, and at times dozens of parachutes of Soviet airmen were floating in the sky. Incidentally, it is possible that the large number of parachutes in the sky gave rise to legends about German airborne assaults right along the border.

In order to correct the artillery fire and to get a sense of the situation on the territory of Central Island, tethered observation balloons were raised in the vicinity of the railroad bridge. Commissar Fomin ordered Sergeant Major Durasov to get rid of the observation balloons by any means. The assignment was rather problematic – of the entire complement of artillery, only two 45mm guns remained intact, and shells for them were sought in the turret of Matevosian's armored car. There they found only armor-piercing shells – Durasov used them to open rapid fire at one of the observation balloons. Before doing so, he had consulted with artillerymen, and they had dug a ditch behind the gun. Then they lowered the gun's trails into it in order to elevate the gun barrel. Durasov recalls,

> However, it was very hard to damage the target, because the shells didn't have time-fuses and we could only count upon a direct hit. After about ten minutes of firing, the balloon dropped: whether we actually shot it down or someone else did is unknown.

However, the main thing going on at this time within the Citadel and on North Island was the organization of defensive strongpoints and the procurement of ammunition by their defenders. Praxa's units had been routed and Oeltze's infantry was pinned down – each minute of respite had to be used. In the Citadel the defenders were busy with this even as Teuschler's group had been driving from the Terespol Gate toward the Trekharoch Gate and the East Fort on North Island. At 0500, the 33rd Engineering Regiment acquired their first cartridges. Dolotov relates:

> We found out that there was an ammunition stockpile somewhere in the 84th Rifle Regiment's barracks. At this time there was really no one in charge; everything happened on the fly by agreement among the junior commanders. That's how I wound up going for the ammunition, having chosen ten men, among which were Sergeants N. Iakimov and A. Gordon, as well as Private Sarkisov. Under the cover of the armoured cars, we made a dash to locate the stockpile. A sergeant major had given us directions to where we could find it. Having loaded ourselves with grenades, we grabbed several boxes of explosives and each one of us shouldered a box of rifle cartridges, before heading back. On the right the buildings of our administrative platoon were burning, and gunfire was crackling all around us. Sarkisov and Gordon were both hit and dropped, then another man. We all hit the dirt. The shots were coming from somewhere behind us. We crawled along on our bellies, each of us dragging two boxes of cartridges. Sarkisov and the other private (whose name I can't remember) were both dead. A. Gordon was lightly wounded in the thigh.

At this time, the second wave of Praxa's battalion was attacking. Dolotov's party was fired upon 'from behind', which means from the church. In the 33rd Engineering Regiment, they would learn that Germans were over there only at 0900. During the day, men of the 33rd Engineering Regiment went repeatedly for ammunition, and also came back with several pistols and PPD submachine guns, with ammunition for them. Soldiers of the 84th Rifle Regiment, who were continuing to exchange fire with Germans on South Island, were being given ammunition from this same stockpile. The Border Guardsmen were still too busy with other things than to concern themselves with stockpiling ammunition – their 10th Company was several meters away, in the sector of the Ring Barracks at the Terespol Gate. Both sides were continuing to fight – after Eremeev's machine-gun crew was showered with grenades, the German grenadier was spotted and the sniper Golubtsov killed him.

A defense was being organized in the cellar of the 333rd Rifle Regiment as well – another ammunition stockpile was nearby in the Ring Barracks, but the ground between it and the regiment's position in the cellar was being swept by fire from the tower of the Terespol Gate. In the 44th Regiment's regimental school and the 3rd Battalion of the 455th Rifle Regiment, the men were continuing to break through walls. However, the men of the 44th Rifle Regiment were tunneling their way toward a growing conflagration in a stockpile of uniforms and equipment, while soldiers of the 455th Rifle Regiment were breaking their way into the bunkers adjacent to the Trekharoch Gate, in order to escape the increasing amount of smoke filling the casemate. More and more men were now occupying the casemates at the Trekharoch Gate – Makhnach encountered a sergeant major that was carrying a German bayonet and wearing a German helmet (indicating that he'd killed one or two Germans), and two commanders as well – Lieutenant Martynenko, and an unfamiliar, severely-wounded senior lieutenant. The third commander he met was a junior lieutenant and military paramedic who had just arrived the day before in the 455th Rifle Regiment, and who hadn't even yet submitted his papers. As the sole medic, he was put in charge of a medical team, but he was shot on 24 June by Red Army men for failing to carry out an order.

Altogether, there were now around 300 men in the casemates of the 455th Rifle Regiment at the Trekharoch Gate. The majority of them were busy with stockpiling ammunition, carrying as much as possible down into the cellars. Wounded men were being carried there as well – the majority through the broad passage of a concrete service pit of the auto repair shop of the 333rd Rifle Regiment.

Then, finally, fighting with Oeltze's battalion was continuing on North Island, and Major Gavrilov, the commander of the 44th Rifle Regiment, was organizing a defense. Petr Mikhailovich Gavrilov just several days before, on 17 June, had turned 41; he was a Tatar by nationality. Gavrilov was rather short, slightly stooped, and deliberate in movement. By the end of the war, Gavrilov in his 40s would be commanding an entire *front* – but in the meantime, here, in the fortress, he was one of the most experienced commanders, with service in both the Winter War and the Russian Civil War. He was also the senior officer on North Island. In the 44th Rifle Regiment, Gavrilov had the reputation of being a very demanding and strict commander.

Gavrilov had divided the numerous Red Army men from a number of different units under his temporary command into groups, and had assigned them to defend three areas: the Main Wall to the left of the Northern Gate, and the East and West Forts. The groups of defenders were relatively sizeable, each with more than 100 men. By this time they were already engaged in fighting and had both weapons and ammunition. Gavrilov himself established his command post 150 meters to the east of the Northern Gate.

Despite the fact that several isolated defensive strongpoints were now coalescing within the Citadel and on North Island, men were continuing to filter out of the fortress. In dozens they were running across the Trekharoch Bridge toward the Kobrin and Northern Gates; many of these men had already received their combat baptism. A portion of the 125th Rifle Regiment was continuing to hold out in the western half of North Island.

By this time, the supply chief of the 6th Rifle Division Major K.V. Lapshin had arrived within the Citadel with a rifle platoon. He was searching for commanders of the 6th Rifle Division's units, in order to give them the order to withdraw to the Peschanaia ridge, 5 kilometers outside of Brest on the road to Kobrin. Amidst the gunfire and flames, he managed to locate Captain Landyshev, the commander of the 125th Rifle Regiment's 1st Battalion. At this moment, the soldiers that had been gathered by Landyshev and the company commanders were pinned down at the Main Wall, opposite the cemetery. Having received Lapshin's order, Landyshev gave directions for a retreat. A large group of civilians and personnel of rear units (150–200 people) moved out together with Landyshev's troops. Covered by fire from the groups and individuals remaining within the Citadel, they and the soldiers of the 1st Battalion exited through the Northern Gate, together with other groups that had linked up with them on their way out (including ten Border Guards). Only half of his group eventually reached the Peschanaia ridge, but this still made it one of the largest groups to escape from the fortress. The fate of the others of his group, who failed to make it to the rallying point, is unknown.

Despite the fact that the majority of men in the fortress were trying to escape it, the remaining men were continuing to struggle: Mamchik's group, which had taken up a defense in the walls at the Trekharoch Bridge, didn't have to wait long – almost immediately, within a matter of minutes, they engaged Oeltze's battalion, which was attacking eastward across North Island along the Muchavec. Oeltze's soldiers were hit by heavy flanking fire from their right – there, across the Muchavec, many trainees of the regimental school and various units of the 44th Rifle Regiment remained in the Ring Barracks. They had rallied and were firing at any of Oeltze's soldiers that they glimpsed through the smoke, trees and willow shrubs. There were few commanders among them – and there was no one to give the order to conserve ammunition. Just a couple of days before, Major Gavrilov had ordered his deputy chief of staff Semenenko to check whether all the units had turned over all their 'excess' ammunition to the stockpile. Semenenko recalls: 'He proposed to keep one combat load per rifle, to remove the cartridges from the belts and drums, and to grease them and turn them into the ammunition supply depot.' Now the soldiers, who'd been 'spared of excess ammunition', were unconcernedly blasting away out the broad windows of the barracks – they were confident that the Red Army would arrive at any moment. In their combat fervor, they were firing freely at any barely visible silhouettes, with no regard for ammunition. Then word was passed down the chain of soldiers that a man in a Red Army uniform was crawling along a wall that ran along the other side of the Muchavec. Their firing subsided, and the soldiers watched as the unknown soldier crawled up to the river, slipped into the water, quickly swam across it in several strokes, and having clambered out of the water, crawled to reach the barracks where he leaped through a window.

The man proved to be Bytko, the chief of the regimental school. Having led the group of trainees to the Northern Gate, he had returned for the rest. New soldiers were gathering in the compartment – having assembled a group, Bytko, carrying a Nagan pistol in each hand, led them toward the Trekharoch Gate. However, they were now unable to cross it. The Germans in the 33rd Engineering Regiment's officers' mess met them with intense fire. Having lost too many trainees killed on the bridge, now covered with their corpses, and in front of the mess hall, and realizing this time they couldn't get through, the soldiers fell back to the barracks together with their wounded. Understanding that they would now be here for quite some time, Bytko as the first matter of business ordered ammunition to be conserved, and to fire only at clear targets. Next he re-positioned riflemen and machine-gunners in light of the new situation, and ordered sentries to be posted at the firing ports in rotating shifts. Having passed through the Winter War with Finland as the commander of a rifle company, having been wounded there and being the first in the 44th Rifle Regiment to be awarded the Order of the Red Star, Bytko remained undaunted. His sangfroid pepped up the others.

* * *

Meanwhile, after mopping up the space between the Kholm Railroad Bridge and Bridge 'Wilka' of straggling groups of Red Army soldiers falling back from the border, and advancing along the eastern bank of the Muchavec, at 0510 the groups of *Leutnants* Kremers, Lohr and Kleine (who was leading a unit of Brandenburg commandos) took Bridge 'Wilka' by storm. In the assault they took eighty prisoners. Kremers, likely under enormous stress after the loss of almost his entire detachment, decided to crown the operation with some dramatic gesture, which might possibly compensate for the casualties. What could be more suitable than raising a flag over the captured objective? Grabbing a flag bearing a swastika, which had been used to mark the front line for the *Luftwaffe*, Kremers headed toward the bridge's railings . . . Lohr, sensing disaster, persistently urged him not to expose himself, but Kremers, caught up in the moment, could not be stopped – he began to raise the flag and probably didn't hear the single shot fired by some sniper. The others ran up to him, but it was already too late – Kremers died, clutching the *Reich* flag, fatally wounded in the head. Kremers, together with Zümpe, was mentioned in a *Wehrmacht* communiqué, but his operation, which had cost so many lives, had been proven to be pointless – not a single one of the bridges had been seized by Kremers' group independently, as had been planned. Lohr himself had taken Bridge 'Kholm' and Bridge 'Hipp', while Kremers took 'Wilka' only together with Lohr and Kleine. Without their support, the outcome of the fighting would have been uncertain. Kremers' death didn't detain Lohr and Kleine for long – almost immediately they captured the railroad bridge 'Kovel', the last one designated to be taken by the 45th Infantry Division.

At 0530, XII Army Corps commander General Walther Schroth arrived at the 45th Infantry Division command post in Terespol. He received a briefing on the situation. Despite the fact that the offensive was going as planned, nests of Russian resistance were noted, especially in the sector of I.R. 135's attack; von Kluge had spoken with its commander Friedrich John half an hour previously. The regiment was persistently requesting reinforcements in order to carry out its mission. Schroth was not opposed to this and ordered the corps reserve (I.R. 133) to be moved up closer to the combat zone. At 0555, Schlieper after a discussion with John decided to commit the 45th Division's reserve. However, *Oberst* Hipp was pleading for the corps reserve to be sent to the sector of his I.R. 130 – with the continuation of the attack to the east, the strength available to defend against Soviet counter-attacks from the north would become inadequate, and it would be impossible to sustain a further advance to the east. One can assume that Hipp was concerned about a counter-attack from the direction of the Citadel; plainly, there were more Russian units inside it than had been assumed. It wasn't clear how much strength the Russians had left on South Island – fighting was still going on there. The Germans had already activated almost all their forces, and a danger existed of a Russian attack out of the Citadel into the

ıe caption beneath this
ıotograph in the journal
gnal reads: 'At a position
ı the Soviet-Russian
order. A battery, well-
ncealed, waits for
X-hour'', the hour of
ıttle.' The photograph
ıows a 150mm sFH 18
owitzer.

'22 June, 0305. As the artillery holds the Soviet-Russian field positions and bunkers under a virtually unprecedented storm of fire, the assault groups everywhere are preparing for the attack,' *Signal*.

ıflatable rafts one after the
her slip into the water of
e Bug, the border river
etween the General-
overnment [occupied
oland] and the Soviet
nion. Soon, once they've
ached the enemy-held
ınk, the assault boats will
llow,' *Signal*.

'Being swept by a hurricane of fire from the heaviest artillery, the Brest-Litovsk Citadel is prepared for the assault. A powerful explosion followed the fall of a shell; a gigantic cloud of dust, earth and smoke remained visible for several minutes from every direction,' *Signal*.

'The effect of our artillery fire was enormous. After it ended, as our soldiers were driving the enemy out of his positions, everywhere fires continued to rage,' *Signal*.

'An assault group has penetrated into the city. The streets and buildings, which were shot-up and abandoned back during the Polish campaign, have been reduced to a state of neglect,' *Signal*.

(*Left*) 'Equipped as assault infantry, gripping a hand grenade, we move rapidly along the streets of the city. A gun and ammunition are being transported in a scrounged handcart. Horses that have lost their masters gallop along the street. Is an enemy air-raid threatened? Again and again, the attacking soldiers search the sky with their eyes,' *Signal.*

(*Right*) 'A Soviet automobile was stopped with several gunshots. Overcome, the driver sits near his vehicle, waiting to be taken prisoner by German soldiers,' *Signal.*

Panzerjägers of I.R. 130 move past a burning Soviet armored car. Note the man in undershorts and undershirt moving with the anti-tank team. According to a number of recollections, the German soldiers forced prisoners to haul ammunition and guns.

'A group of Soviet Russian prisoners. The terror of the German artillery fire is still on their faces. The barrage and German assault went so unexpectedly that several of the Soviet soldiers were not even dressed,' *Signal.*

'An assault group prepares for a final assault on the Citadel's casemates,' *Signal.*

'22.06.1941: Only several hours of fighting, and prisoners are already being led away in columns, appearing as they would otherwise only after the conclusion of an entire campaign,' *Signal.*

Riflemen firing. Likely, they are located in rifle pits atop the Main Wall – it was along its crest that barbed wire ran, deployed either by the Red Army or possibly even by the Polish army. Note the cloth spread out in front of the soldiers in the foreground – likely a recognition sign for the *Luftwaffe*.

Machine-gunners firing from the Main Wall. Above the Citadel and in front of them are clouds of smoke and dust. It seems like there is no longer any enemy there, but it is better not to stick your head up above the edge of the shell hole.

A company mortar takes part in the fighting. Judging from the shells in the ammunition case, the mortar has only just gone into action and thus far only one shell is on its way toward some point on North Island. Note that the barbed wire has already been removed.

(*Left*) A submachine-gunner, possibly a platoon commander, quenching his thirst somewhere on the Main Wall on North Island. On his belt is a cartridge pouch for a submachine gun. In each of the three squads, a cartridge pouch should contain a magazine for thirty-two cartridges. Next to the pouch is a standard leather case for a pair of 6 × 30 binoculars.

(*Right*) He is likely keeping watch through binoculars over a fire on North Island. Judging from the oily black smoke, either a vehicle is burning, or a petroleum and oil stockpile.

ıbove) A German submachine-gunner dashing in front of West ɔrt. It is the only photograph that shows details of this ›rtification. On the right is a dead horse, and beyond the white ates, seemingly a dead man.

ʒelow) They are without their waist belts, but they are carrying ıeir carbines – Germans inspecting one of the officers' ɔartment buildings. In the foreground is a concrete plinth ›resumably for trash cans). Even today it can be seen on North ›land.

ʀight) 24 June: the *Reich*'s flag is raised above the bullet-ddled barracks of the 333rd Rifle Regiment.

(*Left*) The wall at either Point 143 or Point 145. Russians are out in front, 50 meters away, or perhaps even down below, in the lee of the wall. Nevertheless – no longer is everyone in rifle pits, while those left have placed mess tins directly on the breastwork – lunch, in any case, on schedule.

(*Right*) A surrendering Red Army soldier. He isn't young, so he's possibly from the designated personnel. In his hands, in addition to the white flag, is a pea jacket (which was introduced in the spring of 1941), which indicates that he spent several days in the chilly underground cellars. Possibly, this is a gate on South Island.

'The Bolsheviks, of course, were particularly counting upon the underground vaults. They were hoping that from there, they could continue a partisan struggle. However, our soldiers with the use of tested combat means quickly managed to root them out of their shelters,' *Signal*.

'The heavy barrage had its effects. At first only isolated Soviet soldiers, then small groups and finally large throngs of Soviet soldiers emerged from their positions with upraised hands and were searched for weapons. Among them one also encountered political commissars. The image above shows the entrance to a casemate of the Brest-Litovsk Fortress,' *Signal*.

(*Left*) 'This NKVD (formerly GPU) commissar, before his capture, had torn the insignia from his collar and sleeves, thinking it would be better to remain unrecognized. However, he was quickly uncovered and placed under guard,' *Signal*.

(*Right*) A surrendering Russian emerging on the Main Wall. The Germans, without their waist belts and weapons, are standing at full height. A second Soviet soldier is summoning others to surrender. Note the rifle pit – it has been dug on the forward slope of the wall, so that the crest of the wall masks the silhouettes of the riflemen in it.

'These degenerate soldiers in skirts fought with particular savagery in a cunning partisan war against our soldiers; however, soon they were uncovered and disarmed,' *Signal*.

The assault on the Citadel has been crowned with success; despite the desperate enemy fire, our ssault groups pushed forward to the gates of the casemates, forced the garrison back from the ntrance, broke inside and took it prisoner. The defenders had already suffered rather a lot from the oncentrated artillery fire: as a sign of capitulation, a white flag had been hoisted,' *Signal.*

Gorge barracks of the Main Wall. Likely, these are garages of the 44th Rifle Regiment.

'The end of the defenders of Brest-Litovsk: in long columns, with upraised hands they are entering the road leading to a prison camp. The German arms proved to be stronger than their obstinate will to resist,' *Signal*.

;erman commanders – (*Top left*) The commander of the 45th Infantry Division Fritz Schlieper. chlieper believed that his infantry 'would manage everything on its own'. In June 1941, he had to cknowledge the era of infantry attacks without air or tank support was now past.

Top right) The commander of III/I.R. 135 Hans Hartnack. It fell to his battalion to seize the final ocket of resistance on the territory of the Brest Fortress.

3ottom left) The commander of I.R. 133 Fritz Kühlwein. It was Kühlwein's regiment, which had een initially held back in reserve, that was able to change the course of the fighting for Brest in the ;ermans' favor.

3ottom right) The commander of the 81st Pioneer Battalion Alfred Masukh. Masukh's combat ngineers played a critical role in the seizure of the fortified casemates and the multi-tiered nderground chambers and cellars of the fortress.

(*Top left*) *Gefreiter* of 10/I.R. 135 Hans Teuschler. One of the few surviving veterans of the assault on Brest, Teuschler proved to be the only man who left behind eyewitness testimony regarding the circumstances surrounding the collapse of I.R. 135's headlong attack on the morning of 22 June.

(*Top right*) The commander of III/I.R. 135 Robert Praxa. Likely, he was the first battalion commander in the *Wehrmacht* to be killed in Operation Barbarossa.

Russian commanders – (*Bottom***)** The commander of the 44th Rifle Regiment Major Petr Mikhailovich Gavrilov. Thanks to Gavrilov's resolve and firmness, the sector of defense headed by him was able to hold out longer than the others.

(*Top left*) The deputy commander of the 44th Rifle Regiment for supplies Ivan Nikolaevich Zubachev. He became nearly the only one of the commanders who managed to break through to the location of his regiment within the Citadel and to attempt to organize a defense there. He was one of the leaders of the defense of the Officers' House.

(*Top right*) Regimental Commissar Efim Moiseevich Fomin, the deputy political commander of the 84th Rifle Regiment. He was one of the leaders of the defense of the Officers' House, but more likely served as a political motivator rather than a leader of combat operations. However, in the situation that they faced, the word at times played a greater role than the weapon.

(*Bottom left*) Captain Konstantin Fedorovich Kasatkin, commander of the 18th Separate Signals Battalion, who was Major Gavrilov's closest associate and the chief of staff of the so-called East Fort.

(*Bottom right*) Lieutenant Andrei Mitrofanovich Kizhevatov, chief of the 9th Line Border Guards Detachment. Kizhevatov's Border Guards were the first to meet the assault groups of Praxa's III/I.R. 135; unable to prevent the Germans from entering the Citadel, they didn't give them the possibility to get back out of it.

A *Luftwaffe* aerial reconnaissance photograph taken in May 1941 of the central portion of the Brest Fortress (the North and Central Islands). Subsequently, these places saw the heaviest combat in June 1941.

A *Luftwaffe* aerial reconnaissance photograph taken in May 1941. The barren expanse between the town of Brest and the Brest Fortress is distinctly visible. The impossibility of finding concealment in these enormous fields and gardens became a major obstacle for those Red Army men seeking to escape from the fortress.

rear of the regiment's elements that were now approaching the city's northern limits. But how then would things be inside the Citadel? Praxa's situation was unclear, while Oeltze was still involved in heavy fighting on North Island. In the end, the Russians might bleed John's regiment of all its strength, and at minimum place artillery fire on the bridges that had been captured so fortuitously (or at a maximum, recapture them and demolish them). Indeed, if the Russians within the Citadel managed to drive the Germans back beyond the Main Wall, a situation would emerge that would be similar to what had happened back in 1939.

Schlieper, who had been in command of the 45th Infantry Division for less than two months, now faced the need to make a difficult decision. Incidentally, there did remain a hope that everything would be resolved of its own accord – the Russians, recognizing the hopelessness of resistance, might retreat or surrender. Now, though, the division command was confronted with a dilemma: to give the reserve to Hipp would mean to continue an effective attack to the east, acting in accordance with the blitzkrieg's main idea – pushing ahead without halting. Strategically speaking, this was the proper decision.

On North Island Oeltze was again attempting to break the Russian resistance by launching a fresh attack with elements of Major Parak's II/I.R. 135. Launched with determination, the companies swept forward toward the city. Judging from available evidence, they managed to seize the West Fort and that portion of the Main Wall that had been abandoned by Landyshev's battalion. However, during the attack, while attempting to rally faltering elements, Major Oeltze was killed. So was the 4th Company commander *Leutnant* Kimberger at his side – in a dispatch at 1600, Kimberger was still listed among the wounded, but by evening his death had been confirmed. Oeltze's and Kimberger's bodies remained on the battlefield. The 2nd Company lost all of its officers – its commander *Oberleutnant* Bols and platoon commander *Leutnant* Hafner were both wounded. It wasn't clear who was now commanding the battalion! In any event, I Battalion had failed to make a decisive breakthrough. Heavy, attritional fighting continued, despite the commitment of reserves. Paul Orbach, the commander of the 8th (Machine-gun) Company that had been committed into the fortress at this time recalls:

> Meanwhile the Russian fire was coming from every direction and no one had any idea what was really going on. Having set out, I led my company (sometimes at a crawl, sometimes cowering) closer to the Citadel and selected a position that offered a satisfactory field of fire. A group of the headquarters company was already occupying the most advantageous spot.
>
> The Russians were superb shots, and barely had anyone raised his head in order to figure out where they were, bullets were already humming right by it.
>
> The commander of the group of the headquarters company was lying dead right beside me. A shot to the head! Then I directed my machine guns, which were supported by an anti-tank gun and anti-aircraft gun,

> and fired 2,000–3,000 rounds at previously revealed targets. While we were firing, the Russians didn't answer with a single shot, but as soon as we made just the slightest pause in firing, a hail of enemy bullets would force us to drop down into cover. For us it became clear that in these circumstances, we had no way to get inside the fortress. Soon, several wounded men were lying beside me.

At 0600, Zahn's *panzerjägers* were still being delayed – the railroad bridge was impassable because of traffic jams. The situation was alarming – Hipp had already reached a line where Russian tanks might launch attacks, and the *panzerjägers*' high-explosive shells would be useful on North Island as well. However, a discussion with Masuch, the commander of the 81st Pioneer Battalion, didn't inspire optimism – the artillery's crossing still wasn't ready in every sector. Naber's I/I.R. 130, and especially Hartnack's II/I.R. 130, which were holding the bridges on the Muchavec, were at risk of being caught between a hammer and an anvil. In response to a combat alarm, thirty-three guns of the Soviet 204th Howitzer Artillery Regiment had left Kovalevo and had arrived at the river from the west; one battalion was horse-drawn and the other two had mechanized tow. Two of its batteries and the majority of its motorized transport had been destroyed by the early-morning German artillery barrage. Their task under the pre-war plan had been to defend the Brest area. However, only several of its batteries had managed to cross the Muchavec before Lohr and Kremers had taken the bridges – in addition to the German fire, the 204th Howitzer Artillery Regiment's crossing had been disrupted by the 22nd Tank Division: having departed from the South Military Encampment, its motorized vehicles and tanks were still on the move eastward toward the bridges at Zhabinka. As a result, while standing immobilized in front of the bridges, the 204th Howitzer Artillery Regiment suffered heavy losses from *Luftwaffe* attacks and began to withdraw to Radvanichi.

The 22nd Tank Division, as anticipated, attempted to attack I.R. 130's exposed battalions. The commander of I/A.R. 98 *Oberstleutnant* Windmann, whose 2nd Battery of light field howitzers was attached to I.R. 130, provided an account of the first encounter with Red tanks:

> On 22.6 while pursuing the offensive, 6/I.R. 130, which was armed with two anti-tank guns and machine guns, came under an attack by four Russian tanks from the direction of the crossroads lying immediately to the east of Wulka Podgorodnyi. A forward observer and the commander of 2/A.R. 98 directly behind him fired on the tanks with shells that had impact fuses. The shells exploding near the attacking tanks stopped them, and forced the crews to abandon the tanks. The escaping Russian tankers were killed or wounded by shell fragments. As was later revealed, not one of the tanks had any damage. The effects of the shells' nearby explosions were such that the tracks on all four tanks had been blown off and partially ruptured by the blast waves.

In fact, Hipp's 6th Company and Windmann's 2nd Battery had been fortunate – this was the Russian tankers' first battle, and they were in T-26 tanks. Altogether, by 0620 the 22nd Tank Division had lost nine tanks to the fire of machine guns, anti-tank rifles, anti-tank guns of 14/I.R. 130 and the artillery of the 2nd Battery of Windmann's I/A.R. 98.

By 0715, fighting on South Island was intensifying. *Oberst* Welker, the commander of A.R. 98, was wounded, as was *Oberst* Hipp, who had incautiously moved his command post onto South Island. Now *Oberstleutnant* Windmann assumed command of the division's artillery regiment. By 0730, John was getting a clearer picture of the situation facing Praxa's III/I.R. 135: wounded men were trickling back and at last messengers were making it across West Island. There had been no communications with the battalion for almost three and a half hours – for that reason the news was even more stunning: not a single objective had been reached, nor was it clear how to achieve them. Two battalion commanders were dead; one of the battalions had simply disintegrated inside the Citadel, while the second had already been struggling for three and a half hours for 200 meters of land on North Island. The commitment of the division's reserve had yielded almost nothing. The heavy artillery couldn't be used because of the risk of hitting German troops; the anti-tank artillery was stuck at the crossings, while that portion of the regimental artillery that had managed to cross had been ineffective thus far.

In contrast, something was being learned about the Russian units in the Citadel. John reported to the division command post that infantry of the 14th Infantry Regiment were inside the Citadel. The information wasn't complete and moreover wasn't the most accurate, but at least it was something . . .

On North Island, groups of Red Army soldiers were besieged in the apartment buildings housing the command staff's families and in other sectors of its western part, and were trying to break out. Among them was Shablovsky's group, which included Military Doctor 3rd Rank M.N. Gavrilkin:

> Captain Shablovsky wanted to extricate the rest of the military personnel out of the fortress and believed that the defence was senseless. We had tried to make a dash to the Northern Gate, got as far as the park, but there we were fired upon by a machine gun from the Northern Gate. We turned back and returned to our starting point. There were twenty to twenty-five men.

From the Soviet side, even those who had no part in combat operations were trying to make their way through to the apartment buildings of the command staff: their inhabitants, who were searching for food because their children were getting hungry. Dar'ia Prokhorenko:

> When leaving my husband had told me, 'When the fighting begins to die down, run back to the apartment and get something for the children to eat and wear.' Around 7:00 or 8:00 in the morning, things had become completely quiet, so I left the children with the soldiers, asking a soldier

> to keep an eye on them so that the horses wouldn't trample them, because there were a lot of horses in these cellars, and then I left. I got about halfway to our building when I heard 'Halt!' Since I didn't know this word, I thought I had misheard and continued on my way. However, the shout was repeated more loudly, so I looked back and even felt a sense of joy. There were a lot of soldiers in iron helmets standing around the entrance to the cellar that I had just left. Thinking that they were our soldiers, I laughed and wanted to shout something welcoming to them, but just then my voice fell off in apprehension and hatred. These soldiers were gesturing with their hands for me to come towards them. I realized that they wanted me to approach. I walked towards them and tried to grasp what would happen with my children, because it was clear they were going to take me away. As I neared the Germans, I angled towards the corner of a wall that I had passed when leaving, and when I drew even with this corner, I flipped them off with both hands and ducked behind the wall, but a German jumped down from the top of this same wall, and at that moment something struck me on the head so hard that I couldn't see, my vision grew hazy, and I was standing there as if in some big fog with no recollection of myself. I could see that this German had dropped dead next to me. Apparently our guys had been observing me and had killed this German. I don't remember how I made it back to the children, or with whose help; I only remember that on the evening of 22 June I was with my children again in that same basement, where my husband had taken us, and the same soldiers and horses were there, but now my husband was with us.

* * *

At 0730 on the basis of incoming reports, for the first time the impression was forming at the command post of the 45th Division that stronger than anticipated units of the Russian garrison of the defensive fortifications were making a stand in the rear of the division's forward units. The initial idea to come to mind was to use the 45th Infantry Division's indisputable superiority in artillery. However, now artillery support for the troops in the Citadel was impossible, because the German and Red Army positions were too close together.

At 0740, I.R. 130's units were stretched thin, extending from the 'Kovel' railroad bridge inclusively to South Island. Hipp, reporting on the situation to Schlieper, was apparently under the strong impression of the events on South Island and Welker's wounding. The commander of I.R. 130 acknowledged that the Citadel was occupied by a rather strong and courageous defending garrison. Schlieper informed Hipp that I.R. 133 (the corps reserve) would be committed to I.R. 130's sector. Factually this was the first sign that Schlieper was halting the assault on the fortress itself. He couldn't have failed to notice that the introduction of Parak's II/I.R. 135 on North Island had achieved practically nothing. To commit the II Battalion of *Oberst* Kühlwein's I.R. 133 there as well was risky: the overall situation (the destruction of the Russian forces on the border) was unclear on 22 June and remained so over the next several days. Commit Kühlwein's I.R. 133 to West Island? But the situation there was murky, and the regiment risked the loss of several important hours. Thus he decided that the division's sole remaining reserve would support Hipp's success and expand his offensive.

At 0810, more news about III/I.R. 135 arrived, this time from the artillery observers that were attached to it. An officer of I/A.R. 99 was reporting that the soldiers of III/I.R. 135 had stopped and were lodged in front of the fortification of the Central Citadel, having lost approximately 35 percent of its men. At 0830, the battalions of *Hauptmann* Kaehne (Oeltze's replacement) and Major Parak again went on the attack. This time, despite bitter Russian resistance, they managed to reach their goal – the road spanning North Island from north to south, and gained access to the Trekharoch Bridge. In the process, the T-38 tank that had helped Mamchik hold the bridge for more than two hours had been hit and had burst into flames: 'In the flames we could see a tanker who couldn't get out of the vehicle; wounded, he didn't even have the strength to clamber out of a hatch. It was impossible to witness this without tears.' Most likely, the T-38 had been set aflame by a 37mm gun of 14/I.R. 135, whose commander, *Oberleutnant* Wessig, was also killed during this attack.

The remnants of Mamchik's group crawled back into the shrubs around Point 145. From there a level athletics field stretched for approximately 400 meters to the command staff's apartment complex, where the group decided to find shelter. Under scathing fire as they crossed it, the soldiers were dropping one after another as Mamchik led the survivors to the apartment complex. Hurrying after their commander, the soldiers were able to reach the buildings at a run and to exchange fire with the Germans once again, during which Mamchik was killed. However, not all the soldiers had followed Mamchik – several men took cover in the willow shrubs along the bank of the river, under the bridge, and in the casemates of the wall at Point 145. This is the last we know of the fighting for Point 145 and the Trekharoch Bridge from known eyewitnesses among the defenders. All further discussion of the events connected with Point 145, whose defenders resisted right up to the fall of the Officers' House on 26 June, are drawn from German sources. Parak's soldiers mounted the earthen wall contiguous to the gorge barracks at Point 145 and dug several rifle pits atop it. The wall at Point 145, like the entire fortress, had turned into a 'layer cake' of opposing forces.

The remnants of the forces that were fleeing from the fortress and the Northern Military Encampment assembled north and north-east of Brest. Often the soldiers were arriving individually in a half-clad state. The regiments' matériel could not be evacuated from the fortress. The situation proved easier for those units located just outside the fortress. The 6th Rifle Division's 131st Artillery Regiment, which had been encamped on the bank of the Bug River, came out with eight guns of the 2nd Battalion and its regimental school. Two artillery battalions of the 17th Howitzer Artillery Regiment and 19 guns (of the authorized 36) and 300 men of the 447th Artillery Regiment emerged from the Northern Military Encampment.

The latter, which had lost several tractors during the artillery barrage, likely had to abandon some of its guns in the artillery park due to the lack of a means to tow them. Thus, the losses from the artillery fire and the opening hours of the *Wehrmacht*'s attacks were heavy but not catastrophic for those outside the fortress. Much more equipment had to be abandoned later because of the lack of fuel, prime movers and vehicle breakdowns.

The Red Army men striving to escape Brest often were unarmed and were offering practically no resistance. The Germans began to target their transport. Walther Loos recalled:

> Constantly, trucks fully loaded with Russian infantry, again and again were trying to reach the Citadel, or were searching for a way out of the city to the east. In the majority of cases they were shot up by machine guns or destroyed by an anti-tank gun at point-blank range.

At 0840 Masuch reported that Russian reconnaissance armored cars were on the Central Island, some of which were trying to break through: probably, he's talking about Matevosian's armored cars, which had clashed with Teuschler around 0435. Isolated gunshots were still being heard on West Island as well. Because of these and other incoming messages, the impression was forming at the command post of the 45th Division that an increasing number of the bypassed and isolated Russians were rallying and beginning to defend. In particular, the loss of officers was relatively high; for the most part they were being shot by riflemen firing from trees and rooftops.

At 0845, I.R. 130 was given the 45th Reconnaissance Battalion to support the attack against Hill 144. However, the reconnaissance battalion was running behind schedule for the attack. Since I.R. 130 was left with only light howitzers and 37mm anti-tank guns, it requested artillery to be brought up hastily. The 1st and 6th batteries of A.R. 98 began moving up, but they were stopped due to the lack of available bridges.

At this time, the *Luftwaffe* dropped several bombs on the southern portion of Brest. Because of the smoke and haze, the strike hit no particular targets. Gottfried Hammacher recalls, 'From up above, we couldn't see what was happening down below. I only remember that the entire sky was red from the fires. Below us were only scarlet clouds of smoke.' News of the bombing reached the 45th Division command post, which immediately contacted the headquarters of the XII Army Corps. *Luftwaffe* activity was termed 'maximally undesirable', since here 'I.R. 130's transport was already coming up.'

At 0900, the XII Corps operations chief got in touch with the 45th Division's command post with some long-awaited news – the corps reserve (I.R. 133) was being given back to the division. By this time, two battalion commanders and one company commander in the 45th Infantry Division had been killed, and one regiment commander had been wounded. Precisely at 0900, the Brest-Litovsk railroad station was taken by an assault detachment of the 1st Railroad Engineering Regiment's 5th Company led by *Leutnant* Linni. The detachment, arriving at the station, discovered that the basement of the station had already been occupied by the enemy. Three attempts were made to penetrate into the basement, but each time they were beaten back by its defenders with losses for Linni's men. No further attempts were made – the detachment wasn't adequately armed for assaults. Linni reported, 'In the basement, which has been adapted as a bomb shelter, there are approximately thirty-five men.' In reality, there were approximately 100 armed men there: Border Guards who had retreated from the Terespol Bridge; anti-aircraft gunners who'd come to Brest in order to pick up boots for their unit at a warehouse; approximately thirty junior commanders of the signals company of the 45th Aviation Base of the 10th Composite Aviation Division's 74th Ground Attack Aviation Regiment, who'd been heading toward their base in Pruzhany to receive a batch of fresh recruits; and sixteen soldiers of the 66th Fortified Region headed by political instructor F.L. Zazirnyi. In addition, more than a few commanders and soldiers of other units had been caught at the train station that night. Alerted by the explosions on the border and being armed, they stocked up with ammunition that was distributed to them in the police station's duty room from the supplies of the paramilitary railroad security and the local police precinct. Those who didn't have weapons obtained them from those confiscated from border violators.

After bitter fighting on the approaches to the train station, they had fallen back to the station itself, and then down into the basement. Hundreds of passengers (those who had spent the night at the station, as well as more who had come running to the station, hoping to find a way to escape to the east; according to some estimates nearly 2,000 of them) were crowding the basement as well.

At 0915, a new phase of the fighting on North Island began. Now Friedrich John had no intention to continue the attack into the island's eastern portion. Russians in the East Fort, the Main Wall and in other pockets in the eastern part of North Island were securely bottled up. Another attack, for which there was inadequate strength, would only lead to fresh casualties. Now the main task for the commander of I.R. 135 became to alter the situation in the Citadel, which had resulted from the destruction of Praxa's III Battalion. John was intending to break into the Citadel from North Island by concentrating his key force (Parak's II Battalion) against the Trekharoch Bridge. However, just at this moment the Russians launched a counter-attack on North Island, which resulted in the recapture of several points that the Germans had gained with such difficulty. The regiment's reserve – the 9th Company – was thrown into the fighting. It managed to drive the Russians out of the buildings that they had just recaptured, but then the company pushed on, not stopping, and attacked the northern section of the Main Wall. While the 9th Company was assaulting the wall, one of the companies of Parak's battalion launched an attack across the Trekharoch Bridge, taking heavy fire from the 'hold-outs' of Mamchik's group, who'd taken shelter in the gorge barracks (Point 145), and from the windows of the Ring Barracks.

The machine-gunners of 12/I.R. 133, advancing across West Island, took a position to the right of the Terespol Bridge. From this place, Leo Lozert had a splendid view of the sector in front of the company. However, no Russians were visible, even though heavy firing was going on inside the Citadel. Now and then wounded soldiers of the assault groups, who'd survived by some stroke of luck and were exhausted by the night-fighting, came across the bridge, as well as Russian prisoners. Some of the soldiers of the machine-gun company joined assault teams that were combing through West Island, searching for Red Army hold-outs.

At 0930, *Oberleutnant* von Fumetti (I/A.R. 99) reported that his forward observers on West Island had been encircled by hostile forces. Almost immediately there followed the news that the encircled men had been killed. They proved to be *Hauptmann* Kraus, the commander of I/A.R. 99, and two officers of A.R. 98 that had been accompanying him. How this happened isn't known. In the recollections of the defenders of West Island (A.S. Chernyi and M.I. Miasnikov), they only talk about the defense of separate sectors or about furtive break-out attempts. However, there are mentions of the destruction of a tentatively-encircled German group in the barracks housing the trainees of the District driving school. In addition, Chernyi managed to break out by attacking in the direction of the bridge and levees (though of the forty men in his group, only thirteen managed to reach casemates on North Island, and four of them were wounded). It is fully possible that somewhere around the bridge, Chernyi's group had bumped into Kraus and his accompanying officers and had killed them.

Despite Kraus's death, at 0950 John asserted that his regiment now held West Island and the western half of North Island, but added, 'The regiment is trying to rescue the men of the III Battalion who are encircled in fortifications of the Central Citadel, and who are attempting to break out across the Trekharoch Bridge.' This comment is noteworthy – over the last thirty minutes or so, the task of the attack had changed from seizing the Citadel to 'tidying-up' and 'rescuing the encircled'; a significant difference! Judging from everything, John now realized that taking the fortress would be a lengthy job, one that could not be accomplished on 22 June, and now the main goal was to rescue men. It is apparent that the 45th Infantry Division was running out of steam, shuffling reserves around here and there, reaching and cancelling decisions, and was shocked by the casualties over these first hours ...

By this time Parak's attack on North Island toward the Trekharoch Bridge had faltered – extremely heavy defensive fire prevented the Germans from even setting foot on the bridge. The Russians were rooted in along the riverbank, in the East Fort and in the apartment buildings in front of it (Cherniaev); in addition fire at the attacking Germans was coming from the casemates at Point 145. The artillery could provide little help – there was no way to deploy a few anti-tank guns in a good position, while any support from Arko 27 was unrealistic, since the Russian defenders in the Ring Barracks were firing out of the windows that faced north, on the side sheltered from a barrage. Despite the fact that the artillery was now almost silent, the artillerymen were suffering losses. In the wake of Wessig's death, *Leutnant* Zennek of III/A.R. 98, the commander of a signals group that was attached to the infantry, was killed. With regard to the death of officers, II Battalion was at risk of repeating the fate of I Battalion – *Leutnants* Orbach (the commander of 8th Company) and Hatterbauer (the commander of 6th Company) were both wounded. The losses among the junior command staff were also high.

Only 9/I.R. 135 achieved a genuine success. Having captured the northern edge of North Island and the Northern Gate, it was attempting to advance to the east in order to accomplish that which I and II battalions had been unable to do.

Exploiting the collapse of Parak's attack and the stabilization of the situation at the Terespol Gate and Kholm Gate, at this time the Red Army forces inside the Citadel began to try to wrest the initiative away from the Germans. The first order of business was to drive the Germans out of the church and the 33rd Engineering Regiment's officers' mess. Soldiers of the 455th Rifle Regiment initiated the attack. Heavy fire didn't allow them to advance. Russians on the second floor of the headquarters of the 33rd Engineering Regiment supported the attack by firing at the windows of the mess hall and church. There were only a few German defenders in the officers' mess – with little hope to hold the entire sector of the Ring Barracks adjacent to the Trekharoch Gate, they had decided to abandon the first floor and to hold the second floor, and from there they were firing at the attackers. The 455th Rifle Regiment's attack against the officers' mess and soon after it the 84th Rifle Regiment's assault on the church both faltered – the attackers were too few, and the attacks were disjointed. It became clear that the consolidation of forces was necessary.

At 1020 the commander of I.R. 133 *Oberst* Kühlwein arrived at the 45th Infantry Division's command post and received a mission from Schlieper: to be ready by 1300 to begin crossing over to the southern sector of South Island and to attack on I.R. 130's right. However, on the basis of incoming messages, in particular from I.R. 135, about the enemy strength in the Citadel, and after consulting with Hipp, Schlieper realized that John no longer had the strength to get anywhere and decided to change I.R. 133's mission. Now Major Freytag's I/I.R. 133, reinforced by 13/I.R. 133, was first to mop up West Island, before reinforcing John in the Citadel. From there it was to cross over to South Island and clear it of any remaining enemy resistance.

It would seem that 45th Infantry Division's command had rather decisive intentions: to commit the reserves and finish off the enemy. However, it seems that no one had any real confidence in accomplishing this – in order to support the final mopping-up, XII Corps headquarters ordered Schlieper to wait for the arrival of a *nebelwerfer* battery from the 6th Nebelwerfer Battalion (which had to this point been subordinated to the 31st Infantry Division). Its arrival was expected only toward evening. By 1050 it had become clear – the Citadel would not be seized on 22 June with the forces at hand. So now efforts were focused on freeing encircled groups in the fortress and taking the most advantageous positions for forthcoming attacks. Of course, everything wasn't so dire for either XII Corps (the 31st and 34th Infantry divisions were advancing against almost no resistance) or for the 45th Infantry Division: the bridges had been taken, thus clearing the way for Guderian's panzers; the Russians were trapped inside the Citadel; and at any time now the Russian groups on the other islands would be finished off. Schlieper was disturbed by something else – time itself was beginning to work against the 45th Division. This began from the moment when Praxa's and Kremers' men became isolated in the church. They had a radio; with no thought to conceal their presence in the church, they had already begun radioing for help. Both the 45th Infantry Division command post and battalion commander John were waiting for a decision from General Schlieper, who had been in command of the division for less than two months ... However, more men would be killed attacking through the Trekharoch Gate in the effort to rescue them than would be rescued in the church. Artillery fire could be directed only against a solitary Russian machine-gun nest at the Trekharoch Gate; the artillery was impotent against the casemates, the Karl mortars were out of action, and in any case, an attack by them (or by *nebelwerfers*) would only secure a withdrawal of German troops from ground that had been taken with such difficulty. In addition, a *nebelwerfer* attack would blanket the church as well. Incidentally, during subsequent German barrages on the Citadel, striving not to hit the German centers of resistance in the church and officers' mess, rocket-launchers were not employed – yet they still took no less punishment from their own artillery.

The exhausted officers at the 45th Infantry Division command post, dispirited by the death of two of the three battalion commanders, John's fruitless attacks, and Parak's stalemate at the Trekharoch Gate that they could see through binoculars, all came to the same understanding. The encircled Germans in the Church of Saint Nikolai couldn't hold out long.

Chapter 7

The Church of Saint Nikolai

A.I. Makhnach recalls: 'At this time dense blue smoke began rolling across the Citadel's grounds and barracks. Someone shouted, "Gas!" Many of us donned gas masks.' The smoke was signaling Parak's new attack at 1050. Having laid down a smokescreen, probably employing 81mm mortars, a company of II/I.R. 135 managed to dash across the Trekharoch Bridge from North Island. A portion of it burst through the Trekharoch Gate and into the Citadel, while the rest of the company began tossing grenades into the windows of the 455th Rifle Regiment's and 33rd Engineering Regiment's sectors of the Ring Barracks that overlooked the bridge, so that having bypassed the barracks of the latter Soviet regiment along the bank of the Muchavec, they could pivot and re-enter the Citadel through the gap in the Ring Barracks next to the White Palace.

As a culminating stroke, two additional assault groups, having suddenly crossed the Muchavec River over the Brigidki Bridge, broke into the Citadel through the Brigidki Gate on the opposite side of Central Island, hoping the element of surprise would bring them success. It seemed that these events at last signaled II/I.R. 135's long-awaited success. The majority of the Red Army men were still lurking in the cellars, and no one could come to their assistance (German machine-gun fire coming from the Terespol Gate and the church was preventing any movement). The Germans who had penetrated through the Trekharoch Gate had escaped the beaten zone of fire coming from the Red Army men holding out in the casemates of the wall at Point 145 and elsewhere. The situation was hanging by a thread . . .

The Citadel was saved by a desperate counter-attack led by Lieutenant Vinogradov – the chief of the 455th Rifle Regiment's chemical services. Seeing the German breakthrough, in a matter of minutes Vinogradov was able to assemble not more than fifty men – there was little time, and the bunch hastily gathered by him immediately set off toward the Trekharoch Gate. In the smoke, they collided in hand-to-hand fighting with the Germans – there was no other option. The fury of the Red Army men overcame the Austrians' desperation – the troops of the 45th Infantry Division broke and fled back across the Trekharoch Bridge. Those who were advancing along the outer perimeter of the Ring Barracks, tossing grenades into the windows, also met with failure. Russians were firing at them from the semi-tower in the 455th Rifle Regiment's sector and from the gorge barracks (Point 145). Nevertheless, they did manage to reach the windows of the 33rd Engineering Regiment's sector. However, even there the use of grenades brought no results: noticing that the M-24 grenades were exploding only after a delay of five or six seconds, the soldiers scattered mattresses on the floor, which cushioned the landing of the grenade – and then had time to pick them up and toss them back at the Germans.

A handful of Germans nevertheless did manage to break into the Citadel through the gap in the Ring Barracks next to the White Palace – but heavy fire coming from its windows forced them to halt the attack, and they had to swim back across the Muchavec in retreat under the cover of a smokescreen. Several Germans attempting to take cover under the Trekharoch Bridge were killed almost immediately by machine-gun fire from the semi-tower of the Ring Barracks that overlooked the Trekharoch Bridge and Gate. There were no prisoners . . .

Soldiers of Praxa's III/I.R. 135 were continuing to hold out in the mess hall of the 33rd Engineering Regiment. They didn't seize their chance to abandon their position and break out of the Citadel together with Parak's men as they fell back across the Trekharoch Bridge. It isn't known why they failed to do so. Perhaps they had wounded men and couldn't leave them behind; perhaps they didn't have orders to pull out; or possibly they still didn't see their situation as critical.

This was a major success for the defenders of the fortress, which happened only due to their resolve and courage. But it mustn't be forgotten that the German assault groups that had broken into the Citadel from North Island across the Brigidki Bridge were also moving toward the Trekharoch Bridge, and on their way they had seized the casemate of the Ring Barracks that housed the 44th Rifle Regiment's headquarters. What next? Push on through the Ring Barracks' interior? However, first and foremost there were no passages between the casemates; secondly, they faced the resistance of troops of the 44th Rifle Regiment that were there; and finally, the raging fire that had by now enveloped a large section of the casemates overlooking the Muchavec also blocked this possibility. After leaving behind a small force in the burned-out offices of the 44th Rifle Regiment's headquarters, they exited the casemate and hurried on directly toward the Trekharoch Gate – across the parade ground adjacent to the 333rd Rifle Regiment's building.

However, at this moment there was now a more solid defense in the basement of this building than had been there earlier that morning. Machine guns had been set up in the delivery ramps leading down into the basement on both sides of the building. In addition, soldiers had constructed a barricade on the broad steps leading down to the parade ground outside the building, behind which another machine-gun crew was concealed. Finally, in the basement itself, the soldiers had erected firing platforms at the basement windows from the rubble of walls, beams and boxes, upon which riflemen were posted.

It was here, during the attack across the parade ground, that the Germans put into play Paternola's 20mm anti-aircraft gun positioned at the nearby Brigidki Gate – it opened fire at the embrasures of the cellars and the 333rd Rifle Regiment's machine-gun positions. By this time the 20mm gun had already demonstrated its usefulness against ground targets – it could fire both armor-piercing and fragmentation shells, and had a rate of fire of 220 rounds a minute. With a 360° field of fire, the anti-aircraft gunners could rake the entire rear facing of the 333rd Rifle Regiment's building with fire. Positioned in the gateway, its crew was sheltered from fire from both sides. Paternola's bursts of fire inflicted casualties on the defenders of the 333rd Regiment, who hadn't anticipated an attack from this direction. Having witnessed the bounding advance of the German assault groups along the walls of the Ring Barracks within the Citadel, some of the soldiers became panic-stricken. The majority of these men were designated personnel who had recently been conscripted. A.I. Leont'ev, a veterinarian assistant in the 333rd Rifle Regiment, recalls: 'A Pole, who should have been at an embrasure with a Degtiarev machine gun, came running towards me from it with a white sheet shouting "Germans!"' Leont'ev mechanically shot him in the back of the head as he ran past, and having grabbed the Degtiarev, he opened fire at the Germans advancing across the parade ground. Bursts of gunfire rattled from other embrasures as well – nevertheless, the Germans managed to seize a chamber of the Ring Barracks occupied by the 44th Rifle Regiment's regimental school and to penetrate right up to the sectors held by the 455th Rifle Regiment's 8th and 9th companies. The Trekharoch Bridge lay just a bit further ahead – however, Paternola, who was firing at the embrasures of the 333rd Rifle Regiment, couldn't target the 44th Rifle Regiment's soldiers, who were positioned in a corner of the Ring Barracks on the other side of the German attackers. One of these soldiers recalls, 'When the Germans incautiously made a pell-mell attack against the fortress's central area in the sector of the regimental school, we prepared a warm reception for them.'

Attacking along the walls of the Ring Barracks within the Citadel, the Germans practically had nowhere to duck into it, neither in the 44th Rifle Regiment's sector nor further ahead, past the burning section of it, in the 455th Rifle Regiment's sector. Having seized one of the regimental school's chambers, they were unable to hold it for long. Then, caught in a crossfire being placed by the 44th Rifle Regiment's soldiers in the Ring Barracks and the Red Army soldiers in the 333rd Rifle Regiment's building, the basement windows of which were out of sight to Paternola's anti-aircraft gun, they had no choice but to retreat under fire. Those who did manage to get away probably considered themselves lucky.

Having suffered failure in every sector, Parak's II/I.R. 135 was finally played out – this was the only instance when the Germans managed to cross the Trekharoch Bridge, but in fact it was also their last serious attack of the day. The cupola of the Church of Saint Nikolai, a constant reminder of their objective, was visible to them through the smoke of the burning uniform and equipment warehouse and the smokescreen at the Trekharoch Gate, but was out of reach to the II Battalion.

* * *

After Parak's attack, the Soviet defenders reinforced the defenses at the Trekharoch Gate – a 76mm gun from the 333rd Regiment's artillery park was deployed near it, together with twenty to thirty shells. This was done by Lieutenant A.L. Petlitsky, the commander of a 44th Rifle Regiment's anti-tank gun platoon; his group had six men, all junior commanders. The gun was placed in front of the semi-tower in the 455th Rifle Regiment's sector. It was decided to restrict fire to only armored vehicles or to large groups of penetrating infantry, in order to conserve shells. Petlitsky returned to the basements of the 333rd Rifle Regiment – by this time, a perceptible desire was growing there to drive the German 10th Company away from the Terespol Gate, and not allow the Germans a single foothold in the entire western sector of the Citadel.

The opposing side was also giving some thought to artillery support – *Oberst* John, who'd gotten in touch with the division command post, declared that he wanted to try to break the resistance at the Trekharoch Bridge with the single howitzer of III/A.R. 98 that was available to him, in order to extract the encircled Germans in the Citadel across it. In addition, it was stressed that a precondition for successes on Central Island was the elimination of all pockets of Russian resistance on West Island by I/I.R. 133. At 1010, Hipp reported that *Oberleutnant* Miske had raised the banner of the *Reich*'s armed forces above 'a turret' on South Island (probably having in mind the water tower on that island). On this basis *Oberst* Hipp concluded that all resistance on South Island had collapsed, except for exchanges of fire with isolated Russians.

Inside the Citadel, the defenders were preparing to launch another attack toward the Church of Saint Nikolai. This time, the main assault force would come from combat groups of the 84th Rifle Regiment, the 33rd Engineering Regiment, and a Border Guards unit. The attack couldn't count upon cooperation from other units. There were no communications with the 44th Rifle Regiment, while the 333rd Rifle Regiment and Kizhevatov were being targeted by 10th Company machine-gunners and the 20mm gun at the Terespol Gate, which were covering all exits from the basements of the Arsenal and the Border Post. The 455th Rifle Regiment was preoccupied with defending the Trekharoch Bridge, but before the attack on the church, it also had to eliminate the Germans that were still holding out in the officers' mess. Considering that in addition Fomin's group had to keep the Kholm Bridge under fire, the attack couldn't be a large one. Nevertheless, this attack would be the first joint operation involving several combat groups. Ivan Dolotov recalls, 'Our attack began somewhere around noon – prior to this a group of three men had come running over from 84th Rifle Regiment, who tried to give us orders to attack the church in the name of some officer.'

Fomin's machine-gunners from the south and the 33rd Engineering Regiment from the north opened fire at the church's windows, driving the Germans away from them. Immediately the first wave of Red Army men rushed the church, followed by a second. Dolotov continues:

> I was running towards the church with the second line of attackers. The ground between us and the church wasn't wide: just the evening before, tents had been standing on it, and the field kitchens had been growing dark under the spreading branches of large trees. But now there were no tents. Dashing from tree to tree, we reached the walls in bounds, many

> falling under the fire of Germans, who were shooting from windows. We caught our breaths lying behind the wall. Beyond it we could hear shouts, explosions and gunshots. The doors of the church facing in the direction of the 333rd Rifle Regiment were open. Red Army men were running in and out of them.

They managed to break into the church, but the Germans, having fallen back from the windows, were crouched behind columns at the altar and were keeping the entrance under fire. More were located up in the choir balconies perched above the entrance. These Germans could fire on both those running toward the entrance from the direction of the 333rd Rifle Regiment and from behind at anyone inside the church attempting to attack the altar. It was impossible to hurl grenades up into the altar, because the first wave of attackers was already in the church, and besides, there were few hand grenades. Gunfire was coming from every direction. The approaches to the church were covered by fire from the Germans in the officers' mess hall and in the 33rd Engineering Regiment's building. True, the latter were conserving ammunition, but the German machine-gunners at the Terespol Gate were firing actively, even though the flickering figures of the Russian soldiers were poorly visible to them because of the trees in the churchyard.

Some of the Germans (primarily the wounded) were located in the church's large basement – the so-called 'lower tabernacle'. It was difficult to break into it down the sole narrow staircase leading to it. Indeed, generally speaking, this wasn't even necessary – those Germans sitting in the basement's darkness didn't present a danger. However, a no less difficult task was prying those Germans out of the choir balconies above them – a narrow, spiral staircase, like those leading up to a medieval castle keep, led up to them. Only a single file of people could climb up the stairs. The choir balconies themselves were wooden – bullets could penetrate them, and if a demolition charge could be found, the front of the balconies could be undermined. However, the rear portion of the balconies' area rested on the church's stone foundation, and it could be taken only by assault.

Dolotov, dashing into the church, at first couldn't even understand what was going on:

> It was dark inside the church and in the first moments not even people were visible; after the daylight outside it was so dark that you could only see reddish flashes of automatic weapons' fire and hear the din of gunfire, intensified by the high vaulted ceiling. The Germans were up in the choir balconies, while our guys were down below. Soon our eyes adjusted to the darkness and things became more visible, and it seemed to me that there weren't many Germans up there, just five or six submachine-gunners firing down on us.

Maybe they ran out of ammunition, or maybe their nerves gave way – but the Germans lodged in the altar suddenly jumped up and darted for the windows facing in the direction of the Engineering Directorate:

> To shouts from the doors, I dashed outside. It turned out that Germans were jumping out of the windows and running in the direction of a hedgerow growing along the sidewalk outside the former Polish headquarters [the building of the Engineering Directorate]. We opened fire at the fleeing men. However, the main thing was that the Germans were stopped by a barbed-wire fence that was concealed in the hedgerow, which separated the yard outside the headquarters from the road. Rushing along the hedgerow across open ground, the fascists were wiped out by our fire and the fire coming from the Ring Barracks. Obviously, the small [German] group in the choir balconies was covering the withdrawal of the church's main group. The red and black flag no longer waved from the windows of the church.

However, the soldiers who had shot down the fleeing Germans, running together with Dolotov, immediately hit the ground, trying to save themselves from machine-gun fire that was coming from the windows of the 33rd Engineering Regiment's mess hall. They decided to wait for darkness ...

The attack by the Red Army soldiers led to only partial control of the Church of Saint Nikolai. Neither the 84th Rifle Regiment nor the 33rd Engineering Regiment could fire on the handful of Germans holding out in the balconies. Meanwhile, those Germans were still keeping the 333rd Rifle Regiment, the 455th Rifle Regiment and the Border Guards under fire. It was impossible to move into the church, because its interior was being swept by fire from the balconies. The attackers were only able to occupy a small pigeonhole below the balconies, just inside the church's entrance, that was outside the field of fire from the enemy in the balconies. Nevertheless, even though this was insignificant and incomplete, it was still a success. However, there was a cost to be paid for it – of the approximately ninety men of the 33rd Engineering Regiment that attacked the church, not less than 60 percent fell dead or wounded. The commander of one of the attacking detachments, Junior Lieutenant V.I. Prusakov, was severely wounded in the head (he passed away later the same day). The casualties of the 84th Rifle Regiment and of the Border Guardsmen were probably roughly similar.

Around noon, Fritz Schlieper reported to Schroth: after the arrival of both batteries that had been attached for this purpose, I.R. 130 would continue its attack toward Hill 140 east of the Citadel. Bitter fighting was going on inside the Citadel – there were very many KIAs, especially among the officers. Walther Schroth ordered for no more units to be committed into the Citadel, thereby setting aside its capture for the time being, proposing instead to besiege it, to extract the German units encircled inside it, and then to hammer the adversary with heavy artillery. Practically speaking, Schroth was again counseling the initiation of a withdrawal. However, there was no way to extract those Germans still holding out in the Church of Saint Nikolai. Of course, Schlieper understood that to Walther Schroth, the fate of those lodged in the Church of Saint Nikolai simply boiled down to accepting unavoidable costs. However, that which would take place only a year and a half later in Stalingrad, having by then become customary business on the Eastern Front, was still rather unaccustomed in June 1941! Thus Schlieper nevertheless tried to obtain from Schroth some means in order to breach the 'damned Trekharoch Gate' and extract the encircled Germans.

At 1230 I.R. 133 was given an order to assign only one reinforced company to the task of mopping up West Island; having finished this job, it was then to attack the Citadel (if this was possible without heavy casualties). Thus, Schlieper on one hand was for all practical purposes suspending the assault, having assigned not even Freytag's full battalion (I/I.R. 133) to West Island, but only a reinforced company. The maximum it could achieve was to comb through West Island for Russian holdouts and then reinforce the positions of 10/I.R. 135 at the Terespol Gate. All the remaining reserves would be committed to exploit the success of Hipp's I.R. 130. It was time for him to begin mopping up the city of Brest, which seemingly had been abandoned by the Red Army. At 1235, the XII Corps' Ia gave a briefing, emphasizing that the division's first task was to normalize the situation in Brest.

At 1240, the command post of I.R. 130 (together with the command post of A.R. 98) was relocated from South Island to Fort III. The South Island had been almost completely mopped up, but was still receiving fire from the fortifications of the Citadel. The city, it seemed, was calm, although serious resistance was being put up in the vicinities of the train station and the oblast military commission, where a well-armed group of soldiers and commanders was defending. Walther Loos:

> Fire was coming at us from cellars, windows, attics, upper stories, and from construction sites, trees and bunkers. Several of our soldiers were hit and dropped to the ground. In the dense smoke, fumes and dust, with the exploding shells and burning buildings, it was very hard for me to spot the enemy riflemen.

Elements of 13 and 14/I.R. 130, as well as the 1st and 10th companies, swept through the southern part of Brest along its main avenue and linked up at a viaduct on its east side with elements of the 2nd Company, which had been pushing through along the southern outskirts to support the attack against Hill 140. This development was decisive – the Red Army elements within the Citadel were thereby cut off from the city.

At 1300, the German XII Corps commander called the 45th Infantry Division's command post, requesting information for a conference with his superiors about the situation inside the Citadel and in Brest itself. Schroth was demanding the settling of the situation in the Citadel that same day: he was prepared to offer flamethrowers and assault guns to accomplish this. If Brest itself was clear of the enemy, then I.R. 130 should take the Citadel from the east. In addition, it was necessary for reconnaissance to sweep through Brest toward the train station from the south-east. Finally, Schroth expressed the desire that Schlieper himself ascertain the situation inside the Citadel by going there. Thus a happy medium was found with corps headquarters – Schroth was giving Schlieper assault guns, which was just what he needed to breach the Trekharoch Gate. Schlieper set in motion all his remaining reserves toward Brest and to hold the bridges on the Muchavec.

At 1300 officers of a battery of the 201st Assault Gun Battalion, which was attached to the 34th Infantry Division, arrived at Friedrich John's command post. The battery included six *Sturmgeschütz* [*StuG*] III assault guns armed with 75mm main guns. Each had a crew of four and carried a daily combat load of forty-four shells. The essence of the plan, the details of which began to be discussed with the company commanders, was to break into the Citadel across the Trekharoch Bridge and, developing the attack in conjunction with a company from II/I.R. 135, to link up with the assault groups and units of III/I.R. 135 at the Terespol Gate.

At 1350, General Schlieper also arrived at John's command post. Everything was ready for the assault guns' attack and it was set in motion. The battery entered North Island through the Northwestern Gate and headed in the direction of the Trekharoch Gate. It had been decided that one platoon would remain in reserve, in the area of the apartment buildings of the command staff, while a second platoon would attack the Trekharoch Gate with the support of infantry – one *StuG* III would stop short of the bridge and suppress fire from the embrasures of the Ring Barracks across the Muchavec River, while the second *StuG* would pass over the bridge and through the gate and begin firing at the defenders in the Ring Barracks from the rear – thus, the defenders would have nowhere to hide, and they would either be liquidated or be forced to descend into the cellars, where they would have no way to prevent the passage of infantry. The third assault gun platoon would head to the Eastern Gate, where the attack by the 9th Company, which had been making decent progress, was now bogged down by fire coming from the 98th Separate Anti-tank Battalion. A company of II Battalion would support the *StuG* attack.

This was one of the assault's key moments. The rumbling of the assault guns' engines could be heard a long way off. The 3rd Platoon was the first to reach its firing positions – one assault gun advanced across the athletics field, while a second rolled forward to a point between the residential complex and East Fort. Having stopped, they opened fire on the defenders of East Fort from practically point-blank range, thereby covering the infantry that was moving through the complex of apartment buildings. The 2nd Platoon of *StuGs* reached the Trekharoch Gate – one of the assault guns took position at a wall, 6 to 8 meters from the end of the bridge, on the road that led to the kitchen located in Point 145.

I.A. Alekseev was a witness of the assault guns' attack:

> The first tank [sic], moving along the earthen wall, was methodically firing incendiary shells at the quarters of the engineering regiment, the signals battalion and the 333rd Rifle Regiment from its gun. The walls of the mechanics' repair shop, the kitchen and the sanitation unit facing the river were demolished by the tank's [sic] fire, while flames enveloped all the wooden parts of these quarters; a fire also began in the 333rd Rifle Regiment's basement ration depot. The wounded, who were located in

> the service pit of the 333rd Rifle Regiment's motor transport repair shop in the Ring Barracks, all burned to death in this fire.

A.I. Makhnach also witnessed the assault guns' barrage: 'It was terrible to witness our impotence. Our grenades lacked fuses.'

The *StuG* III's shells couldn't penetrate the thick walls of the Ring Barracks, but penetrating the embrasures and windows (from a range of just several meters, it was hard to miss), they inflicted terrible casualties, filling entire casemates, which were jammed with Red Army troops seeking shelter from the raging fires, with killed and wounded. The soldiers were compelled to go down into the basements; just a few isolated men remained on the upper floors. While the first assault gun, which had stopped below the wall at Point 145, kept firing, the second slowly approached the wall near Point 143. Next, with its support, Parak's infantry was to rush across the Trekharoch Bridge. Paul Orbach:

> We greeted the assault gun in our position with joy, as a saviour. Then, two officers and three soldiers, who had volunteered, were to approach the fortress under its protection. We wanted to try, with the assistance of this heavily-armoured gun and under the covering fire of my machine guns that were still in our old position, to prepare an assault on a sector of the Citadel. Nevertheless, as we five were advancing, we came under very heavy fire, though at first we had no casualties, finding a little cover behind the assault gun.

However, the morning scene was repeated. As Friedrich John testified, 'The furious defensive fire deprived [the group of attackers] the possibility of crossing the bridge.' Paul Orbach continues, 'The gun was firing superbly. Nevertheless, as soon as the firing ceased (for a short time, in order to select a new target) the frantic firing of the Russians resumed.' The *StuG* III that had halted in front of the bridge fired ceaselessly, but of Orbach's group of five, which took the risk to cross the bridge, only one man remained unharmed: one was killed outright, a lieutenant and one more soldier were mortally wounded, and Orbach himself was severely wounded (he became an invalid). The identity of the men, who once again stopped the soldiers of Parak's battalion, remains unknown; possibly, they were a few soldiers of the 75th Separate Reconnaissance Battalion. Parak's soldiers, demoralized by the casualties and failures of nearly ten hours of constant fighting, again fell back.

However, the accompanying assault gun continued on across the bridge and through the Trekharoch Gate. Pivoting onto the athletic field, it stopped at a point between the church and the building occupied by the 333rd Rifle Regiment and opened fire at the Ring Barracks. Yet, without supporting infantry, the crews of the *StuG* III assault guns of the 201st Assault Gun Battalion were under the threat of being hit by snipers and grenadiers. When the assault gun commander stuck his head up out of the hatch of the *StuG* III that was firing at the 33rd Engineering Regiment from across the Muchavec River, he was killed by shots fired from the Ring Barracks. Several minutes later, the entire crew of this assault gun was killed.

It isn't known how this *StuG* was destroyed; according to some witnesses, credit belongs to a 45mm anti-tank gun that had been manhandled up into the semi-turret of the north-western corner of the Ring Barracks, while others say the credit belongs to two 76mm anti-aircraft guns of the 1st Battery of the 393rd Separate Anti-aircraft Artillery Battalion, which were firing from the direction of the East Fort at the more vulnerable rear aspect of the assault gun.

The second assault gun that had entered the Citadel, but was left without infantry support, was firing at the Ring Barracks, making sure to stay out of grenade range from its windows. However, it was damaged by a gun that Petlitsky had set up beside the circular public rest room (Point 179). The *StuG*, its engine howling, managed to trundle back through the Trekharoch Gate – accompanied by the anguished gazes from the choir balcony in the Church of Saint Nikolai . . .

The platoon of assault guns that was moving toward the Eastern Gate bumped into the fierce resistance of the 98th Separate Anti-tank Battalion, which had successfully repulsed the attack by the 12th Company's infantry a few hours prior. The *StuGs*, having shot up the headquarters of the 98th Separate Anti-tank Battalion and having expended all their ammunition, began to pull back. Now it was the infantry's turn – but once again, despite advancing to within grenade range, their attack was repulsed by heavy fire and the tossing of grenades.

This latest success encouraged the Red Army men. In the cellar of the 333rd Rifle Regiment's building, they were keeping watch on the Terespol Gate – but it was clear that the Gate couldn't be taken by a frontal assault. After the German seizure of a sector at the Brigidki Gate, enemy machine guns were keeping all the ground around the building of the 333rd Rifle Regiment under fire. It would have been logical to launch an attack from the direction of the 84th Rifle Regiment – there, the casemates of the 132nd Escort Battalion of NKVD troops were adjacent to the Terespol Gate. To send a group there was unrealistic – noticing it, the Germans would easily shoot the belly-crawling group to pieces. So it was decided to replace the group with one capable commander – the choice fell on A.L. Petlitsky, who'd just managed to arrive. He was to organize an attack by the NKVD troops, who judging from the sound of gunfire carrying occasionally from there, showed no intention of surrendering.

Going on the attack on the first floor of the Ring Barracks, the NKVD troops managed to drive back the German 10th Company at the Terespol Gate to a mess hall, where hand-to-hand combat erupted. By this moment, Petlitsky had no more than ten men left with him – having driven the Germans out of the mess hall, they broke into the power plant, where they immediately had to repel a German counter-attack. Grenades flew and a fire started. Finally, Petlitsky had only six men left with him: bringing with them two heavy machine guns and several boxes of ammunition that they had grabbed, they managed to reach the Arsenal building and took cover in the basement of the 333rd Rifle Regiment, covered by fire from the Border Guard Post.

Every German who had any connection with the operation's planning now understood that the matter was being prolonged and had taken a serious turn for the worse. However, the soldiers and junior officers continued to display optimism. At 1610 Major General Schlieper again informed Walther Schroth of his proposals for the next day: an early-morning powerful artillery barrage on the Citadel, followed by an attack by I.R. 133. The task of I.R. 135 for the morrow was to hold their positions they'd achieved with the assistance of the two remaining assault guns.

Even before noon, von Pannwitz's 45th Reconnaissance Battalion had received an assignment to mop up the city of Brest-Litovsk and to keep military targets in the city's nearest surroundings under control. By 1630 the reconnaissance battalion had reached the Central Train Station, where von Pannwitz established his command post and reported, 'The city up to this location is free of the enemy; only solitary defenders have been left behind.'

At this time, however, firing was still going on in various portions of the fortress. In the 45th Infantry Division's journal of combat operations, there is the statement:

> ... approximately at 1700, captured Russians were sent with flags of truce by the regiments to parts of the fortress that were still occupied by the enemy, in order to convince the foe of the uselessness of his resistance. There was little success, and some of the flag-of-truce bearers were killed.

It isn't known why Soviet prisoners and local residents were sent out as negotiators, rather than officers of the division (perhaps their prior experience in the battle had made them reluctant and no one was anxious to take on a suicidal assignment). Located in one of the apartment buildings of the command staff in front of the East Fort, Cherniaev could see a machine gun that was periodically firing from the garret of the 333rd Rifle Regiment's barracks. Suddenly, Cherniaev and his group spotted a motley group of people bearing a white flag making their way toward the 333rd Rifle Regiment: 'They were plainly enemies of Soviet power, who had been lurking in the city before the war. But the traitors didn't manage to get far. They were all cut down by the machine gun firing from the garret.'

The next truce negotiator sent toward the 333rd Rifle Regiment was Valia Zenkina, the daughter of I.V. Zenkin, who was a sergeant major in the 33rd Engineering Regiment's platoon of musicians. During the fighting for possession of the electrical power station, the families of the seven commanders, who before the war had been living in the Terespol Tower and who'd taken cover in the power station, were forced to leave it. They had headed to the bank of the Muchavec River. Here, a German officer approached Valia, and 'in broken Russian language'

> He ordered me to enter the fortress and to pass word to our command for the garrison to surrender. I wanted my Mama to come along, but they wouldn't let her. 'Your mother will remain here. You must come back with the answer of the Soviet command.' A soldier escorted me to the building of the electrical power station and shoved me through the door into the Citadel's courtyard ... The fortress was burning; it was quiet, and the entire area was strewn with dead bodies ...

Valia heard a gunshot and the cries, 'Valia! Get down! Crawl this way!' It turned out that Petia Klypa, a 14-year-old pupil of the 33rd Engineering Regiment's platoon of musicians, recognized her. Reaching the cellar window, Valia clambered through it – soldiers wearing helmets, 'most of them German helmets' – surrounded her: 'They all looked at me quietly, surprised. It seemed to me that they were regarding me as a traitor and would shoot me. Facing them, I felt guilty because I'd been taken prisoner.' As a result, Valia remained in the cellar, where she took care of the wounded.

Approximately the same scene took place in other sectors. For some reason or another, the truce parties never returned, or they never even managed to reach the defenders. The 45th Infantry Division had to think of other ways to persuade the garrison to surrender.

At 1830, General Field Marshal von Kluge arrived at the division command post together with a small escort group. He held a brief conference. In principle, there was nothing really to discuss – the situation was clear. Having received a briefing, the impetuous von Kluge ordered for 'no useless blood to be spilled in fighting around the Citadel' – the battle was of only local significance. Instead, 'the enemy should be starved out.' His order for the night was for the Citadel to be entirely encircled (I.R. 133 from the west, south and east, and III/I.R. 135 from the north), and to thwart any enemy attempts to break out. I.R. 130 received the order to bring about order in Brest. Incidentally, Hipp's regiment (I.R. 130) was currently to the east of the Citadel: that afternoon by 1615 it had attained its objective for that day – Hill 144. However, the idea of 'starving out' as expressed by the inexhaustible and decisive army commander didn't take into account all aspects of the situation. In that case, what would happen to those German troops waiting for help in the Church of Saint Nikolai?

Thus, the decision was amended – on the morning of 23 June, the fortifications of the Central Citadel were to be taken after a ninety-minute artillery preparation between 0300 and 0430. Before it started, word would be passed to those encircled in the church to begin to withdraw to the cordoning line. Their opinion, however, was that another break-out attempt had to be made, while the machine-gunners at the Terespol Gate, who were preparing to withdraw, could still suppress enemy fire or Red Army counter-attacks. Charging down from the choir balconies, they overran the several Red Army men that were still inside the church. However, as they ran toward the Terespol Gate they were spotted immediately. Fierce fire from every direction, which the machine-gunners of the 10th Company vainly attempted to suppress, forced them to drop prone near the building of the Border Guards post. At that point, a counter-attack by the Border Guardsmen forced them to fall back to the relative safety of the church, which was their only reliable shelter. Incidentally, not all of them made it back – in addition to those killed in the attempt, one badly-wounded *feldwebel* fell into the hands of the defenders. Junior Political Instructor Kalandadze spoke with him:

> He was terribly afraid and prayed for us not to kill him, saying that his father was some high-ranking officer of the Nazi Army. He said his father

> would show his gratitude to us for sparing his son's life: 'You'll get several of yours back in exchange for me.' I interrogated the feldwebel, but he couldn't give us anything sensible that was useful for us.

At 1900, the 45th Infantry Division began to pull back its units to positions to cordon off the Citadel: III/I.R. 130 yielded its sector of defense on South Island to Major Eggeling's II/I.R. 133, and was pulled back into the city of Brest. Eggeling's soldiers, who still hadn't taken part in the fighting, began to act with great energy – especially the 14th Company, *Hauptmann* Watzek's *panzerjägers*. Doctor Watzek was known for his energy, and he didn't waste any time on this occasion either. Having rolled his guns up onto an embankment, he began to fire at the Ring Barracks at the point-blank range of just 150–200 meters. The fire coming from the windows and embrasures of the barracks died down – the defenders had nothing with which to oppose the fire of the anti-tank guns. The gunfire on South Island fell silent, but even so the Germans hesitated to storm the Kholm Gate, especially since the withdrawal of their troops to the cordoning positions was still under way. Instead, the Germans withdrew their 20mm *FlaK* 38 guns and Engelhardt's anti-tank gunners, on the heels of which several machine-gun fire bursts rang out from the 44th Rifle Regiment's semi-tower, and the anti-tank gunners fell back across the Terespol Bridge to West Island and continued on into the German rear. Almost immediately, Bytko's Red Army men took full possession of the semi-tower, which had once held the now burned-out headquarters of the 44th Rifle Regiment.

Now the German infantry elements at the Terespol Gate had to be withdrawn – and the commander of the 10th Company did this with utmost reluctance, as Lozert confirms: comrades of the battalion were still holding out literally just 100 meters away in the Church of Saint Nikolai. Only solitary white flares that sometimes soared above its damaged cupola testified to the fact that they were still alive. But an order is an order, and the 10th Company began to fall back across the bridge. The machine-gunners, having given a parting burst of fire at some 'diminutive Russian' who was trying to make his way to the Ring Barracks at a crawl, set out along the narrow passage from the Terespol Tower and ran across the bridge ... they couldn't be seen from the Border Guards posts or the 333rd Rifle Regiment's basement, but those in the Church of Saint Nikolai had a much better field of view. Probably conserving the radio set's batteries, the Germans encircled in the church launched a full cluster of white flares. Spotted from *Oberst* John's command post, they didn't add to the equanimity of the colonel, who now knew that he could do nothing further for them on that day. The Red Army defenders in the Citadel also perfectly understood the desperate implication of the flares. I.A. Alekseev recalled, 'The enemy located in the church, seeing their own looming deaths, were launching illumination flares in greater numbers ... calling for help.'

However, many could no longer count upon assistance, only on mercy: numerous wounded Germans remained where they had fallen. One of those forgotten unfortunates, who was lying among the corpses around the position of the anti-aircraft gun at the East Fort, began to stir – Hans Teuschler, who had finally regained consciousness. Having spent hours in a state of unconsciousness, a terrible scene opened before him, one which Teuschler could long recall in detail:

> On the forward edge of the FlaK position was the half-constructed tripod of a heavy machine gun. Behind it lay its gunner, mortally wounded, gasping with a severe gunshot wound to the lung. His eyes were glazed over and he groaned with pain and thirst. 'Have you anything to drink, *Kamerad*?' he asked me. I passed him my canteen with difficulty. To my right a machine-gunner sat bolt upright, unmoving. There was no response when I spoke to him. In the immediate vicinity a sad concert of cries from the helpless wounded could be heard from all sides. 'Medic, medic, God in Heaven, help me!' The sniper had been particularly effective in his work.

In reality, it hadn't been a solitary sniper, but riflemen firing from the East Fort, the 98th Separate Anti-tank Artillery Battalion, and remnants of Mamchik's group occupying buildings of the apartment complex for the command staff. Teuschler continues:

> At the last of my strength, I was able to roll over onto my side, in order to rest a bit more comfortably and not on the ammunition boxes. My chest felt as heavy as lead and my shirt and tunic were soaked in blood. As my first act I began to search for where I'd been hit, until I finally found the tiny entrance wound under my left collarbone. I applied a field dressing to 'build up a crust'; the exit wound in my back had already congealed in my previous position, lying on my back. Feeling myself rescued, I began wandering through a wonderful dream world. Gradually, the terribly hot day came to an end, and a hopeless night fell upon the still raging battlefield.[1]

However, it is possible that Teuschler was only lapsing back into unconsciousness – nighttime was still a long way off.

The aforementioned 'diminutive Russian' was the 14-year-old pupil of the 333rd Rifle Regiment's band, Petia Klypa. Throughout the entire day he had been conducting a search on the upper floors of the Arsenal, but now he and his age peer and fellow classmate Kolia Novikov had crawled out of the basement window nearest to the Ring Barracks. Silence had fallen over the fortress, disrupted only by the sound of gunfire coming from the Kholm Gate. Coming under the burst of machine-gun fire, Klypa rose and darted toward the Ring Barracks, while Novikov turned back toward the basement. Passing through the stables of the 333rd Rifle Regiment's battery of 76mm guns, Klypa reached the south-western corner of the Ring Barracks untouched by the machine-gun fire, where he ducked into a stock-room of ammunition and weapons. Grabbing a PPD-40 machine pistol for himself, Klypa glanced out the window – everywhere he could see, Germans were falling back beyond the river. Klypa hurried back to the basement and this time made it back without being fired upon. Moreover, judging from the silence in the Ring

Barracks, the Germans had already pulled back from it. He reported this news right away to Potapov.

The news instantly flew around the basement. Now other soldiers were emerging and taking a look around. What was this – war? Had this just been some sort of border provocation? An incident? Soldiers clambered out of the cellar – had they been victorious? From a distance they could hear the clatter of a BA-10; it approached and soon stopped at the gate, and a regimental commissar with a bandaged head climbed out of it: it was Matevosian. He held a short meeting at the Terespol Gate with the commanders of the defense – Potapov, Kizhevatov, Sanin, Semenov and others. Opinions differed on what should be done next – the situation was too unclear, but everyone agreed that it was necessary to make another attempt to drive the remaining Germans out of the fortress – connection with the 455th Rifle Regiment had still not been established because of the threat of gunfire from the officers' mess.

At this time the defenders became aware that the Germans hadn't completely departed. Several soldiers who had incautiously run up to the bank of the Bug River had been fired upon from the vegetation lining the bank on West Island. Clearly, the 'border conflict' had not yet been settled.

The result of the officers' discussion was that the 333rd Rifle Regiment (first of all Potapov's group) would attempt to reach the encampment of the 22nd Tank Division (South Military Encampment) by crossing over to West Island, and from there cross over to South Island before heading south to the encampment. They couldn't exit through the Trekharoch Gate: the mess hall of the 33rd Engineering Regiment, Point 145, the Main Wall and the moat presented too many obstacles for Potapov's small group. Moreover, the city of Brest was now likely in German hands. The only feasible path was through the bushes on West Island or along its levees paralleling the Bug River, and then to swim across to South Island. The Border Guards would remain behind, as would many men of the 333rd Rifle Regiment and other units. It had been decided that it was also necessary: (1) to lay in a supply of cartridges and grenades; (2) resolve the problem at the 84th Rifle Regiment's club (the Church of Saint Nikolai); and (3) to gather volunteers and to attempt a break-out. Unfortunately, there was no unified leadership.

The first item on the list was quickly carried out: the entire regimental stockpile of weapons and portable ammunition was moved into the basement. V.I. Sachkovskaia recalls though that the soldiers brought back shells without mortars, submachine guns without drums of ammunition, grenades without fuses, but among all this they did come back with the most vital item – cartridges. Immediately, the grenade and ammunition boxes were dragged over to the cellar's windows, and several soldiers with light machine guns were now posted at them. Approximately forty men, among them Junior Political Instructor Aleksandr Kalandadze and Lieutenant Aleksei Naganov, moved into positions to defend the Terespol Gate – Naganov and his men in the semi-tower, Kalandadze and his men, above the gate itself. As the ammunition and weapons were being lugged down into the cellar, simultaneously soldiers of the 333rd Rifle Regiment were readying artillery to support an assault against the officers' mess and the Church of Saint Nikolai. In addition, it had been resolved upon to try to harass the Germans' return crossing of the Bug, which was quite visible from the windows of the Ring Barracks – for this, 120mm mortars that had been found in the regimental stockpile would be brought up.

There remained only thirty-seven of the Border Guards. Leaving behind several riflemen in the ruins of their post, they moved over into the basement of the Arsenal to join the 333rd Rifle Regiment. Worn out by the long hours of fighting, shaken by the deaths of their comrades and the wives and children of the commanders who'd been living in the building, there they encountered a prisoner that had been taken that morning – by this time, the only one still alive. S. Bobrenok recalls:

> In the cellar, soldiers were crowded around a captured Nazi, a tall, well-fed Obergefreiter ... It was strange to see the freshly-shaven, plump mug of the fascist ... The sleeves of his dusty tunic had been rolled up almost to the elbow ... The Obergefreiter was plainly frightened. His little eyes behind puffy eyelids were darting around in a cowardly fashion, meeting the gazes of the silent defenders of the fortress ... The commanders arrived. The first questions were given to him. The Obergefreiter straightened up and he froze like a statue. His thick lips were striving to form a dismissive smile. He refused to answer the questions. Then suddenly, in an unexpectedly high voice quivering with hatred, he shouted – '*Alles kaput*!' ... He was shot like a stray dog not far from the entrance to the cellar.

Several more or less intact regimental 76mm guns and 45mm anti-tank guns that had been scrounged were aimed at the church and the officers' mess. I.A. Alekseev:

> When we found a [76mm] gun among the ruins of the artillery park, I didn't notice that its sight had been damaged. The irreplaceable commander of the gun was the deputy political leader of the 333rd Rifle Regiment's 76mm battery [Shcherbakov]. He took upon himself the servicing of the gun and the loading, aiming and firing of it. A crew of three men handled the gun trails, and the duty of bringing up shells and passing them to Shcherbakov.

By firing at the upper level (the garret) of the officers' mess and the choir balconies of the Church of Saint Nikolai, the plan was to force the Germans to descend to the main level of each, and there to destroy them. The 76mm shells couldn't penetrate the thick walls of the church, but those walls had small arched windows and shell holes; a couple of direct hits in them would cut down all of the Germans huddled in several nooks of the balconies and on the staircase leading up to them. In addition, a significant portion of the roof above the balconies had also been destroyed, and there was an enormous window above the church's entrance that was level with the balconies. It was possible to hit these openings even without the use of the damaged sight, simply by pointing the gun barrel.

Likely, the operation was coordinated in some fashion with the 455th Rifle Regiment. A 76mm gun crew (which included Alekseev) practically at point-blank range opened fire at the officers' mess and virtually demolished it – but as it subsequently turned out, some of the Germans with the very first explosions had descended into the cellar, which was out of reach for the artillery fire, while others dashed over to the church.

However, assault groups of the 455th Rifle Regiment were already hurrying toward the officers' mess. They included Border Guardsmen, who had likely taken shelter in the casemates of the 455th Rifle Regiment's sector during the opening artillery barrage. Machine guns supported the attack, firing from the Ring Barracks not only at the officers' mess, but also at the windows of the church.

In addition to the Border Guards, one assault group included Lieutenants Eslannikov, Usov, Tereshchenko; Political Instructor Koshkarov, who had arrived in Brest only on 18 June after finishing training; and several other soldiers and junior commanders. The assault group ran up to the officers' mess, whereupon the machine guns in the Ring Barracks ceased fire. Grenades flew into the windows of the building, which had been half-destroyed by the fire of the 333rd Rifle Regiment's guns. Usov and several Red Army soldiers, who had rushed into the mess hall, were once again sweeping through the premises – it became clear that Germans were still lurking there. The assault group managed to break into the cellar as well: pressed back into one corner, the Germans were still offering fierce resistance. Having laid a demolition charge at the entrance to the cellar and having lit the shortened fuse, Usov and Koshkarov barely had time to make it to the building's entrance when the explosion came, which collapsed the remnants of the walls of the officers' mess and knocked the political instructor unconscious. Men grabbed Koshkarov and dragged him back to the 455th Rifle Regiment's cellar – he regained consciousness only the next morning.

If there were in fact any Germans left in the cellar of the officers' mess, they sought to keep out of sight, hoping to wait until help arrived. The officers' mess would really offer no further trouble to the 455th Rifle Regiment, though Alekseev recalls that on the morning of 23 June, he did take fire from there.

Meanwhile, soldiers of the 333rd Rifle Regiment and the small group of Border Guards with them were to wipe out the remaining Germans encircled in the Church of Saint Nikolai. However, once the crew deployed the 76mm gun and opened fire at a 'window beneath the church's cupola', from which German fire could sweep the entire western half of the Citadel, it was only able to fire a few shells (and obtain two hits) before a radio team with the German infantry in the church established contact with their artillery, and directed its fire onto the gun that was targeting the church. Shells began to explode around Alekseev's gun, and the crew hastened to take cover in the cellar – one shell splinter split the lower lip of the gun commander, the deputy political instructor.

The attempt to use the regimental 120mm mortars to shell the German infantry that was withdrawing across the Bug also ended in failure. They only managed to fire a few rounds before the German artillery blanketed their positions, and the mortar crews also barely had time to make it into the cellars. One of the mortars was destroyed. The rifle and machine-gun fire that opened up on the crossing almost simultaneously was merely a morale-booster; it was more than 3 kilometers to the German crossing site.

It became clear that the effort to harass the German crossing with rifle fire would be possible only by approaching it across West Island, while to pound it with mortar fire would require first the elimination of the Germans still holding out in the church, who were directing the German artillery fire. Thus the artillerymen ran out of the cellar and up to the 76mm gun once again; Alekseev was among them: 'We brought up shells on skids, the deputy political instructor aimed the gun, loaded it, and fired it at the church. After several rounds struck the church's cupola, its upper portion collapsed and forced the enemy to abandon the balconies.' However, the shell hits didn't signify the deaths of the Germans encircled in the church. Plainly, they had descended from the balconies – but since the radio communications were continuing, they were able to place a barrier of artillery fire in front of the church, which hindered any attack. Still, at the very least the 76mm gun crew had forced the German machine-gunners in the church to abandon their advantageous positions in the balconies, so they could no longer keep the entire fortress under machine-gun fire. Thus it was now possible to assemble a large group at the Terespol Gate for the break-out across West Island.

Potapov entered the cellar to recruit volunteers for the break-out group – according to what he told the soldiers, the situation had become serious, there was hardly any prospect of help, but the tankers of the 22nd Tank Division were likely still fighting at the South Military Encampment. There was hardly anyone then within the Citadel who suspected that the tank division might also have been destroyed by the Germans on the very first day. Potapov found quite a few volunteers: more than 100 men.

Potapov's plan was quite risky. Both the German strength and positions on West Island were unknown, not to mention on South Island, and before reaching the latter the men would have to swim across the Bug. Moreover, the encircled Germans in the church couldn't be forgotten. They might be fully able to report over the radio about the concentration of Russians at the Terespol Gate, which was plainly preparing for a break-out.

. . . The first soldiers leapt up onto the causeway that paralleled the Terespol Bridge – among the break-out group was the 14-year-old Petia Klypa, who was running with a pistol in his hand and who quickly surged ahead of the rest. The first machine guns opened fire at them only when the leading group of soldiers had almost reached the opposite riverbank. Once across the river, without stopping, Klypa and the other soldiers veered to the left, just as Potapov, who was now running alongside them, had ordered. Scrambling through the bushes, which proved to be below the machine-guns' beaten zone, they strove to reach the bank opposite South Island as quickly as possible. Those trailing behind the lead group, who had been caught atop the causeway at the moment the German machine guns opened fire, were riddled by machine-gun fire and plastered with mortar fire. Disoriented, the groups of men scrambled to take cover behind a low embankment that ran along the opposite riverbank. Having lost their commander Potapov, who had rushed on ahead, the surviving soldiers continued to lie prone there for several minutes, before the majority of them turned and fled back across the causeway under heavy machine-gun fire. Only a handful of men managed to make it back to the Ring Barracks. That evening, Kalandadze returned to the cellar for a short while: 'However, a glance was sufficient to notice that the garrison had lost half its men.'

Meanwhile Potapov, Klypa and the other men had reached a point on the Bug opposite South Island. Petia Klypa, who was a fine swimmer, dove into the water, clad in his boots, trousers and undershirt, with his pistol clenched in his teeth. They had almost managed to reach the seeming sanctuary of the willow thickets along the far bank when machine guns opened up on them. Only thirteen men managed to make it across to South Island. Along the river's edge on South Island ran another embankment and those who had managed to swim close enough to the opposite bank were covered by the dense willow thickets growing atop it. However, Lieutenant Potapov wasn't among them, and his fate is unknown. The next morning, nine of the survivors who made it to South Island were taken prisoner.

While Potapov was attempting to break out to the south, on the east side of the fortress, the Germans were pulling back. At 2000, *Oberst* John transferred his command post to the south-western corner of a food warehouse outside the boundaries of the Central Bastion; his units took up a defense along the Main Wall. Friedrich John recalled:

> In the afternoon, the division was given an order to evacuate North Island and the centre of the fortress at twilight and to go on the defence at the exterior walls to prevent any break-out by the encircled Russians. I.R. 135 took up a defence along the northern walls between the Bug and the Northern Gate. I Battalion was replaced by other troops in the city of Brest-Litovsk and took over the eastern part of the North Island's walls; II Battalion occupied the western portion of the walls. North Island was evacuated practically without any sort of opposition.

Likely, John was holding the western portion of the Main Wall, including the Northern Gate that had been seized by the 9th Company. Further to the east along the wall, huddled in the rifle pits that still remained of the Polish defenses, were Red Army soldiers from various units, who Major Gavrilov had merged into two composite companies under the command of Lieutenants Iakovlev and Samoilov. Next to them in the rifle pits and partially in trenches were artillerymen of the 98th Separate Anti-tank Artillery Battalion. The positions were quite adequate for repelling an attack by infantry units with infantry support weapons, but hadn't been constructed to provide shelter against heavy artillery. However, beyond the 98th Battalion was a small but key sector held by the Germans on the Muchavec River itself. Thus, almost the entire eastern portion of the Main Wall was in Soviet hands, but key sectors (the Northern Gate and the Wall at the Muchavec), which controlled both movement to and from North Island and prevented possible break-out attempts or bringing fire to bear on the main highway, were held by the Germans. The interior of North Island was now a no-man's-land of dying fires, already cold corpses and unconscious wounded men.

At 2100, von Krischer presented a plan to the 45th Infantry Division command for the next day's preparatory artillery barrage. The planned artillery fire would begin at 0300 and end at 0430 – three times longer than it had been on 22 June. This would allow the avoidance of numerous mistakes as far as possible – the targets were already well-known, and now there was no need to hurry. It is not insignificant that the fire would now be observed and directed by the Germans still holding out in the Church of Saint Nikolai, from their vantage point in the heart of the Citadel. In accordance with the plan, the mortar battalions (Galle's and the 854th) would fire at the maximum possible rate, with a total expenditure of 644 shells; 3/6th Nebelwerfer Battalion would fire 900 shells (1/3 high-explosives with delayed-action fuses; 2/3 – smoke); 1/A.R. 99 1,440 shells. The 8th Nebelwerfer Battalion and batteries of the 833rd Heavy Mortar Battalion would conduct fire according to a special plan. The rocket-launchers would begin firing at 0259, launching salvoes at the eastern portion of Central Island. The batteries of the 833rd would fire on the western portion of the island at a rate of one shell every five minutes. The plan would go into effect with the special code word 'Blücher', which would be transmitted prior to midnight. The artillery barrage would begin with the code word 'Augsburg'.

At 2215, a summary report from the command post of 81st Pioneer Battalion (on the eastern outskirts of Malashevichi) arrived at the 45th Infantry Division's command post, which had been sent by *Oberstleutnant* Masuch at 2045:

> We caught the Russians unaware. After overcoming the initial shock, they put up resistance with part of their strength ... The effective combat strength of the 1st Company of Pionere Battalion 81 has changed very greatly; a significant portion of the lead assault detachment hasn't returned. They're in the centre of the fortress.

At this time, fighting was continuing on the Central Island, to where a few of the survivors of Potapov's break-out group had recently returned. I.A. Alekseev recalls: 'We manhandled the 76mm gun over to the Terespol Gate ... We set it up here, pointed in the direction of West Island. The deputy political instructor loaded the gun and began to fire shells at West Island.' The result was the same as had happened previously – the crew was blanketed with mortar fire. The artillerymen darted toward the windows of the cellar, but Alekseev tarried and was wounded in the head by a shell splinter. He was dragged into the cellar and taken to the casemate below the 333rd Rifle Regiment's club, closer to the 455th Rifle Regiment. This turned out to be reliable shelter ... It was now conclusively clear that there would also be no success targeting the German withdrawal across the Bug River with mortars – the Germans, using their fire superiority, were suppressing any attempt to employ the mortars.

Now as the fighting was quieting down, disorganized groups and dozens of solitary men were beginning to search for their units, striving to break through to the remaining major defensive strongpoints at a crawl or by making dashes. Having noticed the German withdrawal on North Island, the survivors of Cherniaev's group, which was still defending in the apartments of the command staff standing in front of East Fort decided to make their way to that fort. By day's end, there were only four left in the group. Cherniaev recalls:

> In the twilight at a crawl we made it across a more exposed area to a different cluster of apartment buildings, and under their cover we ran the final 200 metres to the gate of the East Fort at full height, crying 'Friendlies!' We were escorted into one of the chambers. I spotted Political Instructor Skripnik . . . He presented me to Major Gavrilov, and the Major placed me in command of a group of soldiers in the second and third chambers. I took charge of the group of twenty-seven men and their equipment: one machine gun, two submachine guns, and rifles.

Cherniaev recalled that the fort's garrison had only 170 rifles, two Degtiarev light machine guns ('one infantry, the other likely taken from a tank (without a bipod)'), and two submachine guns. If one can believe this information, then almost half the defenders of the East Fort (which numbered approximately 400 when the defense ultimately collapsed) were unarmed.

Likely at this time Captain Zubachev, who had been fighting all day at the Trekharoch Gate, situated with machine guns that were firing from the cellar beneath the 455th Rifle Regiment's kitchen, took advantage of the fact that German fire from the officers' mess had ceased and made his way back to his own 44th Rifle Regiment. There he found preparations under way for a break-out attempt, being led by the energetic V. Bytko. Zubachev didn't approve of the idea – a break-out without prior reconnaissance might lead only to the complete destruction of the already thin garrison. But as the regiment's deputy commander of administration, Captain Zubachev couldn't give orders to the chief of the school for the junior command staff Senior Lieutenant Bytko. Bytko continued to prepare a break-out through the Northern Gate, designating it for 2300.

. . . Ivan Dolotov spent the entire day pinned down with the remnants of his group in the park area between the Church of Saint Nikolai and the 33rd Engineering Regiment's barracks. In the darkness, Dolotov's group finally made its way back to the barracks. At the moment of Dolotov's return, the duty officer for his bridging company on the night of 21 June, Sergeant Lerman, decided to take upon himself the task of assaulting the 33rd Engineering Regiment's mess hall, having assembled a group of twenty-five volunteers. There were three Degtiarev light machine guns to cover the assault. The soldiers, each taking two grenades along, crawled along the walls on both sides of the building. Staying low, they couldn't be reached by fire from the mess hall, while the Degtiarev machine-gunners kept an alert watch over the church and walls. They crawled up to the entrance, where they tossed grenades into it and into the cellar windows. After the grenades went off, Lerman's assault group rushed through the door. They were greeted with fire – the courage of the Red Army men couldn't compensate for their lack of experience in close combat. Some of the group were killed, while the rest retreated. Lerman was lightly wounded in the head and the left arm. 'Thus ended the first day of the war in the fortress,' Ivan Dolotov sums up; 'I didn't feel like eating, but I was tormented by a terrible thirst. There was no water in the taps – only in the Muchavec.'

At 2300, Bytko's group launched its break-out attempt. More than 200 men quietly slipped past the 455th Rifle Regiment's sector of the Ring Barracks, and having turned left, passed through the Trekharoch Gate to the Trekharoch Bridge, which was now strewn with corpses. There was silence in the fortress. Just as the first soldiers crossed over the bridge, the Germans opened up. The group with Bytko at its head hurried down an alley between the stadium and the apartment buildings of the command staff, which led to the Northern Gate. The German fire intensified – they were firing from the Northern Gate, and the alley was completely exposed to the fire. In matter of minutes, Bytko's group suffered heavy casualties. Understanding that the break-out attempt had failed, Bytko issued an order to run to the left, into the cover of other apartment buildings of the command staff. There they waited until everything had quieted down, and in the darkness the survivors returned to their starting-point. The first break-out attempt had ended in failure.

* * *

At the 45th Infantry Division's command post, the evening summary reports were arriving from the regiments. Schlieper, who had thrown all his reserves into the fighting on the first day, still was unable to determine the full magnitude of his losses. The most accurate data on the casualties of the 45th Infantry Division on 22 June would be the figures in the XII Corps' summary of losses, compiled by the corps headquarters. According to them, on 22 June the XII Army Corps suffered 58 men killed-in-action, including 6 officers. Practically all of the killed (55 men, of which 6 were officers) were from the 45th Infantry Division. All the men listed as missing-in-action (15, including one officer) belonged to it as well. On 22 June the XII Corps lost 313 men wounded, including 14 officers – 138 of these men (including all 14 officers) were from the 45th Infantry Division. But this includes only those wounded men who were hospitalized on 22 June. A number of men had to wait for several days before medics could reach them on the battlefield, and their number gradually added to the initial list. Altogether, according to the data of Rudolph Gschöpf, probably obtained by him after the battle for Brest ended, the losses of the 45th Infantry Division on 22 June in killed alone amounted to 21 officers and 290 non-commissioned officers and men. In comparison, the XII Corps' 31st Infantry Division on 22 June lost 12 killed and 72 wounded. This division had no losses in officers.

Note

1. Gschöpf, R. *Mein Weg mit der 45 Infanterie Division* [*My Way with the 45th Infantry Division*] (Linz, 1955), pp. 156–57.

Part III

Mopping Up

Chapter 8

Leutnant Hurm's Operation

The longest day of the summer had finally come to an end – there was hardly any other time which had so many people waiting for darkness to fall with such impatience. Finally it arrived, though only quite provisionally so, because of the fires that continued to rage in various sectors of the fortress. However, the darkness was immediately further attenuated by illumination flares soaring above the walls: the break-out attempts undertaken by the Russians until 2330 alarmed the Germans. This night was no less tense for the defenders of the fortress, who were in constant expectation of a German attack. Exhausted men fell on their weapon and immediately fell asleep. However, many were unable to do so, fearing creeping Germans with grenades. If 'snipers in the trees' appeared to materialize in front of the men of Freytag's and Gerstmeyer's battalions, then to the defenders, who were straining to hear any nighttime rustle, it seemed that Germans were sneaking toward the Ring Barracks from every direction, hoping to finish them all off with grenades.

However, in addition to defense, the defenders' main task became obtaining water. Hunger hadn't become a problem yet, but thirst had already seized them by the throat. I. Dolotov:

> We were extremely thirsty. Groups of two or three men who made it to the river with buckets or pots brought back a little water, but it all went into the cellar for the wounded. When a group of fifteen to twenty men who wanted to quench their thirst gathered, they inadvertently revealed themselves, and immediately an illumination flare was hanging in the sky, and a fierce fire-fight erupted with Germans firing from the sections of the Main Wall to our north.

Many of the Red Army soldiers crawled around, checking the bodies of the dead Germans – by morning, Sergeant Lerman of the 33rd Engineering Regiment already had a German field pack on, a pair of binoculars dangling from his neck, and was gripping a German pistol in one hand and a German compass in the other. But Sergeant Lerman wasn't only busy with searching for trophies – he decided that artillery would be necessary to take back the 33rd Engineering Regiment's mess hall, so he sought to remove the main gun and ammunition for it from a damaged BA-10 that was standing next to the 33rd Engineering Regiment's building (right up against its wall). Grabbing a few volunteers, he accomplished this while it was still dark. It turned out that there were only a few shells – just ten or twelve, but they were enough to give it a try when it became light.

There were actually few who got any sleep that night. It was necessary to use the several hours of darkness to maximal effectiveness: stockpile water and rations, and establish contact with the neighboring sectors of the defense. Unfortunately, almost nothing is known about the attempts on the night of 22 June to establish communications among the defenders. Centralized command and control existed in only a few of the defensive pockets, and where it did exist, primarily attempts were made to contact those who were in an adjacent casemate by breaking through walls or exploiting the darkness, but not with those in a neighboring building. It is notable, for example, that one of the defenders of the East Fort, V.Ia. Sisin, only found out after the war that soldiers of the 125th Rifle Regiment in the apartment complex of the command staff and artillerymen of the 98th Separate Anti-tank Battalion were holding defensive positions next to the East Fort on North Island.

Still in the evening, seeing the difficulty of the situation, in East Fort on North Island Major Gavrilov also had given thought to a break-out attempt. The situation was unclear, so he decided to send three groups out in different directions – one to make contact with the defenders inside the Citadel, the second to contact the defenders still holding the eastern walls, and third to clarify whether or not a withdrawal in the direction of the city would be possible. Lieutenant Ia.I. Kolomiets, the commander of a 125th Rifle Regiment mortar battery, who'd been fighting in the East Fort, was sent together with ten men into the Citadel. This group only managed to reach some of the apartment buildings of the command staff. From there, having lost several men after coming under heavy fire, they had to turn back to the East Fort. Having heard Lieutenant Kolomiets' report, Gavrilov decided to prepare a break-out, without waiting for help. The other two groups didn't return.

To the west of Gavrilov, Shablovsky's group remained in the attic of Building No. 5 of the command staff's residential complex right up until evening. From an attic window, they could see the Trekharoch Bridge, which was piled with corpses, as well as Germans and Red Army men who were trying to break out. The defenders of Building No. 5 were practically out of ammunition – their situation was hopeless. Several times, Captain Shablovsky intended to kill himself, but he was talked out of that idea with difficulty. That night a group of soldiers made their way to Building No. 5 from the 125th Rifle Regiment's area – through a joint effort they again tried to escape, but realizing that the walls were occupied by Germans around the entire perimeter, they rejected the idea of a break-out attempt.

At 0030, no one was sleeping in the command post of the 45th Infantry Division either; the command post was working in shifts. Among those still awake was *Generalmajor* Schlieper. He decided to cancel the order for Arko 27, which had been issued at 2100 on 22 June. Having received the report about attempts by the Russians to break out in various directions (up until 2330), Schlieper understood that a fresh assault, even one with a more prolonged artillery preparation, would lead only to higher casualties, which was contrary to the Fourth Army commander's directive. The Russians were still strong and active. The new decision was to withdraw the units to safe zones on the outskirts of the fortifications of the Central Bastion prior to 0500, and then to subject the Citadel to constant harassing fire, for which purpose the *nebelwerfer* battalions subordinate to both of the neighboring divisions would be attached to Arko 27. Immediately von Krischer issued the corresponding order.

... Dawn was approaching. In this pre-dawn hour, several shadows were seen dashing across the Terespol Bridge from West Island. Kizhevatov's group, ensconced in the nearby semi-tower of the Ring Barracks, managed to recognize their fellow Border Guardsmen just before opening fire. The guardsmen reported to Kizhevatov: 'On West Island the Germans are falling back to the Bug; we still have some of our guys on the island. We're running out of ammunition.' Kizhevatov made a quick decision – they'd gather ammunition, and while it was still the pre-dawn hour, they'd cross over to West Island. Once across, they'd make another attempt to harass the Germans' river crossing from the northern edge of the island. Several Border Guards among those who'd been fighting at the Terespol Gate went with Kizhevatov's group. The majority of the guardsmen, however, would remain in the cellars of the 333rd Rifle Regiment's building, where the Border Guards had sought shelter following the destruction of the building that had housed the Border Guards posts and their commandant's headquarters. Only one machine-gun crew remained in the ruins of the building opposite the Terespol Gate.

Wasting no time Kizhevatov's group made its way to the northern edge of West Island. From this vantage point, the German crossing site lay in front of them as if on an open palm. The cartridge belts had been filled. The morning silence, broken only by the rumble of German transport vehicles on the temporary bridges across the Bug, was shattered by the first bursts of machine-gun fire. It was 0500 – a new day of fighting had begun.

It was most important news to the 45th Infantry Division's command post: Kizhevatov's fire for some time made the 8-ton bridge on the western side of the Citadel impassable, and the division was once again taking casualties. It was becoming clear that Russian forces moving out of the Citadel were able to filter back into the areas of West and South Island that had been abandoned by his division's units. For all practical purposes, this meant that it would be necessary to sweep West and South Island clear of Russians once again.

Now, too, the Citadel and North Island had begun to quake – the German artillery had opened up a harassing fire. The Russians began to come down off the Main Wall, trying to take cover in the casemates below it. On top of the wall, they were terribly exposed under the mortar fire, not to mention that of a more powerful weapon. Because now the 833rd Heavy Mortar Battalion's 2nd Battery joined the barrage – the prior afternoon, the sweating crewmen had managed to free 'Thor' of the shell that had become jammed in it. 'Odin' was still out of action – although they'd managed to extract the shell with the assistance of a winch mounted on a semi-tracked prime mover, the heavy mortar still couldn't be fired because the electrical ignition device wasn't working. However, the seven shells fired by 'Thor' on this day had their effect – one shell struck the probable route of the assault groups that had been assigned to free the encircled Germans in the church. A thunderous explosion shook the entire western side of the Citadel when a shell fired by 'Thor' struck the semi-tower at the Terespol Gate, demolishing it almost down to its foundations. No one survived – those who weren't blown apart by the explosion were crushed under the rubble or were flattened by the powerful blast wave of the explosion, which struck the entire sector of the Ring Barracks adjacent to the semi-tower. The remaining standing walls of the Border Guards' building collapsed, and the cellar in the 333rd Rifle Regiment's sector was rocking in different directions from the nearby explosions.

Then suddenly the cellar's walls buckled, and the sounds of its collapsing ceiling muffled the screams of those who were under it. It had been a direct hit on the structure! The cellar ceilings collapsed in several places, burying a portion of the field hospital beneath it. It was located beneath the regiment's club in the largest chamber, where wounded men had been laying directly on the floor in tightly-packed rows, while soldiers just below the ceiling had been laying prone on ammunition boxes at the narrow cellar windows, keeping watch. Now only the sound of muffled groans was carrying from there. A.P. Kalandadze recalls:

> Many of the soldiers were bleeding from the ears and nose ... Not everyone's nerves held out. One of the soldiers rushed to the exit ... We grabbed him. He was shouting, 'Let me go! Everything is about to collapse!' He was struggling to break free, striking us with his fists. We had to tie him up with belts.

The powerful explosions from the shells fired by the Karl heavy mortars were also shaking the cellars in the 455th Rifle Regiment's sector. A. Makhnach recalls, 'Blood streamed from the ears and nose from a blast wave. You had to keep your mouth open.'

The White Palace also collapsed. This building was a key position, because it covered the gap in the Ring Barracks, and because it was rather tall, it allowed fire to be placed as well on the 'eastern walls' on North Island adjacent to the Muchavec. Red Army men ensconced in it had spent the entire day before exchanging fire with Germans occupying the eastern walls. They possessed only a few individual packages of bandages for the wounded, so they had resorted primarily to bandaging wounds with sheets and shirts. One of the men there recalls, 'In order to ease somehow the suffering of the wounded, we carried them down into the White Palace's cellar, where ice had been made for food items that would spoil rapidly. Chipping pieces from it, the wounded men quenched their unendurable thirst.' One can assume that wounded men from the sector at the Kholm Gate were also carried into the cellar under the White Palace. One witness to the building's collapse was Senior Sergeant S.M. Kuvalin, who decided to crawl over to it together with a comrade in order to find something to eat – in the daytime, the artillery fire and the threat of fire from the Church of Saint Nikolai prevented anyone from moving around at full height. Having found a little bread, the soldiers started crawling back. Kuvalin relates:

> About 150 metres from our objective, the deafening whistle of an incoming shell flattened us to the ground. Placing the sack of bread on my head, I took cover in a crater and waited for whatever would happen; the shell exploded quite nearby. My comrade was killed by a large stone fragment. Glancing out of the crater when everything had quieted, I saw the White Palace entirely shrouded in smoke. Having waited for the smoke to dissipate, I started moving towards the building. It seemed to me that anyone located inside it had been killed: the shell had penetrated all the floors of the Palace.

When working to clear away the ruins of the White Palace in 1959, forty-eight sets of human remains were found in its cellar. A bit earlier, in October 1958, an inscription had been found carved into one of its walls: 'We die without shame . . .'

* * *

Although it was not according to his wishes, the wounded Hans Teuschler, lying on North Island, had spent the night once again in practically the center of events, under the machine-gun bursts that were lashing across the entire island:

> That night again and again there came the terrifying artillery fire, which seemed never to want to end, and now and then gunshots sharply rang out in the impenetrable darkness. Never had I had a more burning desire to see the coming day. However, the dear sun became too good to us. The heat rose until it was almost unbelievable. From the rucksack of the dead non-commissioned officer, I took bread and cheese and began to busy myself with preparing a little snack from them. I divided the rations precisely so that I could hold out for four or five days, since after all the misfortunes I had no desire to die from hunger.

. . . At 0745, after a harassing fire that had continued for almost three hours, a barrage from all the artillery was called down upon the eastern and southern portions of the fortifications of the Citadel – however, without any perceptible results. Its only effect became the fact that shielded by the division's artillery fire, some of the men encircled in the Church of Saint Nikolai managed to do what they had not been able to do over the entire preceding day: break out to West or South Island. It is readily understandable how they were able to reach West Island. The Border Guards building and the semi-tower at the Terespol Gate had been totally demolished, and the few survivors were obviously waiting out the rest of the artillery barrage in the Ring Barracks; from the windows of the cellar of the 333rd Rifle Regiment's building, it would have been difficult to spot fleeting figures. In fact, all of the surrounded Germans in the church could have escaped by the same route, but because of disorganization or their reluctance to abandon their wounded, most preferred to remain in the church. Incidentally, a relief attempt might have succeeded had it been conducted from the direction of the Terespol Gate on this day – but now, it seems, the divisional command, recalling how stubbornly the Russians had fought the day before, opted not to press matters.

But why were other Germans able to escape to South Island? Most likely, they exited through the Kholm Gate, and they were able to do so primarily because over the night, the sector of the Ring Barracks at the Kholm Gate had been abandoned by its defenders. The leader of the defense in this sector, Regimental Commissar Fomin, had decided to pull back to the barracks of the 33rd Engineering Regiment. Various reasons have been offered for this decision. For example, some have argued that the Germans' employment of their anti-tank guns had in fact rendered an effective defense of this sector impossible. However, the more likely explanation is the fact that although under pre-war plans, it was the 84th Rifle Regiment's 3rd Battalion that had been designated to defend the fortress, the war had started in such circumstances that to defend it had become senseless, even suicidal. Thus on the previous afternoon of 22 June, realizing *what* had started, Fomin didn't hesitate – a break-out was the only realistic course, and an attempt had to be made as soon as possible, having assembled forces for this in the barracks of the 33rd Engineering Regiment. There was still a chance for this break-out to succeed. Possibly, this is exactly why Fomin had in fact ordered Sergeant Lerman on 22 June to drive the Germans out of the 33rd Regiment's mess hall – to attempt to break out, while having enemy in your rear firing at point-blank range, would have been ill-advised. However, the attempt to clear the mess hall of Germans had failed – all the approaches to the mess hall from the 33rd Engineering Regiment's barracks were exposed to German fire, and there was no covered route to it available. Lerman's failure had disrupted Fomin's plans, but he had no intention of abandoning the idea of a break-out.

It is possible that the abandonment of the Kholm Gate sector had started during the daylight hours of 22 June. A.M. Fil' recalls, 'At noon, Commissar Fomin ordered us to abandon our combat positions without being noticed, and to make our way to the engineers' building.'

However, the main forces weren't withdrawn until the night of 22 June, and it was still necessary to hold the sector at the Kholm Gate for some time. A.I. Durasov remembers:

> Fomin ordered for the German advance from the direction of the hospital [on South Island] to be kept in check for as long as possible with two or three machine guns, while the rest of the defenders withdrew to the barracks of the sapper battalion [sic]. I set up a Maksim machine gun at a window. Among the remaining soldiers there were no machine-gunners, so I had to operate the machine gun myself. Because of the ceaseless firing, the water in the jacket was boiling. Fortunately, in one of the corners of the room we found a bucket of water, which we used to refill the jacket. After some time had passed, we had used up all of the available reserve cartridge belts. The barracks emptied [of its defenders].

There could be no talk of bringing the severely wounded along in the break-out attempt. The majority of the lightly-wounded men were still fighting. Nevertheless, while there was still no pressure from the Germans, and while not everything was ready for the break-out attempt (the Germans hadn't yet been driven out of the 33rd Engineering Regiment's mess hall), the 84th Rifle Regiment's field dressing station (the so-called 'regimental infirmary', located in the cellar of the building of the Engineering Directorate) was continuing to function.

Ivan Dolotov recalls Fomin's arrival in the 33rd Engineering Regiment:

> In the morning a man showed up in a private's uniform, but it was obvious that he was a commander. With him were two or three Red Army soldiers, who'd been under our command yesterday morning. One of them was an ethnic Caucasian. For the rest of the day, they took charge of all further actions and everyone in our barracks. Later we learned that this commander was the regimental commissar of the 84th Rifle Regiment, Comrade Fomin. They had brought with them several heavy machine guns, and one of them was set up at a window overlooking the gap in the Ring Barracks and facing the Muchavec.

It is possible that it was A.V. Zhigunov's machine-gun crew that was manning this weapon. He remembers, 'Regimental Commissar Fomin gave us an order to take up a firing position on the second floor. We set up our Degtiarev machine gun on the staircase and covered the Eastern Bridge across the Muchavec River.' Considering that Dolotov called it a heavy machine gun, and Zhigunov says he deployed a Degtiarev, we can assume that it was the 7.62mm DS-39 heavy machine gun. A not insignificant detail: this was an air-cooled machine gun, not water-cooled, but at the time it was still sensitive to dust.

Perhaps from this point on, it would be more correct to name the sectors of the Citadel's defense or the defending combat groups that had spontaneously emerged, not according to their unit designations, but according to the last names of their leaders (Fomin – the 33rd Engineering Regiment and the 84th Rifle Regiment; Bytko – the headquarters and regimental school of the 44th Rifle Regiment; and Vinogradov – the 455th Rifle Regiment). However, because it still isn't clear who was leading the 333rd Rifle Regiment, it would be best to refer to it by its proper designation. The Consolidated Combat Group was Captain Zubachev's composite combat group; Gavrilov's Combat Group was holding the East Fort, while the 98th Separate Anti-tank Artillery Battalion practically fought as a separate unit right up until the last moment. Ivan Dolotov describes:

> From this day, we had a headquarters of the defence of the Ring Barracks that had emerged, and a command post appeared. Fomin spent all his time located at the entrance of a left-wing corridor on the first floor . . . of the 33rd Engineering Regiment's building. He sat on the floor and there received reports and issued orders.

Nevertheless, having abandoned the Ring Barracks at the Kholm Gate, Fomin was taking a great risk – what if the Germans seized it before Lerman could drive the

Germans out of the 33rd Engineering Regiment's mess hall? For all practical purposes, the entire Citadel would then be ensnared – the disconnected Red Army men in the several different sectors would be deprived of both any hope of a break-out, as well as indeed virtually any way of fighting on. But so far, the Germans hadn't detected Fomin's withdrawal from the Kholm Gate, so there was still time. Lerman, having assembled volunteers, launched another attack against the mess hall – but this time with 'artillery' support. The cannon that had been removed from the damaged BA-10 was deployed next to a lavatory – the closest vantage point to the mess hall. Sighting on a window, they opened fire, but all the fired shells had no effect – because of the sharply-oblique targeting angle to the Ring Barrack's wall, all the shells struck the side facing of the targeted window opening. However, apparently the 45mm shells shook some of the Germans inside, because several Germans leaped out of windows facing the Muchavec River on the opposite side of the Ring Barracks, where they were shot down almost instantly. The morale of the remaining Germans, worn out by two sleepless nights, plainly plummeted – after witnessing the death of their comrades who had tried to escape, it had become clear that no break-out attempt could succeed.

At 0845 on 23 June, the 45th Infantry Division's journal of combat operations recorded that thus far, approximately 2,000 prisoners had been taken. Over the preceding two hours, the number of prisoners had doubled. Most likely, these additional 1,000 prisoners were Red Army soldiers, who the day before had gone into hiding in Brest and outside the city limits where units of the division had been deployed. On the morning of 22 June, they had fled the fortress half-dressed, and with no weapons or commanding officers, they had sat out the night in various shelters; now, in groups or as single individuals, they were surrendering to the first German soldier who happened across them.

However, the main result of the artillery barrage on the morning of 23 June was something else – taking advantage of the fact that the Russians, seeking shelter from it, had taken cover, German assault groups achieved the swift seizure of almost the entire length of the Main Wall, save for a small sector at the Eastern Gate. The ring around the defenders became much stronger.

At 1130, a vehicle from a German propaganda company arrived in the 45th Infantry Division. Using a loudspeaker, it began to call upon the Russians to capitulate. At first, at least on West Island and in the sector of the 333rd Rifle Regiment, it yielded no tangible results. Leo Lozert:

> At noon, the propaganda company broadcast appeals to surrender through a loudspeaker. At first there was no success. Only seven Russians, in small groups or alone, emerged from the Citadel and crossed over to the island ... Suddenly a Russian armed with a machine gun appeared from behind a hedge. I didn't shoot, he surrendered, and explained to me that the remaining men in the fortress wouldn't surrender, but were continuing to fight.

The appeals by the propaganda vehicle's loudspeaker were clearly audible to Shablovsky's group in Building No. 5 of the command staff's apartment building complex – they were practically right next to where the vehicle was parked: the situation was hopeless – imprisonment was unavoidable. The loudspeaker announced that the Russians would have one half-hour to come over to the German positions. Now there were no further orders, each person made his or her own decision. Two of the officers committed suicide. Captain Shablovsky told everyone to go outside. Taking his little daughter into his arms, he kissed her and gave her back to his wife. The soldiers and officers of I.R. 135 watched as a file of people emerged from the building – first military men, then their wives and children. M.N. Gavrilkin:

> We were surrounded and shown where to go. A hush had settled over the entire fortress. We were escorted to the wall. There they made us sit, while the women and children were led down the slope to the bank of a canal. Submachine-gunners approached us and ripped off our rank insignia. Then they left our families alone, while we were taken down the slope from the wall and lined into a file, with Shablovsky in front. We approached a little bridge, where the canal enters a pond, and the depth of the water was about 1.5 metres. The footbridge was wood-planked, without railings. Shablovsky shouted 'After me!' and dove into the water. There was motion to follow him, but submachine-gunners intercepted us. They were firing at Shablovsky. The place was shallow, just 1.5 metres of water, and you could see his tunic and blood.

To an Austrian soldier of the *Wehrmacht*, this made a strong impression. It was the second day of the war . . . despite the fact that now and then prisoners were coming up, *Oberst* John remarked, 'Hardly any of the Russians thought about surrender. They courageously fought to the last man.' The combat engineer Heinz Krüger also testifies to this:

> A fantastic thing, *Ja*? – the fortress at Brest-Litovsk. And the men that fought there, they didn't give up. It was not a question of victory – they were communists – it was more one of annihilation. And it was exactly the same for them – we were Fascists! It was some battle. A few prisoners were taken, but they fought to the last.

At 1400, another propaganda vehicle arrived at the 45th Infantry Division command post, one with a more powerful loudspeaker. After the text of the propaganda was prepared and approved by General Schlieper, both vehicles were sent into the sector of I.R. 135. There, the following surrender appeal went out to those encircled inside the Brest Citadel:

> Comrades! Those besieged in the Citadel of Brest-Litovsk! Attention! Attention!

The German command is appealing to you for the last time and is calling upon you for your unconditional surrender. Your situation is hopeless. Don't spill your blood in vain, since there is no way out of the siege. You've been cut off from the others. More than 100 kilometres separates you from them. Your forces are hastily retreating, and several military units are running away. No one will come to your relief.

Comrades! Today, 23 June 1941, the beginning of the Citadel's bombardment has been set ... X-hour, Moscow time.

Nevertheless for reasons of humanity, the German command has postponed the bombardment until ... Y-hour, in order to spare your life and once again return you to your families and your homeland intact and unharmed.

Comrades! Commanders ... and soldiers! Fighters!

You have fought honourably – we will deal with you in accordance with this. You're given one hour to think it over.

If by Y-hour Moscow time on 23 June you haven't surrendered, your fate is sealed.

Red troops! Send flag-of-truce bearers! Lay down your weapon! Further resistance and bloodshed is pointless. Show compassion for yourself and for your families!

Around this time, a fresh message from the city of Brest shook the 45th Infantry Division's command post – approximately at 1400, the commander of the 45th Panzerjäger Battalion *Oberstleutnant* Paul Zahn was critically wounded when a Russian train loaded with ammunition exploded near an overpass bridge on the western outskirts of Brest. They managed to bring the badly-wounded commander back to the division's medical aid station, but there Zahn, one of the division's oldest veterans, who had participated in all its campaigns, passed away.

The situation was sufficiently quiet for *Oberst* John, whose troops of I.R. 135 were holding the pocket closed around North Island. At 1430, the remnants of the 10th and 11th companies and the headquarters of III/I.R. 135, now numbering around 100 men, were withdrawn to the area of John's command post for rest. In the meantime, they were combat-ineffective. The regiment's immediate objective was to keep North Island sealed. The condition of the enemy troops hadn't changed. Just as before, the adversary was savagely fighting with their former methods, immediately moving back into the territory that had been mopped up the day before. Russian tanks were located in the center of the fortress (and after the German withdrawal, possibly on North Island as well). John noted, 'It is still impossible to estimate the enemy casualties and amount of captured equipment. The number of military prisoners isn't great.'

For I.R. 133, this day of 23 June became an introduction to the 'harsh realities of the Eastern Front'. Although this regiment had been committed to the fighting on 22 June (except for the machine-gunners, who had arrived on the battle line that morning), it was only on 23 June that its combat became genuinely serious – as well as its casualties. The adjutant of I.R. 133 *Oberleutnant* Dedekind sent a provisional report from the regiment command post, which was located 1,200 meters to the south-west of the Terespol Bridge:

> Because of the withdrawal of II and I Battalions to South and West Island respectively for the planned artillery attack at 0500, the Russians managed to re-establish themselves there with weaker forces. Thus the battalions are again under heavy machine-gun fire and rifle fire, although the islands had been absolutely free of enemy forces yesterday evening. The regiment is preventing, nevertheless, any attempt by the enemy to break through or to escape from the encirclement.

Although the first surrendering defenders had already exited through the Terespol Gate, others, who had no intention to surrender, passed through them moving in the opposite direction – from West Island, Lieutenant Kizhevatov and several men had returned to the cellar of the 333rd Rifle Regiment's building, having crossed the causeway and then over the embankment to the Terespol Gate. The Citadel continued to quake from occasional explosions of heavy artillery shells – which was precisely why *Oberst* Kühlwein units that had been sealing the Citadel on its western side had been withdrawn from the bridge. That is also precisely why it was possible for Kizhevatov's group to escape West Island 'to the rear' – to Central Island, which was reverberating with explosions.

Though Kizhevatov had been able to hold up the German river crossing (and this was no small result!) with the fire from his position on the northern edge of West Island, the Germans nevertheless had resumed it. With no intention of retreating, Kizhevatov, exploiting the absence of Germans along the eastern bank of West Island, decided to repeat his fire attacks on the river crossing, once having stocked up again with ammunition. At this moment, one of the commanders of the Belorussian Border District driving school Lieutenant A.P. Zhdanov was continuing to command the Border Guards who had remained on West Island, occupying a defense along the wall on the Bug, from a pillbox north of Point 242. Despite the numerous sweeps of the island by Freytag's battalion, they were continuing to hold out, firing both at the bridge, and at elements of I.R. 133 that were on the island – and were waiting for Kizhevatov to return with ammunition.

Even after midday, the 45th Infantry Division continued to place targeted artillery fire on the Citadel in order to destroy its fortifications. Meanwhile, the men of Fomin's combat group, tormented by thirst, were continuing to attack the 33rd Engineering Regiment's mess hall in the Ring Barracks. The next attack was being led by the same Sergeant Lerman, and this time he decided to attack from the direction of the Muchavec. Three sergeants – Dolotov, Iakimov and the third, unknown – and one Red Army man were ordered to provide covering fire for Lerman. Along the entire wall of the barracks, the most advantageous firing position in order to cover Lerman both from the right (from fire coming from the eastern walls) and from the left (from the walls at Point 143) was the entrance to a boiler room in the cellar. The four men crept into the position from the interior side of the barracks through a window well in the boiler room. The private was armed with a PPD, while Dolotov had a Degtiarev light machine gun.

Once again, though, Lerman failed to break into the mess hall – with the fire from Dolotov's machine gun, it was hardly possible to suppress fire coming from both directions of the 33rd Engineering Regiment's barracks. It had become clear by now to Lerman that further such attacks would lead to nothing, so a different solution to the tactical problem was proposed: from the corridor of the 1st entrance, which led upstairs to the regiment headquarters, break a hole through the wall into the mess hall's kitchen, using engineering equipment, through which it would be possible to make entry. Then the assault group wouldn't have to expose themselves to fire from both sides of the Ring Barracks – from sections of the Main Wall on North Island and from the Church of Saint Nikolai. In order to prevent the Germans from shooting the men as they entered the kitchen through the gap, the kitchen had to be cleared of Germans. This they decided to accomplish by creating an opening in the ceiling above the kitchen (which was located directly beneath an office of the 33rd Engineering Regiment's headquarters), through which they could toss grenades down into the kitchen below. When the Germans fell back, the assault group would break into the kitchen through the wall opening and then wipe out the remaining Germans in the mess hall itself.

Work immediately got under way – those Germans located in the mess hall listened to the blows against the wall and the ceiling with anguish and alarm. At this time, the kitchen staff and two or three women (likely wives of the command staff who'd sought shelter in the mess hall) were in the cellar below the mess hall after being forced into it by the Germans. There was a similar situation in the Church of Saint Nikolai, where by the end of its siege there were nearly as many Russian prisoners inside the church as there were Germans. It is interesting to note that neither in the mess hall nor the church, despite the hopeless situation, the Germans made no effort to 'deal with the problem with the prisoners' by radical measures.

Lerman's last unsuccessful attack had yielded positive consequences – water was found in two boilers in the boiler room. Already within a half-hour, it was being passed up to the first floor in buckets through a hole created in the floor. Primarily this water was used to refill the cooling jackets of the machine guns, or was given to the wounded men, and the women and children located in the cellar.

At 1700 a storm of artillery fire was raging inside the Citadel – the Germans were conducting an intensified barrage using all their available artillery. Again, just as happened that morning, the walls of the 333rd Regiment's building and of the Ring Barracks in the 44th and 455th regiments' sectors, as well as in Group Fomin's position, began to rock. Lerman's men continued to work to create an entry into the kitchen, while the encircled Germans in the church were waiting with excitement, anticipating that a relief attack would come to their rescue as soon as the barrage ended.

However, instead of this, again the loudspeakers on the propaganda vehicles started up. The propaganda officers had added another line to the surrender appeal:

'Major General Puzyrev, the chief of the Brest Fortified District, is drinking vodka with German officers, while you're continuing senseless resistance.' In fact, Puzyrev avoided being taken prisoner.

This broadcast managed to prompt a certain number of defenders in every sector of the Citadel to surrender. Numerous reports coming in from the units encircling the Citadel about surrender talks and the capitulation of entire units, and later the interrogation of the prisoners, created the impression among the officers of the 45th Infantry Division that the garrison's morale had weakened perceptibly.

So, what was going on inside the Citadel? Several riflemen and machine-gunners were still occupying the sector at the Kholm Gate. The Germans had still made no attempt to attack it – there'd been no order to do so. Indeed, those few men still holding the Kholm Gate through rare exchanges of fire were giving the appearance that the barracks there were still being held. It must be said that Fomin had yet another reason to abandon the Ring Barracks at the Kholm Gate, which was the disintegrating discipline among their defenders. Possibly, it was under the influence of this factor that he had in fact reached the decision to break out of the Citadel as quickly as possible. Those surrendering to the Germans were leaving the Citadel using three routes, but primarily via the Brigidki and Trekharoch Gates. Many had also left through the Terespol Gate, though now, in the daylight hours, the resolute actions of the Border Guards had in fact lessened their flow. Those leaving through the Brigidki Gate (there, they were loaded into rubber dinghies and taken across the Muchavec) were laying down their weapons in the sector of II/I.R. 135, while those leaving through the Trekharoch Gate were surrendering to I/I.R. 135, where the propaganda vehicles were parked.

In numerous eyewitness statements, it has been noted that the recent conscripts of the designated personnel displayed the least resolve (and often alarmism and a straightforward desire to surrender). These soldiers were for all practical purposes still civilians or were former soldiers of the Polish army who were still going through training. The matter reached the level of fire-fights with 'friendlies', which in fact gave rise to many rumors about German infiltrators wearing Red Army uniforms. Junior Sergeant S.T. Bobrenok of the 17th Red Banner Border Guards Detachment exemplifies this: 'We had to clash with infiltrators in Red Army uniforms more than once. They were dastardly, killing soldiers by shooting them in the back, were on the hunt for our commanders, and as a provocation were the first to surrender.' On this day, the 'infiltrators' wounded A.I. Makhnach as well. He had crawled out into a courtyard and had started to sight in a new PPD:

> Suddenly I felt something like an electric current running through my left leg. Overcoming the sharp pain, I glanced around. Behind me I saw some soldier lying prone with a pistol in his hands. I was just about to ask him what he could shoot when firing in the direction of our barracks, when he again shot at me. Without aiming, I fired off the entire drum toward him.

In the sector of the 44th Rifle Regiment, the surrender appeals by the propaganda company also generated a response. Although the majority of the soldiers decided to continue fighting, as A.N. Bessonov writes:

> There were also those with weak nerves. Several sought to swim across the Muchavec and surrender to the Germans, but they all found a resting spot on the bottom of the Muchavec. We had to deal with some within the fortress . . . If the Hitlerites hadn't been so timid, and had launched an assault against the western segment of the [Ring] barracks in the same spirit as they'd shown on the first day, they would have finished us all off without any difficulty. However, the fascists overestimated our strength and our capability to resist, apparently because they'd taken so many casualties, so they were hesitant to make new attacks.

Despite the difficult situation, the majority of the defenders didn't even think of surrendering. A.I. Makhnach relates: 'At this time, up to a regiment of our aircraft flew past the fortress to the south of us. This inspired confidence in us that our victory was close at hand.' I. Dolotov adds:

> There was not even thought of surrender; in the north beyond the walls that ran alongside the Muchavec, all the time we were hearing intense machine-gun and rifle fire, intermixed with the sound of artillery fire, and we were confident that our own forces were breaking through to us from Brest, and that fighting was going on somewhere already near the Main Gate.

Dolotov was hearing the fire-fight between the defenders of the 98th Separate Anti-tank Artillery Battalion and the East Fort on one side, and the Germans occupying positions along the Main Wall on the other. The artillery fire was the reports of the anti-tank guns when they fired.

Despite the fact that the Citadel's defenses were crumbling, Kizhevatov had no intention to drop his plan to disrupt the Germans' river crossing again. Loaded with cartridges, he was preparing to leave together with several Border Guardsmen. Again he planned to cross the causeway over to West Island, and there move along the bank, under the cover of the embankment, to the north of the island. There was now nothing that could be done for the Citadel – at any moment the Germans would either overrun the handful of defenders still holding the Kholm Gate, or penetrate the Citadel through the ruins of the Terespol Gate. Now that the Germans had ceased the artillery barrage and were collecting prisoners, and hadn't yet appeared again on the eastern bank of West Island, it was time to leave. So Kizhevatov left.

Remnants of the 84th Rifle Regiment and solitary men were continuing to converge on the barracks of the 33rd Engineering Regiment. S.M. Kuvalin, who at this time was at his machine gun in the ruins of the White Palace, recalled:

> Five or so soldiers went running past me; I recognized Sergei Volkov among them, who had been training in the armourer workshop. I asked

> him, 'Where are you running?' He replied that Germans had seized the headquarters of the 84th Rifle Regiment ... Remaining alone, I crawled over to that part of the building on the bank of the Muchavec River, where Sergeant Major V.E. Meer was directing the defence; there were around fifty men there. From them I found out that our guys were occupying this entire building, and that here was the defence's headquarters, which Fomin was directing.

At 1815, a fresh artillery barrage started to fall on the Citadel, which continued until 1855. Again, appeals to surrender rang out from the loudspeakers on the German propaganda vehicles. Some of the defenders were continuing to trickle out of the Citadel, laying down their weapons on North Island. John, on the basis of their interrogations, came to the conclusion that the garrison was exhibiting a clear desire to surrender, but according to the prisoners, commissars were preventing it from doing so. It was decided to designate a new surrender deadline, pushing it back until 2030. Incidentally, so many Russians were now coming out, is it possible that the new barrage wasn't even necessary? Obviously, it was during the confusion that was reigning in the Citadel that several German soldiers had managed to break out of the fortifications of the Central Bastion, which the German command took as a further sign that the morale of the Russian garrison had been plainly weakened. Leo Lozert also observed the escape of these trapped Germans, obviously at the same time as the surrendering defenders: 'Remnants of I.R. 135 and wounded men were also still coming out.'

By 1900, Lerman had completed the preparations to storm the mess hall. The wall between the kitchen and the corridor off the 1st entrance had been broken through. The commander of the 44th Rifle Regiment's regimental school walked up to a group of trainees and proposed, 'Anyone desiring to drive out the Germans, follow me.' Six or seven of the men followed him; altogether, ten or twelve men gathered for the assault against the mess hall. With grenades and pistols, they descended the staircase to the first floor and took position in front of the almost-finished breach in the wall into the kitchen. Another group placed two grenade bundles into a small hole that had been created in the floor of the headquarters office above the kitchen, and having covered them with mattresses, detonated them, blowing a gaping hole in the floor. Immediately, grenades went flying into the opening, while almost simultaneously, powerful blows of a pickaxe broke through the wall, and soldiers burst into the kitchen, having first tossed grenades through the opening. The now shattered kitchen was empty, but passing from the kitchen into the service section, the Russians spotted figures in the direction of a door that led into a pantry. Several grenades were tossed in that direction one after another, and a minute later, a female's voice rang out: 'They're coming out.' Three Germans, covered with plaster dust, emerged from the pantry with upraised hands, followed by a woman who was carrying a child of three or four years of age in her arms.

However, it turned out that the remaining Germans had taken cover in the cellar beneath the mess hall, where there were also two women and the kitchen staff, who'd been taken prisoner the previous morning. It was decided to force the Germans out by tossing grenades through the cellar windows. N.M. Morozov, one of the assault team members, recalls:

> After the first explosion we heard a woman's voice: 'Don't toss any more grenades! The Germans are surrendering!' Then we told this same woman to direct the Germans to strip to their underclothing, and to climb out of the cellar one by one through the window. We watched as six Germans in their underclothing began to emerge from the cellar one after the other. We asked the woman if there were any others. She replied that only two dead Germans were left inside.

Likely, the resolve of these nine or eleven Germans in the mess hall had been broken by almost two days of combat, and this eased the task of Lerman's group, which it had been given more than once. Having searched the prisoners, they were escorted by guard up to the second floor for interrogation, where some wounded lieutenant was lying; he had arrived only on the eve of the war from a military school and knew the German language. After interrogating the Germans, they were locked into a store room beneath the staircase. In the kitchen, the Red Army men were able to scrounge some food – sugar, bread, vegetables and some raw potatoes.

At 1912, the command post of the 45th Infantry Division in Terespol radioed XII Corps headquarters about the beginning of the garrison's capitulation under the influence of the artillery fire and the propaganda broadcasts: 'Fortress Brest starting at 1830 under the influence of artillery fire is beginning to capitulate. Trapped German soldiers have been freed. The conditions for conducting negotiations and for accepting prisoners have been transmitted to the regiments.' In order to get a sense of the extent of the Soviets' capitulation, Fritz Schlieper and Armin Dettmer at 1945 were about to leave by vehicle to visit I.R. 135. However, at this time several messages arrived, which gave them to understand that several Russian units were continuing the fight.

Toward evening, Loertzer's machine-gun company again took position to the right of the Terespol Bridge. Soon the surrender deadline expired, after which a new barrage on the Citadel was forthcoming. Lozert and his squad were located directly at the bridge. He was taking in prisoners and pointing out positions for his machine-gunners. Lozert informed an approaching officer that a wounded German, who was unable to walk, was lying in an enemy fortified position on the other end of the bridge. He requested the officer's authorization to go bring the wounded man back, before the next artillery barrage, which was to begin in ten minutes, finished him off. The rescue mission went smoothly.

At 2040, the German artillery again began to pound the Citadel, and by 2100 Dettmer had prepared the daily summary report for corps headquarters. At this time, considering that over the day 1,900 prisoners had been taken, the impression was prevailing in the division headquarters that the next day, after a new, heavy artillery barrage, they'd be able to take the remaining parts of the Citadel that were still in enemy hands with only insignificant losses. Although the evening summary report carried an optimistic tone, it did stress the point that because of the events of the day, the relocation of the division's command post hadn't taken place. Dettmer also couldn't give any information about the division's losses, nor about any captured enemy matériel.

Because of the unexpected hitch in taking Brest, various units of the division had to free up cargo space for ammunition, which was achieved only by unloading the column of trucks that was standing ready to move out. That night, ammunition repeatedly had to be brought up to the front-line units. A shift in the position of Galle's mortar battalion and the need to deliver ammunition to the newly-attached *nebelwerfer* battalions also placed increased demands on the division transport. On this day, movement on all the roads in the division's sector practically froze due to traffic jams. It was particularly difficult for units of the division that didn't have any priority of transit, as distinct from the vehicles of the panzer divisions. Nasty traffic jams obstructed the road movement of the motorized supply units on the highway, while the march of horse-drawn supply columns bogged down because of the prohibition against their use of the Zales'e–Brest highway. The traffic jams on the roads in the sector of the panzer group became a problem that became known all the way up to Army Group Centre's commander von Bock. In his diary on this day, he noted, 'Difficulties in crossing at Brest ... have impeded delivery of fuel.'

After the completion of the latest artillery barrage, Loertzer's 12th Company again resumed taking in prisoners at the Terespol Bridge, although the 3rd Company, which had previously been located in the reserve, had now also been brought up to the bridge. Leo Lozert remembers:

> Suddenly I saw that approximately 100 surrendering Russians were running in the direction of 3/I.R. 133, which had fully been committed into the fighting on this day. I immediately understood that it was necessary to inform its commander Oberleutnant Kushorek about this as quickly as possible, so that he could give the order to his company not to fire. Since the 3rd Company had been committed for the first time earlier that day, it was still firing all along the line. Suddenly approximately 500 surrendering Russians marched out of the Citadel in a column. I went to meet them. A feldwebel of the 3rd Company (he'd received a Knight's Cross on Christmas Day) accepted their surrender before I could reach them. He informed me that German soldiers in the church in the Citadel had been caught by the Russians. Military inspector Manharstberger, believing that the war was over, had already left to take command inside the Citadel, but he was shot by the Russians and his body remained lying there.

According to some testimony, by this time the situation in the cellar of the 333 Rifle Regiment's building had deteriorated to the point that commanders were sitting at the entrances with pistols at the ready, preventing anyone from surrendering.

When one of them was killed by a shell splinter during the artillery barrage, a crowd desiring to surrender pushed past his body, emerged on the surface, ran across the bridge and surrendered to the first German soldier they came across.

In Order la/op. No. 11/41 regarding the mopping-up of the Brest Citadel, which was prepared at 2330 in the command post of the 45th Infantry Division, in particular the following points were mentioned:

> (1) The enemy forces in the Brest citadel have been defeated or rendered incapable of further resistance by the exemplary attacks of the 45th Division on 22 June and the extremely effective encirclement and barrages on 23 June, so on 24 June one can count upon their complete destruction. This day will crown the division's savage and costly struggle.

The division was preparing for the final assault. The night promised to be quiet – it was believed that the Russians were demoralized, depleted and exhausted by two days of fighting, and thus it was possible to give the men some rest before the next day's assault. However, this illusion was soon shattered. At the same time the Germans were preparing for the final attack, Fomin's entire combat group was poised to launch its attack – Fomin was still set upon a break-out. Dense groups of soldiers were waiting in the 33rd Engineering Regiment's mess hall, which had recently been taken by Lerman's soldiers. Now the path to the Trekharoch Bridge was clear. They were only waiting for the signal. In the cellar of the Engineering Directorate, where the field dressing station of the 84th Rifle Regiment was located, the medical staff and mobile patients, who were leaving to join the break-out, were saying farewell to their comrades that would be left behind. Among those being left behind in the cellar was the 84th Rifle Regiment *Komsomol* organizer Matevosian, who'd been wounded in both legs. Many of them were still hoping to avoid being taken prisoner – the Red Army would come at any time! Matevosian said, 'Break through to our army and come back to get us.'

At this moment, Fomin was now also in the mess hall. He looked extremely exhausted. Now and then, group commanders were coming up to him. It was noticeable that something special was being prepared. Everyone was full of nervous tension. Concealed behind chimneys, marksmen were prone on the roof, and machine-gunners had taken position at the window openings. They'd begun preparing for the break-out ahead of time – likely as soon as the mess hall had been cleared of Germans. The assistant chief of staff of the 33rd Engineering Regiment Lieutenant Shcherbakov concealed the regimental banner in the cellar. All of the 84th Rifle Regiment's documents had been destroyed back during the abandonment of the sector at the Kholm Gate. A different problem had now arisen – what to do with the German prisoners? Ivan Dolotov relates their fate:

> Fomin ordered Dolotov to 'complete the operation'; in other words, to shoot the Germans, since in our situation we had no other option. Lerman at first refused to carry out the order, but after a second and categorical

> order from the regimental commissar, he complied. All of the fascists were shot in the stock room below the staircase leading to the second floor.

It was decided to break out in the direction of the Kobrin Gate: judging from the sounds of battle, units of the Red Army were counter-attacking from Kobrin toward Brest. Since the Kobrin Bridge was exposed to fire from the walls, several of the break-out group decided to cross the Muchavec by either swimming or using hastily-built rafts. However, it is difficult to swim with a weapon and in a uniform, so they fashioned rafts from pieces of tables and chairs, parts of doors and door frames, and other woodwork. Empty suitcases served as fine flotation devices. They decided to break out in groups of thirty to forty men each. The first, armed with light machine guns, would dash across the bridge and cover the rest who were swimming across. The break-out groups couldn't count upon surprise – illumination flares dangling from parachutes were constantly suspended above the river. However, several minutes, if only for the purpose of assembling in the dark apertures of the Trekharoch Gate in the failing light, was all they had available.

So now jackboots and shoes began to pound across the bridge – the first break-out group was in motion. Fomin remained at his extemporized command post, anticipating that the eastern wall on North Island would be seized and it would become possible to organize an evacuation of the wounded. It was approximately 2330, around the same time that the 45th Infantry Division's command staff was putting the finishing touches to the order for the next day's assault.

Only the first men had time to reach the opposite bank – suddenly several flares soared into the sky. Simultaneously, dozens of Red Army soldiers began rushing toward the Muchavec with their makeshift rafts. Just then, machine guns opened up at the crossing site from both directions (the eastern walls and Point 143), and mortars began dropping rounds on and around the bridge. Dolotov, who at that moment was running across the bridge, threw himself prone among the dead and dying. Those who remained alive (and there weren't many), began crawling back under the machine-gun fire toward the Ring Barracks. But bursts of machine-gun fire were sweeping the bridge, which was perfectly visible from the walls, like a scythe. In fact, no one was able to make it back to the barracks – the few terrified survivors had flattened themselves against the bridge's surface among the corpses, feigning death. I. Dolotov:

> The tracer streams from the storm of machine-gun fire kept us flattened. Moans of the wounded, cries for help and desperate appeals to be delivered from the agonizing pain ... You couldn't hear any commands. The gunfire would subside, but after a few individual rifle shots, the machine guns would open up again.

A.I. Durasov's stark testimony regarding the break-out attempt stands out among the recollections:

> It is very hard to describe the images of this combat. The Germans illuminated the small stretch of the river with special parachute flares,

> and opened the heaviest machine-gun fire at the soldiers in the water. The bulk of them in fact never reached the opposite bank, having died in the waters of the Muchavec under the hailstorm of machine-gun bullets.

It became clear that the break-out attempt had failed. However, there were also those who didn't realize that – a few managed to break out across the bridge or to make it across the Muchavec. Keeping their heads down under the machine-gun fire, some were able to crawl to the wall at Point 145, where other Red Army troops were located. An attack against the 'eastern walls' was next on the agenda.

Immediately after the Germans had opened fire, the machine guns of the defenders on the roof and second floor of the 33rd Engineering Regiment's barracks began working, covering the crossing, firing at the visible muzzle flashes of the enemy machine guns on the walls. Riflemen opened fire. V.S. Solozobov:

> From the defence's command post located down below, we were warned that we had to increase our fire. I guessed what was happening: our men were sallying to break out. Here, on the second floor, enemy shells were penetrating the roof and ceiling. There was a dense cloud of dust from chips. I got excited and was firing enthusiastically.

It was 2345. The fire from the Russians covering the crossing from the roof of the 33rd Engineering Regiment and those prone atop the wall at Point 145 proved to be rather effective – Kühlwein, the commander of I.R. 133, who immediately got in touch with the division's command post, reported that on the eastern outskirts of the Citadel, the men of Gerstmeyer's III/I.R. 133 who were holding that sector were pinned down under heavy rifle and machine-gun fire.

Meanwhile, seeing no movement on the bridge, the machine-gunners of Kaehne's I/I.R. 135, who'd been firing from the wall near Point 143, held their fire. The cries and groans of the wounded gradually subsided. Still lying on the bridge, Dolotov caught the sound of shouts intermixed with automatic weapons fire and grenade explosions from somewhere to his right beyond the bakery (they were the sounds of combat at Point 145), as well as individual rifle shots. It was a group that had launched an attack in a desperate impulse, trying to escape via the walls at Point 145. Probably, they managed to penetrate to within grenade range of the eastern walls. But the combat was fleeting – the attacking force was too small. Soon they began falling back at a run, falling under the machine guns of Kaehne's and Gerstmeyer's men. A few of them ran into the casemates at Point 145, reinforcing the defenders there.

Those survivors of the break-out attempt in ones and twos, waiting for pauses in the fire, returned to the barracks, cautiously crawling back across the bridge or silently entering the Muchavec. Lieutenant L.A. Kochin, the deputy commander of the 84th Rifle Regiment's signals company, had to lay on the bridge for up to forty minutes; Ivan Dolotov, together with a group of five or six men (some of whom were wounded), was able to return to the Ring Barracks only just before sunrise.

By 2350, the 45th Division headquarters had already informed the subordinate unit commanders of its intention to attack in the morning. However, the written orders for the attack still hadn't gone out: the Russians' energetic attack, which had been accompanied by heavy rifle and machine-gun fire, made it clear that they were still strong in force. Just as the previous evening, events had again gotten ahead of the order. Nevertheless, the attack order still hadn't been cancelled either – it was decided to wait on further developments.

At 0200 on 24 June, Bytko's group launched another sally – toward the Northern Gate. His group was much smaller than it had been the previous night, but he still had a chance to succeed. Kaehne had fallen back to the Main Wall, and Gerstmeyer's machine-gunners had no clear view of targets flitting among the trees of the alleyway leading from the Trekharoch Bridge to the Northern Gate. It was necessary only to make it through the gate – but illumination flares suspended overhead soon revealed the attackers. Again, machine-gun fire swept down the entire alleyway, and mortar shells began to explode. Having lost many men in the scything machine-gun fire that seemed to be coming from every direction, Bytko was forced to retreat. *Oberst* John reported that a lively fire-fight had developed on North Island as well, with an enemy that seemed to be attempting to break out to the north. Speaking on the plans of the attack that was designated for the morning, John stated that he believed it would only lead to heavy losses; in addition, he emphasized the ammunition shortage, especially confronting the small arms.

Meanwhile, fire at the Citadel, seemingly prompted by Fomin's and Bytko's break-out attempts, could now be heard everywhere – flares were soaring upwards, and tracers of machine-gun fire were streaming through the darkness. The 45th Infantry Division's war journal had the following to say about this night: 'Enemy attempts to break out of the encirclement are being repulsed everywhere.' Noteworthy is the morning report from Kühlwein, which arrived at the division command post at 0410: 'In the course of the entire night, Russian break-out attempts, especially in the eastern direction against III/133, as well as to the south, especially in the western portion of South Island. All these attempts were successfully repulsed.' Who could have attempted to break out to the south on that night? It could have been Potapov's small band of men or a different group of the 333rd Rifle Regiment trying to break out to the Southern Encampment, or perhaps one of the groups of Border Guards trying to escape West Island after the energetic actions of Masukh's pioneers the previous day. Further on, Kühlwein's morning report states:

> The regiment is holding the positions achieved by the evening of 23.6. On South Island, several bunkers and buildings occupied by the enemy were blown up with demolition charges by the combat engineers of an infantry unit. West Island is firmly in our hands. Its north-western portion should be cleared by dawn in view of the anticipated barrage.

It is a pity that almost nothing is known about the fighting on South Island – on 22 and 23 June, combat had been raging there that was no less fierce than the fighting for the Citadel or the East Fort. Remember, only a platoon of the 84th Rifle Regiment's regimental school, the medical-sanitation battalion of the 95th Rifle Regiment, and several Border Guards were on South Island ...

Oberst John, in his morning report, confirmed what he had already said in the telephone conversation just an hour before: 'Frenzied activity of the Russians, including attempts to break out to the north (evidently in small detachments). They were all driven back. The Russians are still obstinate and not ready to surrender.'

At 0330, an engine suddenly began to rumble in the Citadel – a Russian tank attack! This couldn't be ... but in the deathly light of the illumination flares, the shadow of a small Russian tank could be seen. Heading out of the Citadel, it turned between the apartment buildings of the command staff and was moving at top speed toward Brest. The guns of the *panzerjägers* of Wetzel's 3rd Company tardily opened fire at the tank that was quickly receding in their rear – their reaction had been too slow. The tank clattered through the gate and drove into Brest, toward a road that was jammed with motorized supply units that were on the move that night. There is evidence that its appearance prompted a wild commotion – in the end, the Germans used logs to trap it at an intersection and tossed a tarpaulin over it, forcing the crew of two to surrender. The prisoners were taken to the command post of I.R. 130.

At 0400, in connection with the reports that the Russians' activity hadn't flagged, and moreover guided by the conversation that had taken place the day before with General Blumentritt on keeping casualties to a minimum, Schlieper again, just as he did the night before, decided to cancel the prepared order to launch a fresh assault on the Citadel. It was decided as the first order of business to clarify the situation by contacting the commanders of the front-line units and von Krischer, which the staff officers of the command post were busily doing. Schlieper himself contacted the XII Corps commander. After a detailed and thorough discussion of the situation, an order was issued – a new version of Nr. 11/41. The division was now expected to prevent any enemy influence on the *panzer rollbahn* and to continue to grind down the Citadel's defenders with artillery fire.

The neighboring divisions by now had advanced far beyond Brest and had been drawn into fighting, leaving the 45th Infantry Division essentially alone in their rear. In Schlieper's detailed discussions with General Walther Schroth about the situation, it became clear that pursuant to the commander's orders, the seizure of the fortress by assault was now impossible, and that the Citadel's mopping-up would require several more days.

Just before morning there occurred another event of no little significance in the history of the Citadel's defense – taking advantage of the pre-morning darkness and a lull in the fighting, Zubachev and Vinogradov, together with their men, managed to cross over to the barracks of the 33rd Engineering Regiment, where they met with Fomin. The circumstances behind this meeting are not fully known, but it is possible to speculate that after the unsuccessful break-out attempts between 2330 and 0030, Fomin decided to unite the defenders and sent messengers out to the other sectors of the defense.

Zubachev and Vinogradov both had combat experience from the Winter War with Finland, while Fomin's own experience was more modest. He had only participated in the 'liberating campaign' in the western Ukraine in the wake of the Ribbentrop–Molotov Pact. According to his rank and position, the commissar outranked both Zubachev and Vinogradov – however, the calm and collected battalion commander Zubachev had passed through the fighting at Trångsund [now Vysotsk, a town that was the scene of fierce fighting during the Winter War], and at one time the Russian Civil War itself, so he was a much more suitable commander to direct the defense. Of the many descriptions of their encounter, the most reliable appears to be that offered by Lieutenant Vinogradov:

> We gathered in a small room with window openings that faced the Muchavec. We exchanged greetings. Fomin requested that we present our personal documents. I was in full uniform with an Order of the Red Star on my chest. Our appearance was so unusual, that it was difficult even to recognize familiar faces: reddened eyes and uniforms covered with a thick layer of dust and ash. After the brief introductions and clarifying the situation in the different sectors, Commissar Fomin reported that the existing situation demanded a more rapid, better organized and operational leadership of the defence, and gave us our orders: to find out about the availability of ammunition and food, the condition of the wounded, and moreover, to make contact with our neighbours to propose that they do the same ... and then to return to him with a report.

It is noteworthy that it was Fomin, not being the formal leader of the Citadel's defense, who was the one issuing orders.

At this time on West Island, where the darkness still reigned over the river-bank thickets, again, for the third night in a row, Lozert was keeping vigil: 'That night I again didn't have the slightest desire to sleep; I was checking the outposts, and since everyone else was fatally tired, I was receiving the food, which was delivered around 0200.' At dawn, Loertzer's company again fell back from the eastern edge of the island and took position along its western bank, at the site of the old crossing. Now, thanks to the combat engineers, a ferry was operating here. The machine guns were pointed to the east – soon again the artillery would begin working, and the possibility of another break-out attempt couldn't be excluded.

Hidden in the willow thickets, several men with faces that had been scorched by gunpowder and bore signs of burns were keeping close watch over Loertzer's withdrawal – these were the Border Guards who had interrupted the German river crossing to the north of West Island the day before. There were now much fewer of them. One, in a blood-soaked uniform, was lying unconscious on the riverbank sand – it was the mortally-wounded chief of the 9th Border Post, Lieutenant Andrei Kizhevatov. He wouldn't survive, but the Border Guardsmen nevertheless decided to drag their commander back to the cellar of the 333rd Rifle Regiment's building. There was now no one to whom to report. The cellar was full of wounded and those concussed by the shell from the Karl heavy mortar the day before – today would be worse, no one doubted.

They carried Kizhevatov into the westernmost chamber of the cellar, and laid him in the corner closest to the Terespol Gate. Here he died several minutes later. Having wrapped his body in sheets and blankets, they left him there – in the place that was nearest to the Soviet state border. They placed the body of Junior Lieutenant Zinov'ev next to Kizhevatov's. After this, some of the soldiers of the 333rd Rifle Regiment headed over to the 33rd Engineering Regiment.

At 0600, the first shells exploded with a roar. The surrender deadline had expired – the loudspeakers, the work of the propagandists, fell silent. Again there were explosions and clouds of dust and smoke rose above the Citadel. First of all the heavy artillery and the heavy mortar batteries set to work. Lozert recalls:

> That night the heavy artillery (210mm) fired for a long time. Every third or fourth shell proved to be a dud. This was good for us, because often the shells were dropping short. The closest shells landed just 20 to 30 metres in front of me next to the levee.

A.P. Bessonov, who had formerly been located in the sector of the 44th Rifle Regiment among Bytko's soldiers, also confirms the dud shells: 'One shell, which had crashed down next to a brick wall or had burrowed into the earth, failed to explode ...' Between 0800 and 0805, the Citadel was shaken by the explosion of the Karl heavy mortars' 600mm shells; over the entire day, 'Thor' would fire eleven shells, 'Odin' six.

In these hours, which were filled with the thunder of the shells that were battering the Citadel, the commanders of the combat groups, Fomin, Zubachev and Vinogradov, again came together in the barracks of the 33rd Engineering Regiment. This time, because of the unceasing barrage, they met in the cellar. A.A. Vinogradov relates:

> It was a small chamber in the cellar, which had a small half-window that faced the Muchavec. On the opposite side of the room, soldiers at Fomin's order had created another opening in the wall that faced the White Palace. Soldiers and junior commanders with Degtiarev light machine guns were posted at both openings. There were a lot of ammunition boxes lying around, the majority of which were already empty. There was a little table in the middle of the space. Fomin invited all of those who had arrived for the meeting to take a seat at it. He gave me a notepad and asked me to take notes. Then each one at the table was asked briefly to present his ideas regarding the further course of actions. After the brief presentations, this was the situation as it was seen then, on 24 June: (1) Very heavy casualties in killed and wounded; (2) Little availability of Soviet-manufactured ammunition; (3) The situation with the wounded, the children and women was exceptionally difficult, due to the lack of proper conditions, medical personnel, and medications and bandages

> for the wounded soldiers and officers. The heavy scent of the decaying corpses was oppressive to the weak and lightly-wounded soldiers and commanders; (4) The food reserves, which we had managed to create on the first day, were almost exhausted.

In a word, something had to be done. The conclusion was one – to break out, now with a unified force. Thus, on the morning of 24 June, after the previous unsuccessful attempts to act with scattered forces, it was decided to create a single composite combat group. Its commander at Fomin's suggestion became Captain Zubachev, while Fomin took the role as its commissar. As its chief of staff, Ivan Zubachev proposed to appoint his fellow officer from the 44th Rifle Regiment, Senior Lieutenant A.I. Semenenko, who was the assistant chief of staff of the 44th Regiment. In addition, as the first order of business, it was decided to take a roll call in order to get an accurate count of the soldiers and to form one company of four platoons (one machine-gun and three rifle platoons). This company, commanded by Lieutenant Vinogradov, would constitute the break-out attempt's spearhead. It was here, at the small table, using three sheets of the notepad, where Vinogradov then compiled Order No. 1, as dictated to him by Fomin and Zubachev. This surviving document became a key source, which to a great extent was destined to shape the history of the study of the defense of the Brest Fortress.

In addition to Order No. 1, two other documents have survived to give us some picture of what was happening within the Citadel at this time. One is a list of the wounded men of one of the companies that has been preserved. More information about those events is also contained in a surviving source which has become known as the 'Notebook of an unknown commander'. This document likely belonged to one of the commanders of the 44th Rifle Regiment, who was primarily occupied with the baggage train – its pages are riddled with notes about procuring fodder, harnessing horses, and other related items. Then suddenly there is an abrupt transition to the following:

> Plan of action
>
> 1. Hvy MGs
> 2. Finish organizing
> 3. Measures to overwhelm a sector
> 4. Organize a guard
> 5. Observation
>   1. Tidy up sectors
>   2. The deceased – collect
>   Ammunition

That is all ... the following pages in the notebook are blank. Note that 'the deceased' was written, not 'the killed' or 'the dead'. Judging from everything available, the author meant those who had died from mortal wounds. The fatality rate among the wounded, who for all practical purposes received no aid whatsoever, was horrifying. Their bodies were lying everywhere; no one had time to remove them from buildings and cover them with earth in the shell craters at the walls.

However, after the writing of Order No. 1, which envisaged a rapid escape from the fortress, an argument erupted again among the commanders – should they break out or should they continue to hold out and wait for help? Zubachev with unexpected heat spoke out against a break-out attempt:

> We haven't received an order to withdraw and must defend the fortress! It cannot be that our guys have retreated very far – they will return at any time, and if we've abandoned the fortress, it will have to be re-taken by assault. What will we then say to our comrades and command? And enough with the senseless waste of lives like tonight ... Of course, it is worthwhile scouting out the possibility of a break-out, but the main task now is an organized defence until the arrival of help.

At Zubachev's insistence, the phrase 'rapid escape' was replaced by the words 'organized combat operation'. Further discussion was interrupted by the tumultuous events of the afternoon.

While the commanders were meeting, in the casemates of the 33rd Engineering Regiment, which were quaking from the barrage of the heavy artillery and to where a few of the survivors had returned after the unsuccessful break-out attempt, the mood was somewhat depressed. Even on 22 June, they hadn't taken such casualties as they had that night. Then, at least the enemy was visible – and it had been shown that it was possible to defeat him. But now for the last forty-eight hours, there had only been the thunderous explosions of shells in the daytime, illumination flares at night, and bursts of fire from invisible machine guns, which prevented them breaking out across the bridge or even from obtaining water. I. Dolotov:

> After the failed break-out attempt, the men were noticeably depressed. In the corridors, there appeared only individual Red Army men who were running along them. Everyone was at the windows, which were piled high with broken furniture and mattresses almost to the top. Underneath the mattresses, bricks had been piled, which created unusual embrasures that allowed one to see everything and to sweep the ground out in front with fire. From the outside they concealed movement and everything that was going on inside the barracks. Sometimes a shell explosion would blow this entire structure out of the window and a fire would be ignited inside, but this was now just a trifle among everything else going on all around.

Again it seems that the artillery fire was eroding the garrison's morale – once again, surrendering men were heading toward the German positions. The first of them was already at the Main Wall. There they were searched for weapons. Standing on top of the wall next to Germans, some of them were shouting loudly to those who were still fighting, 'Come! Come here!' Once again, separate groups of men with upraised hands were running up to the wall at the double-quick; some of the surrendering men were still in their underpants, and their faces bore the imprint of the terror of the last thirty minutes. They were bringing out some of their own wounded, and German medics immediately began tending to them.[1]

However, there was no one to care for the German wounded, who were still lying in various places around the Citadel. The third day of Hans Teuschler's 'struggle for life' was under way; he was still lying where he'd been wounded at the East Fort:

> The second night was terribly unpleasant. On the third day, when the sun was at its zenith, it was so hot that it seemed it was possible to boil in one's skin. With the start of the work of loudspeakers, which were broadcasting in the Russian language, the gunfire was gradually stopping; possibly, surrender negotiations were going on. Foreign male voices and the piercing cries of women and children were all around me. Ten Russians, deserters, went running past me in terror just 10–15 metres away. I quickly closed my eyes and opened them again only when the clamour had died down. Suddenly, a Ukrainian and a Mongol, both armed from head to toe, stopped in front of me. They leaped for me in the pit, their pistols at the ready. 'Oh, you poor gefreiter!!' I thought, 'Now your hour has arrived!' I only had a little time to think, so I shook my head and hands, before pointing to the blood that was covering my chest and face. The Ukrainian said to his partner, '*Tschui*!' Thus this danger also passed.[2]

* * *

At the 45th Infantry Division command post, they believed that the first half of the day was going according to plan. The enemy in the Citadel was being worn down by the destructive artillery fire, which twice intensified to heavy barrages. At 1105, there was a radio contact with the encircled Germans in the Church of Saint Nikolai: they reported that they had approximately fifty men left, under the command of a *feldwebel*. They still had Russian prisoners with them. Having received this information, Schlieper resolved upon more decisive action than had been directed by von Kluge and Blumentritt. He decided to cancel the next propaganda broadcasts that had been planned for 1145 (for which purpose there was to be an interruption in the artillery fire), and instead opted for a local attack that would start at this time in order to free the encircled men in the church.

It was decided that Freytag's I/I.R. 130 and Eggeling's II/I.R. 130 would launch the assault from the West and South Islands respectively. Leo Lozert recalls:

> That morning we were again positioned on the western side at the ferry, when once again a ten-minute cannonade against the Citadel was announced. I immediately took a quick bath in the river (these summer days were brutally hot; we were servicing our weapon in the scorching heat in the presence of such an abundance of bodies of water), when suddenly I was summoned to the commander of II Battalion Major Freytag [Lozert is mistaken – Freytag commanded I/I.R. 133] (our 12th Company

> of heavy machine guns had been assigned to him), who asked whether I would like to free the trapped Germans. I immediately and eagerly agreed, because I was surprised that the infantry companies had so far made no attempt to do so. From my experience, the time (after the artillery barrage) was also opportune. I was assigned an assault group from the 1st Company under the command of Leutnant Hurm, and at my suggestion, a section of heavy machine guns of the 12th Company led by Leutnant Schultz. After a short discussion, in particular, about securing this undertaking with Hurm's men, it was agreed that he would take position to the right of the church, defending the section of two heavy machine guns, which would be positioned to the left of it. The assignment of our machine-gunners was to silence the garrisons of the Russian casemates that were 400 metres to the left of the church, and correspondingly give covering fire in case of necessity to Leutnant Hurm's assault group and suppress the expected threat from the casemates on the right of the churchyard.

At 1130, a particularly heavy artillery barrage began. But the roar of the gigantic Karl mortars muffled even this hellish sound – enormous columns of smoke could be seen rising above the fortress, and the earth was shaking. At 1145, the guns fell silent. From West Island Lozert led the assault group toward the church across the Terespol Bridge – along the same route that he'd taken the day before when rescuing the injured German. Cautiously, leaving behind outposts at key places, Hurm's group made its way to the Church of Saint Nikolai in short dashes. At 1200, Hurm and Lozert reached the church – accomplishing that which hadn't been able to be achieved in the two previous days. The evacuation of the freed German soldiers began, and the wounded were carried out. Approximately fifty men of III/I.R. 135 and the 81st Pioneer Battalion were again on the rosters of the living.

At 1210, German flags appeared above the Terespol Gate and the Arsenal building holding the 333rd Rifle Regiment. The rest of Freytag's battalion crossed over the bridge, and Major Freytag established his command post in the arc of the Terespol Gate. At 1215, a strong assault group led by *Hauptmann* Dr. Watzek (the commander of 14/I.R. 133) also managed to break through the Kholm Gate to the center of the Citadel. Here's how Lozert describes this episode:

> In the middle of the action, Hauptmann Dr. Watzek appeared together with two signallers to discuss the matter of employing an anti-tank gun and ordered a halt to the operation because of the danger of encirclement. I reported to him on the actions and the situation of the assault group, and informed him that I had an order to free the encircled Germans, so then he agreed to let the operation proceed. After Leutnant Hurm left with the last wounded men, I also shouted to the machine-gun section about the withdrawal, after the latter [Hurm's men] had left the church and the grounds of the Citadel.

Meanwhile, assault groups of I/I.R. 133 were cautiously advancing along the walls of the casemates on either side of the Terespol Gate, clearing them of any remaining defenders. Here and there were the sounds of grenade explosions – they were flying into the windows and gate opening. Surrendering Russians were emerging with upraised hands, but it seems that there were a lot of Russians still in the cellars, who were trying to return fire. The first German soldiers cautiously penetrated into the cellar of the 333rd Rifle Regiment's sector through gaps in the deployment of its 2nd Battalion.

At the Terespol Gate, Lozert reported to Major Freytag on the full evacuation of the wounded and the encircled soldiers of I.R. 135, which was conducted without any casualties. Thus the epopee of the Church of Saint Nikolai came to an end, one of the more dramatic episodes for the *Wehrmacht* of those June days. For the first time in this campaign, German soldiers had been encircled. For a little more than two days, it hadn't been possible to free them, located as they were practically in the rear of von Kluge's Fourth Army, because of the fear of heavier casualties. The bitter resistance of the Red Army soldiers twice forced the cautious Germans to cancel an order to seize the fortress by storm, which for all practical purposes also meant the cancellation of attempts to rescue the trapped Germans. On 24 June this was at last accomplished, moreover without any particular difficulties. To distant observers of the events, it seemed that the rest of the Citadel would be taken without difficulty. But this proved to be an illusion.

Notes

1. *Signal*, No. 15 (1941). Editor's note: *Signal* was a magazine published by the German *Wehrmacht*, intended for audiences outside of Germany, and designed to show the lives and conditions of Germany's combat troops at the front. At its height, this propaganda tool was printed in as many as thirty different languages.
2. Gschöpf, *Mein Weg mit der 45 Infanterie Division*, p. 157. Note, the word '*Tschui*' said by the Ukrainian, as distorted by Teuschler, is one of the Russian uncensored expressions which are equivalent to 'Damn him'. The 'Russians running past him in terror' were probably one of the groups of soldiers that had been defending the command staff's residential complex and had decided to move to the East Fort.

Chapter 9

The Officers' House

The *Wehrmacht*'s red recognition flags, bearing a swastika inside a circle, that were visible far and wide, marked I/I.R. 133's new line of defense. Now the line ran across the middle of the Citadel, but its commander Freytag had no intention of stopping. Schlieper, having received a report on the large number of prisoners coming in on North Island, and another report on the successful link-up with the encircled Germans in the Church of Saint Nikolai, gave the order to take the rest of the Citadel. Having seized almost the entire southern half of Central Island, Freytag began to prepare an assault against the sectors of the Ring Barracks held by the 44th and 455th Rifle regiments. The commander of 14/I.R. 133 Dr. Watzek began to act in concert with him. Appointed, at his request, as the commander of an assault group, Watzek's mood had changed and he was now determined to seize the rest of Central Island. The enemy now seemed completely stunned and demoralized – it seemed likely that a renewed attack wouldn't generate heavy additional casualties.

In order to reduce the remaining Russian strongpoints in the Citadel, it was planned to bring up the guns of I.R. 133's anti-tank company – it was decided to employ the 50mm guns of *Leutnant* Schneiderbauer's platoon. Since his platoon had to move up to its firing positions through the combat zone on South Island, Schneiderbauer was able to see much, which promised serious trials in front of them: 'The whole route showed the bitter fighting that had taken place here over the first few days. Buildings were for the most part destroyed, and brick rubble, dead Russians and horses covered the roads. The oppressive stench of burning and corpses was all-pervasive.'

Oberst John on North Island had also gone over to decisive operations – Russian deserters were indicating that the defenders of the fortress still hadn't recovered from the highly-effective artillery fire. An attack was necessary – so John ordered his regiment to take the rest of North Island. Parak's II Battalion, attacking to the east along the Muchavec, was halted 50 meters short of the Trekharoch Bridge. The furious fire from the flank gave the attackers to understand that an attack across the bridge would be just as costly as it had been on 22 June. As a result, Parak had to be satisfied with having once again seized the casemates to the north of the Trekharoch Bridge.

Hauptmann Kaehne's I/I.R. 135, attacking down the road leading southward across the island from the Northern Gates, managed to link up with Parak. But the major news of the hour was a report from Kaehne that his battalion had captured the East Fort (Objective 609)! The announcement was even more remarkable for the fact that it was precisely the East Fort that the regiment kept attempting to take for several more days, right up until 30 June ... Then what in fact had Kaehne's battalion captured? Based on independent sources, it appears that the Germans had seized the top of the inner wall – a key position, from where it was possible to prevent any movement both within the inner yard of the East Fort and along the alleyway between its inner and outer walls. Possession of this position also opened a fine possibility of firing at the windows and embrasures of the fort's interior and outer barracks. In short, the East Fort had instantly lost its impregnability. Moreover, it was now possible for the Germans, covered by fire from the top of the inner wall, to access the top of the outer wall, which would place them above its casemates – for example, in order to dig a hole atop the casemate and place a demolition charge in it. After which, still out of the line of any return fire, it would be possible calmly to blow up the casemates within the wall one after the other.

The German infantrymen, however, didn't have the necessary amount of explosives – until combat engineers were committed to the task of reducing the casemates of the East Fort, the infantry was limited to tossing fragmentation and smoke grenades into the space between the inner and outer walls. This only affected the morale of the defenders within them, but couldn't inflict any harm to them otherwise. However, a lot of demolition charges would be needed, so subsequently they were brought up by trucks.

In fact, though, the position which initially seemed to signify 'the end of the East Fort' also had a lot of shortcomings, as it turned out. The most substantial of them was that the Germans were now in close contact with the enemy, which excluded the possibility of artillery support. Secondly (as the author was able to determine for himself, having spent time crawling along the top of the inner wall), the entire summit of the wall was quite exposed to fire from its gorge barracks. This created a lot of problems, for example, with the supply of food and ammunition and the evacuation of the wounded. The position seized by Kaehne wasn't bad, but it would have been far more effective if the Russians, realizing the situation they were now in, had capitulated right away. In the opposite case, during a long siege, something similar to the situation at the Church of Saint Nikolai would come about – having seized the central core of the defense, the German assault group itself wound up enveloped by fire from every direction, and in addition, became a 'living shield' that protected the Russians from artillery barrages.

On 24 June, though, the taking of the summit of the inner wall seemed to indicate the seizure of the entire East Fort, the speedy reduction of which no one doubted – thanks to which at 2110 a corresponding message went out to the division command post. This, despite the fact that on this day nothing was yet known about the size of the defending garrison of the East Fort, or about the number or size of the fortified chambers within the walls. Nevertheless the Germans, having captured the top of the walls, sincerely believed that the East Fort was finished.

By this time, the defenders of the fortress practically had no hope left that the Red Army was coming to their relief, or hopes that they could hold out for a fairly long time. A break-out had become necessary, but on the other hand, after the loss of the summit of East Fort's inner wall, it had become almost impossible. However, Gavrilov still resolved to make another attempt that evening. It was planned to conduct the break-out in three groups: Lieutenant Domienko would lead his own group toward the Eastern Gates; Kolomiets into the city, toward the railroad station (where judging from the sounds of gunfire, a battle was going on). The commissar of East Fort Skripnik would lead the main group, which would include Gavrilov himself and his chief of staff Kasatkin, toward the Northern Gates, and from there into the Bialowieza Forest. Skripnik's group would also include approximately forty wounded men, women and children. They would travel on several horses that had survived.

Skripnik's break-out attempt was complicated, because Germans on the summit of the inner wall made it difficult to assemble. They would have to run out of the doors of the stables, and this would significantly impede the attack. Moreover, from the top of the inner wall it would be possible to fire at the backs of the Russians that were attempting to escape, and Gavrilov's soldiers would have nowhere to hide. Fire support for the break-out was also excluded – the German machine-gun positions couldn't be hit from the barracks of the inner wall, where the quad-mounted Maksim anti-aircraft machine gun continued to stand. Nothing was known about the enemy strength or the layout of his positions; reconnaissance had broken down and it was impossible to conduct observation of the enemy.

Meanwhile, Freytag's I/I.R. 133 had by now taken the building of the Engineering Directorate and the ruins of the White Palace, from which point it was only approximately 10 meters to the entrance of the 33rd Engineering Regiment's sector of the Ring Barracks. Quickly the Germans rolled up the guns of their *panzerjägers* to the White Palace, and an infantry gun opened intense fire at the windows and embrasures of the 33rd Engineering's barracks. Watzek's anti-tank guns were pounding it from a range of just 300 meters. One lucky shell wounded Fomin in the arm and Zubachev in the head: with this one shell, Watzek had managed to cripple the entire command of the defense in this sector. Having quickly bandaged his arm, Fomin headed down into the cellar. There amidst the moans and screams, he quietly sat on a stool, waiting his turn. However, at this point, the real objective of Freytag's attack was not the barracks of the 33rd Engineering Regiment, but to crush the resistance of the defenders in the sectors of the Ring Barracks occupied by the 44th and 455th Rifle regiments.

By this time there were not so many soldiers left in the 44th Rifle Regiment's sector (the casualties during the two attempts to break out had been heavy). Many had also moved to different locations, for example, to the cellar of the 333rd Rifle Regiment's building, and many were also wounded. To top it off, the defenders of the 44th Rifle Regiment were virtually out of ammunition. Private S.T. Demin, a 44th Rifle Regiment ambulance driver, states, 'By this time we had run out of cartridges. We didn't even have any for the TT pistols; Bytko, who was armed with a Nagan revolver, only had two rounds left.' According to survivors' recollections, V.I. Bytko was intending to commit suicide – but this would have totally undermined the morale of the soldiers, so they talked him out of it, insisting that he was obligated to share the same fate that was awaiting his men … The next evening, when the prisoners were being marched toward Biala Podlaska, Bytko escaped from the column together with the commander of the 455th Rifle Regiment's 4th Company Junior Lieutenant I.V. Sgibnev. Reaching the Bug River, they dove into it not far from each other, trying to swim across to the eastern bank. Germans opened fire at them. Nothing more is known about the fate of the commander of the 455th Rifle Regiment's regimental school; Sgibnev was re-captured on 27 June, and after a savage beating, he was taken back to the camp, where he also ultimately went missing.

A.N. Bessonov also recalls the final minutes of the 44th Rifle Regiment's defense:

> In sum, the end was nearing… We realized the situation and sensed this, but what was waiting for us next, we didn't know. Of course, we couldn't break out. The senior lieutenant's last words to me were, 'Well, that's it, there's nothing more I can do.' He was no longer wearing his Order on his tunic and didn't have his field pack, and all his symbols of rank had been removed. He had prepared for something. I asked him about his decoration and field pack, since the pack contained orders and his personal notes; he told me that they'd both been hidden. After this I never saw him again.

Thus, the defense of the north-west corner of the Ring Barracks had collapsed. Without stopping, Freytag pushed his attack. However, the fight for the 455th Rifle Regiment's sector of the Ring Barracks, which was a key position that covered approaches to the Trekharoch Gate, was unexpectedly prolonged. Freytag's attack from the direction of the 44th Rifle Regiment's sector gradually bogged down into a smoldering fire-fight. Now, when the fortress was about to fall, there was no longer any sense in launching impetuous attacks, as had been made on 22 June.

On this day, a small scandal also flared up on the German side due to the lack of clarity in the lines of command – the highly-energetic *Oberst* John had issued an order for a half-platoon of the 818th Security Battalion's 4th Company, which had been acting as a group to receive and process prisoners on the islands of the Citadel, to join I.R. 135 as replacements. This prompted a sharp rebuke from the commandant of *Frontstalag* 307, which subsequently (on 28 June) sent an official letter of protest to Major Dettmer:

> Doubtless, it is an honour as well for the soldiers of the rear security to fight like regular soldiers, but nevertheless I request a ban on their further use in a combat role. I have a categorical order from my supreme commander that the rear area security soldiers should not be committed to combat operations, since they are absolutely not trained for this.

John's measure is readily understandable – over the first three days of the war, the casualties of his I.R. 135 amounted to 250 killed (including two battalion commanders and several company commanders) and 260 wounded. It no longer had enough men.

Meanwhile, *Generalmajor* Schlieper set out to make a visit to the fortifications of the Citadel. Inside it, now strong garrison units were surrendering, but even so, enemy resistance hadn't yet been stamped out. Gunfire was still being heard even on the repeatedly-swept West Island, so a battalion of combat engineers spent that afternoon mopping up the island once again.

At 1500, Arko 27 was ordered to unload the artillery barrels, but for the meantime to leave their guns in their firing positions. *Oberst* Galwitz, who had left the headquarters of the commander of Army Group Centre's artillery, was able to reach the firing positions of the 2nd Battery of the 833rd Heavy Artillery Battalion after a long delay, having been caught in a massive traffic jam, which began 10 kilometers short of Biala Podlaska. For several hours, traffic had been paralyzed, and only after making a wide detour was Galwitz able to find the firing positions of the Karl heavy mortars, the command post of Arko 27, as well as the headquarters of the 45th Infantry Division, between 1500 and 1600. There he learned that the prevailing impression that existed in the headquarters that were located far to the rear was that the Karl heavy mortars had only fired two or three times, which was incorrect. On the contrary, by this time the heavy mortars had nearly exhausted all their ammunition – 31 of 36 shells. The Karls had worked in the following manner: the No. 3 mortar ('Odin') had fired 4 shells on 22 June and 6 shells on 24 June; the No. 4 mortar ('Thor') fired 3 shells on 22 June, 7 on 23 June, and 11 on 24 June. Five shells remained, three of which were defective. In the assessment of the battery commander *Hauptmann* Meesman, the effect of the salvoes had been devastating. Galwitz decided to remain in Terespol until the evening, believing that the expected formal capitulation of the Citadel would take place here at 1800, and the next morning he would have an opportunity to examine the destruction wrought by the Karl heavy mortars. Meesman's battery, having carried out its assignment, began preparations to depart: its personnel and equipment had been ordered by the Army Group to move to Bergen.

Meanwhile, the de facto leaders of the Citadel's defense – Fomin, Zubachev and Vinogradov – had gathered once again in the cellar below the 33rd Engineering Regiment's sector of the Ring Barracks. Zubachev was calm. Fomin's wounded arm was troubling him. To everyone it was clear that the situation was sharply deteriorating. In a matter of hours, having broken the desperate resistance of the 455th Rifle Regiment, the Germans would be able to take the Trekharoch Gate. In this eventuality, a break-out, which had previously been a most difficult task, would become fully impossible. There could also no longer be any talk about holding out in the barracks – the day or two left for the defenders could hardly allow them to expect help to arrive. It had become clear that the situation at the front was developing not at all as had been assumed just a couple of days ago.

As a result, the choice standing in front of the defenders over these hours was simple: escape or imprisonment. Each hour was precious, and under the influence of the recent developments, there was now nothing left for even Zubachev, who had recently advocated the continued defense of the fortress, but to agree to a break-out. They decided to attempt to break out following the example of the previous attempt – first a vanguard (shock group) of approximately 120 men, led by Vinogradov, and then, under its cover, the main forces would follow. One feature of the operation was that it, most likely, would have to be implemented in daylight – the 455th Rifle Regiment likely wouldn't be able to hold out until nightfall. It was risky; the element of darkness wasn't much, but it would have aided the break-out groups. However, in the first place there was no other choice, and secondly, the Germans had already superbly demonstrated the capabilities of their illumination flares at night. Remembering how many lives the machine-gun fire from the wall near Point 143 had taken the night before, it was decided first to suppress these firing points and to seize the wall, which would cover the exit of the remaining forces. Then, having linked up, the combined group would head past the gorge barracks (Point 145) toward the 'eastern walls' – it was hoped that machine-gunners posted on the roof of the 33rd Engineering Regiment's barracks would somehow be able to suppress the fire coming from the 'eastern walls'. Having reached the 'eastern walls', the break-out group would consolidate and wait for the arrival of the rearguard – the machine-gunners on the roof of the barracks – before they all headed to the east, along the Muchavec. The vanguard's own attack was planned as follows: a machine-gun platoon would dash across the bridge, while the remaining three rifle platoons would cross the river using rafts, flotation devices or simply by swimming.

Vinogradov collected twenty-five to thirty *Komsomol* membership cards from the men of the forming rifle platoon, with which he would move, and placed his own candidate's card for membership in the All-Communist Party (Bolshevik), his Order certificate, his Order of the Red Star and two identification documents on this pile. Then he and the deputy political instructor Smirnov, having placed the pile of documents and the banner of the 455th Rifle Regiment in a pouch, wrapped the pouch with a sheet, and hid the bundle in a pipe that led from one of the cellars of the 455th Rifle Regiment out to the Muchavec. They then blocked the pipe's entrance with rubble. After the war, this hidden bundle could not be found …

Zubachev also assisted Vinogradov in forming the shock group. Primarily it would include soldiers of the 44th and 455th Rifle regiments, who had been fighting at the Trekharoch Gate and who were already quite familiar with the location. Senior Sergeant Filipp Laenkov, an assistant platoon commander of the 455th Rifle Regiment's regimental school, recalls:

> In the middle of the day, Captain Zubachev assembled some sort of council, where Radchenko and several other junior commanders were present. Zubachev told them that it was necessary to make contact with neighbouring elements and to attempt to break out of the fortress in order to link up with friendly units. He was proposing to advance a group of soldiers

> headed by Radchenko (a sensible commander of a department of the regimental school) across the bridge. The group's task included seizing a line on the opposite side of the Muchavec and covering our break-out.

Ivan Khvatalin, who'd been fighting at the Trekharoch Gate, was also preparing for the break-out attempt; he joined the group, the path of which headed directly across the Muchavec. A Border Guards corporal took command of it. Having concealed the documents and the regimental banner, Vinogradov again met with Zubachev at their improvised command post, and they came to an agreement on signals and the supporting fire of the covering group. Having said his farewells to Zubachev and Fomin, he then left to join his platoons.

At 1730, the headquarters of the 45th Infantry Division, including its logistics section and the command post itself, shifted to Brest. But at 1800, machine guns began to chatter from the roof of the Ring Barracks – Vinogradov had launched the break-out attempt. Covered by the fire of the machine-gunners, the first group – Radchenko's machine-gun platoon – dashed onto the Trekharoch Bridge. However, the covering fire wasn't sufficient to suppress the German fire, and Parak's machine-gunners, positioned just 50 meters from the Trekharoch Bridge, shot down almost everyone running across it. There Radchenko was killed as well. Only a few individuals reached the northern bank, where they huddled up against the saving steep angle of the wall near Point 143. Vinogradov: 'Confusion set in. I appealed to Captain Zubachev to give more supporting fire. The fire increased.'

With a battle-cry, Vinogradov rushed across the bridge, followed by the 4th Platoon. They were more fortunate: the Germans opened aimed fire only when Vinogradov and the 4th Platoon had already reached the northern bank and had joined the remnants of Radchenko's 1st Platoon in the dead angle below the Main Wall.

The 2nd and 3rd platoons, which were fighting to make their way across the currents of the Muchavec itself, next came under Parak's fire – the majority of their soldiers were killed in the river. Ivan Khvatalin: 'Only two of a group of forty men succeeded in swimming across the small river. Many were killed, and the rest turned back.' The few survivors of the 2nd and 3rd platoons who made it across the Muchavec assembled on the opposite bank – today it still isn't clear whether they'd succeeded in consolidating at the eastern end of the Main Wall near Point 143, or whether they were holding a line along the riverbank in front of Point 145. I.R. 135's daily report says only, 'Russians broke through to North Island and tried to break out to the north.'

Exchanging fire with Parak's soldiers, Vinogradov now waited for the main break-out forces to emerge. However, for some unclear reason Zubachev delayed, after which it was now too late: German artillery began pounding the Ring Barracks, while mortar rounds were dropping on Vinogradov's vanguard group. Possibly, Parak's companies that were defending along the Main Wall had received reinforcements. It became clear that if the main force moved out now, it would only lead to a slaughter. Zubachev issued a code signal to Vinogradov: 'Continue advancing along the designated route.' Realizing that the break-out of the main forces had been cancelled, Vinogradov's vanguard group, at his order, began to move east, to an area in the lee of the wall at Point 145 on the other side of the Trekharoch Bridge, where they prepared for an assault against the outer wall, which as before was being defended by Gerstmeyer's men.

Their egress from the Citadel to the east was reflected both in the 45th Infantry Division's war diary, which noted that I.R. 135 had successfully repulsed a break-out attempt, and in John's daily report, which mentioned a break-out attempt by the enemy in an eastward direction.

Fortuitously for Vinogradov's group, Schlieper had decided to commit III/ I.R. 133 (reinforced by three flame-thrower teams from the 81st Pioneer Battalion), which had to this point been sealing the eastern outskirts of the Citadel, to mopping up North Island. *Hauptmann* Gerstmeyer received an order to sweep North Island from the east along the course of the Muchavec, linking up with the attack by I.R. 135's I and II battalions. Gerstmeyer's main task was to seize Point 145 and wipe out the final pockets of the 98th Separate Anti-tank Battalion's resistance.

The three flame-thrower teams of the 81st Pioneer Battalion had been assigned to I.R. 133 that morning. The *Flammenwerfer* 40 *klien* ('small') was a difficult weapon even for those who used it. The operator carried a tank on his back that weighed more than 21 kilograms. It contained a sticky blend of combustible viscous petrol mixed with tar (*Flammöl* 19), which was specially developed to envelop the victim in flames when sprayed. The flame-thrower was vulnerable to enemy fire, so the operator was part of a team consisting of a commander, the operator, and escorting infantry. Helmuth Böttcher, a combat engineer of one of the assault groups, was assigned to one of the flame-thrower teams:

> The equipment itself produced a flame about 30 metres long at a temperature of 4,000° C. When one came up to an angled trench system the flame could be directed around corners, of course liquidating anything in there. The inflammable fuel was launched by compressed gas (nitrogen) through the nozzle of the hose, which had an ignition device that generated a spray of flames, against which there was absolutely no sort of defence. Each tank carried enough fuel for a 10-second stream of fire. They sucked the oxygen out of cramped shelters, scorching and destroying the lungs of the defenders, together with the waves of red-hot air. The majority of them were quickly consumed by flames, or, at the very least, left blinded ... These devices were horrifying ... It is awful to think of such work, but I should point out that the flame-thrower operators were never allowed to surrender. They were immediately shot ...

Thus, at the moment when Vinogradov's group moved to break through the positions of Gerstmeyer's battalion along the Main Wall, the 9th and 10th companies that had been defending the sector of the wall targeted by Vinogradov themselves were moving out for their attack across North Island. The elements of the 45th Reconnaissance Battalion still hadn't arrived to replace them by the time of

Vinogradov's attack at 1800 on 24 June, so the walls there were probably being held only by a few machine-gun crews and small reserves. Of I.R. 133's two companies, one moved westward, bypassing the East Fort to the south, while the second attacked to the south-west against Point 145.

At this same moment, Vinogradov's group was moving into the vacuum they had left behind, slipping between the apartment buildings of the command staff and across the athletic field, and hurrying toward the 'eastern walls'. This was a model example of a lost opportunity – the entire break-out group might have been able to advance into the void created when the two attacking German companies moved out, and having breached the weakened positions left by them at the Main Wall, escaped from Brest. Indeed, that which couldn't be done the day before succeeded now: Vinogradov, having breached the cordon while losing many men of his vanguard group, broke out across the Main Wall! The remaining seventy men of his group emerged at a point near Panzer Rollbahn No. 1 . . .

However, why hadn't Zubachev and Fomin followed in the wake of the shock group? Likely, the main reason was because the Germans themselves had launched an attack within the Citadel just as Vinogradov's vanguard group moved out on its attack – and by this time the Germans had seized the sector of the 455 Rifle Regiment as well. This occurred because the majority of its soldiers had left to spearhead the break-out attempt. Moreover, this likely occurred just before Vinogradov had nevertheless taken the eastern corner of the Wall near Point 143. However, he accomplished this just a few minutes too late – now Zubachev's escape was impossible, because in addition to the gauntlet of fire that Vinogradov's men had passed through, now Zubachev's men would also have been struck by machine-gun bursts from behind, from the direction of the 455th Rifle Regiment's sector.

How did the seizure of the 455th Rifle Regiment's sector happen? P.P. Koshkarov, in particular, who at that time was already located in the barracks of the 33rd Engineering Regiment, testifies to the fact that the attack against the last remaining pockets of resistance on Central Island began simultaneously with Vinogradov's break-out attempt. Koshkarov, describing the German attack, states that it came from the direction of the White Palace and the Church of Saint Nikolai. I. Dolotov also recalled the Germans, who were approaching from the direction of the White Palace:

> The Germans went on the attack from the direction of the 84th Rifle Regiment. The attack was stopped by machine-gun and rifle fire. A few of the fascists were within about 100 metres of the barracks, and were halted not far from the circular restrooms. I remember how they rushed behind a circular concrete septic tank that was standing on the side of the road leading to the 84th Regiment in order to take cover against our murderous fire. Some of them fled towards the White Palace.

Freytag's attack to seize the barracks of the 33rd Engineering Regiment was foiled. Things went differently in the sector of the Ring Barracks held by the 455th Rifle Regiment, which had been weakened by Vinogradov's departure together with a number of its men. A. Makhnach testifies, 'The Germans stormed into the fortress [sic] from the direction of the White Palace.' In the given case, Makhnach is referring to the Ring Barracks as a 'fortress'. The White Palace is located on the eastern end of the Citadel's grounds. Within the barracks, bitter fighting erupted. In addition to gunshots at practically point-blank range, there was a furious exchange of grenades – one of the grenades tossed by the Austrians exploded in the above-ground garage practically under the feet of Lieutenant Nikolai Egorov – the same one who had hidden in the kitchen of the 455th Rifle Regiment in the first minutes of the war. Egorov lost an eye and was wounded in both legs. Later, he was taken prisoner among the number of wounded.

Private I.F. Khvatalin, who shortly before had received a concussion during a break-out attempt, turned out to be a witness to the final minutes of the 455th Rifle Regiment's defense. When the Germans burst into his compartment, Khvatalin was in one of the cellars, where the wounded and shellshocked defenders of the Ring Barracks were lying. He remembers:

> The firing never slackened. Suddenly in the afternoon, several men came running to us, shouting: 'The Germans are here; whoever has cartridges, give them here.' They collected the cartridges and left. An explosion thundered above the cellar and several minutes later, the Hitlerites burst into the cellar. They ordered everyone to get up. The severely-wounded who couldn't were immediately executed with pistol shots.

Here, too, in one of the cellars next to the Trekharoch Gate, A.A. Makhnach was captured, and together with him, approximately fifty soldiers and junior commanders. However, despite the fact that most of the 455th Rifle Regiment's sector had been overrun, in some places resistance still continued – shoved back from the Trekharoch Gate, Red Army troops were still holding out in those compartments that were adjacent to the burning baggage warehouse. Who these men were isn't known.

Meanwhile, the 9th and 10th companies of Gerstmeyer's III/I.R. 133 were attacking across North Island from the east. Primarily they were assaulting buildings, where remnants of the 98th Separate Anti-tank Artillery Battalion were lodged and the gorge barracks of the Main Wall, in many of which members of the command staff's families were located. Gunfire gradually transformed into grenade exchanges. The defenders were being pressed steadily back. In the south-west corner of North Island, two captured Russian reconnaissance armored cars crewed by *panzerjägers* of Watzek's company (14/I.R. 133) were supporting the attack. They were practically invulnerable – the Soviet side at this moment no longer had any anti-tank guns left. Motion picture film operator Corporal Nikolai Sokolov of the 98th Separate Anti-tank Battalion was one of those who fought in this sector up until the final moments of its defense:

> A group of Nazis had already broken into the premise. A final hand-to-hand combat erupted. Step by step, the Germans were driving us into a

> corner. A tanker sergeant major from Central Island shouted, 'Farewell, Mama! Take revenge for me!' – and having widely opened his mouth, fired a bullet into it. Deputy political instructor Shiriaev was killed in the hand-to-hand fighting. They had us surrounded and began to beat us brutally with their rifle butts. Then, prodding us with bayonets, they led us out into the square, where several dozen disarmed prisoners were standing ... Filthy, ragged, with sunken, reddened eyes and grizzled cheeks, we stood quietly, dejected by what had happened.

The total number of prisoners taken in this sector is not known. The morning report from I.R. 133 mentions that the crews of the captured armored cars took 142 prisoners. But were these prisoners taken just by them, or is this the total number? In addition, according to this same report, a Soviet armored vehicle (probably an ordinary *Komsomolets* prime mover) was destroyed by the crews of the armored cars. However, despite the support of the armored cars, I.R. 133's operation didn't fully succeed as planned – resistance was still continuing both in Point 145 and in the East Fort. One of the reasons for this, in the assessment contained in the 45th Infantry Division's war diary, is the fact that III/I.R. 133 no longer had sufficient strength to ensure its successful conclusion.

Having bypassed East Fort as it pushed northward to the Muchavec, Gerstmeyer's battalion took possession of territory, where there had been savage fighting on 22 June. Among the already decomposing corpses of the soldiers of Praxa's III/I.R. 135, the wounded Hans Teuschler was also found. However, he refused to leave his shelter, fearing Russian snipers:

> I nevertheless asked to postpone my evacuation to the division's medical station until the saving darkness of night, in order not to become a victim of incaution at the last moment. Only when I arrived in the field hospital in the city of Brest-Litovsk did I finally relax, since in the final analysis, I'd still come out alive.

With the large number of dead bodies recovered and the approaching end of fighting in Brest, the 45th Infantry Division command began to ponder the establishment of a divisional cemetery. Rudolph Gschöpf:

> Of course, we wanted to create a single burial ground, so it was with just this aim I selected the park next to a Russian Orthodox church in the southern portion of Brest-Litovsk. As soon as combat operations began to allow the paying of last respects to the fallen, their bodies began to be brought here, and with our modest means, we created a worthy place of final rest for them.

On this day, Eggeling's II/I.R. 133 finally finished mopping up South Island – since 22 June, Red Army personnel, patients of the demolished hospital, and whoever else able to make their way to them were sitting in underground casemates there. The director of the Brest Military Hospital, Military Doctor, 2nd Rank B.A. Maslov:

> My family, several officers and many members of the officers' families, and several wounded soldiers were together with me. On the afternoon of 24 June, the doors of the casemate were opened, and we were given an order by German soldiers to come out of the casemates. When we emerged, thirty German soldiers led our group of approximately fifty doctors, wives, children and the wounded in the direction of the Bug River . . . After some time passed, our wives and children were separated from us and led off to somewhere else, while we were united with military prisoners, and on that same evening we were directed into the prison camp in Biala Podlaska.

Here was where the Germans in fact conducted their first 'special measures' – initially this was probably more like a spontaneous reprisal, a payback to the 'commissars' for their killed and wounded comrades. Brutalized by sleeplessness, two days of combat, the gunfire from every direction and the Soviets' desperate and ferocious combat, they had to find some 'guilty parties' for all of this. Thus, in fact, Senior Political Instructor I.P. Zazulin and Political Instructor S.T. Zyskavets didn't make it far and were shot just beyond South Island's Wall. Despite the earnest advice of his comrades, Zyskavets (the director of the Brest Military Hospital's club) before being captured had refused to take off his tunic with the red stars denoting a political staff member, and had thereby inadvertently signed his own death warrant.

A similar thing happened on North Island as well; however, here the victim of the reprisal was not a commissar, but the leader of the defense in the sector of the 98th Separate Anti-tank Battalion, its chief of staff Lieutenant Ivan Akimochkin. During the search, his Party membership card was found; he'd only recently joined the Communist Party. 'Did you find this somewhere?' the German officer who was conducting the search asked ironically. 'It is mine,' replied Akimochkin. Leading Akimochkin out of the crowd, he was shot in front of all the other prisoners.

At the command post of the 45th Infantry Division, which was now located in Brest, summary reports from the units began to arrive. In Brest itself there was calm: only the movement of separate units and the reshuffling of their subordination were taking place. However, around 1900, Wetzel's *panzerjägers* successfully eliminated another break-out attempt – this one now beyond the borders of the fortress, at the Muchavec. Vinogradov and his soldiers had not managed to get very far – having broken out beyond the Main Wall, they wound up confronted by Panzer Rollbahn No. 1, which was jammed with columns that were moving to the east. In front of it, guarding the traffic from possible break-out attempts of the Russian garrison, one of the 45th Panzerjäger Battalion's platoons had taken position. As a rule, each platoon was equipped with three 37mm anti-tank guns (with a crew of six for each), one light machine gun (with a crew of three), and a headquarters section of seven men.

In the vicinity of 'Hipp's Bridge', in the wake of 'attempts to break out to Panzer Rollbahn No. 1', Wetzel took prisoner approximately 100 men of Vinogradov's group – the only one which had managed to break out beyond the Main Wall. Vinogradov himself describes the end: '... the fascist command assigned a spare unit of infantry to the highway, and deployed artillery guns together with it, which opened fire at us over open sights. There was nowhere to hide.'

At 2110, the evening report from *Oberst* John arrived at the command post of the 45th Infantry Division. The plans for 25 June were to protect and defend the occupied positions, mop up the territory, and clear the Russians out of the several casemates that were still occupied by them. At 2140, Armin Dettmer, the chief of staff of the 45th Infantry Division, transmitted a summary report for 24 June to corps headquarters. Telegram No. 2 was laconic: 'Citadel at Brest taken!'

It is difficult to say what caused Dettmer, not the division commander, to send such a bold message: none of the commanders of the units still engaged within the Brest Fortress would have confirmed such a report. However, most likely Dettmer and Schlieper, in distinction from the battalion commanders, decided to assess the situation more generally. In the first place, almost 90 percent of the fortress's territory had been taken by the division, and almost all the known pockets of resistance had been liquidated. On Central Island, the Russians were still holding out only in several portions of buildings and in the so-called 'Officers' House', and on North Island – in the area east of the road that splits the island from north to south, primarily in the gorge barracks of the Main Wall at the Northern Bridge (Point 145) and East Fort. The remaining Soviet units were in such a plight that their further resistance, as well as any break-out attempts, was doomed beforehand. Of course, over these days the 45th Infantry Division command had become convinced that the frenzied fanaticism of the Soviets prevented their sober assessment of the situation. However, it was perceptible that the Russians' combat spirit had dropped markedly: 1,250 prisoners had been taken when I.R. 135 took the western part of North Island, followed by II/I.R. 133's seizure of South Island. In these hours, the 45th Infantry Division command sincerely believed that the Brest Fortress was finished. The fact that the battalion commanders hadn't announced this was probably a consequence of the fact that they were looking at the situation from their more limited point of view.

However, already by that evening, the division command was beginning to share that point of view, having altered its assessment of the situation in a more expanded version of the daily report from 24 June:

> With two powerful artillery barrages, which were conducted in the morning, the Russians that were still stubbornly defending in the cellars and buildings were so worn down that in places they responded to the loudspeaker's appeals to surrender... As a result, we succeeded not only in freeing the encircled men, but also in capturing a significant portion of the Central Island... Simultaneously the North Island was seized, and the mopping-up of it will likely end in darkness ...

Even so, the report about the capture of the Brest Fortress managed to make its way up the chain of command.

At 2200, the silence was shattered by the sounds of rifle and machine-gun fire on North Island – the defenders of the East Fort had also resolved upon a break-out. Bursting out of the stables at a run, they were striving to escape from the fort. However, what happened was just what they'd feared: machine guns opened up at them both from the apartment buildings in front of the forts and the medical station of the 125th Rifle Regiment, as well as from behind them, from the top of the inner wall. The defenders were caught in a pocket of scathing fire; they milled around under the fire and dropped prone, trying to find cover – but there was hardly any available. Then mortar rounds started to fall, placing a barrier barrage in front of the apartment complex. Leaping to their feet, the soldiers rushed back, falling under the machine-gun fire. The cost of the break-out attempt was several dozen killed and wounded.

Although the fortress had in fact not fallen, after the day's failures, all the defenders sensed that the end was approaching. Now, as the third day came to a close, tormented by hunger and thirst (a well, that had been dug into one of the cellars, yielded no more than a kettle of water a day), it had become fully clear to them that no help would arrive. But hope, no matter how slight it was, stayed with these people to the end.

By the end of the day, despite the slaughter that had been inflicted by Gerstmeyer's and Kaehne's machine-gunners, it was decided to make yet another attempt to break out. I. Dolotov reports, 'That evening, some of the commanders gathered around Fomin. The possibility of breaking out of the fortress was discussed. Some of those gathered referred to the probable success of Sergeant Lerman's group, which had sallied the day before.' When speaking of 'Sergeant Lerman's group', Dolotov most likely has in mind one of the groups of Vinogradov's ad hoc platoon. Dolotov didn't know that several groups had sallied simultaneously (Radchenko, the Border Guards corporal and Vinogradov himself, who was at the same time in command of all of them). Dolotov would soon meet again with Lerman himself:

> In July, I spotted Lerman, who was lying next to an outhouse in the Biala Podlaska camp among a group of wounded; both his arms were wrapped with filthy bandages, and clotted blood was in his hair. We were both very happy to see each other, because there were few of us from the fortress. The fascists had smashed their shock group with fire from the exterior side of the eastern wall [probably, Dolotov means the interior side] in the open ground between the bakery and the Kobrin Gate. Apparently, Lerman soon thereafter was shot by the fascists, because about three weeks later he disappeared. Prior to this he had expressed his suspicions that they would likely execute him, because several of the 'westerners' [referring to the conscripts that had arrived from the recently-acquired areas of western Belorussia and eastern Poland] had recognized him

> and were talking openly and audibly about how he had disposed of the Germans [the prisoners].

The majority of the men were in a resolute mood – the soldiers themselves began approaching the defense's command post with requests to be assigned to the next break-out group. V.S. Solozobov: 'This time the preparations were troublesome, because the majority of the soldiers didn't know how to swim. Men were searching for wooden items and boards. Commissar Fomin began trying to dissuade some of those who didn't know how to swim, proposing that they wait.' However, now there was no longer any use in waiting.

Around midnight, the first elements of the 45th Reconnaissance Battalion, which had been switched from subordination to I.R. 130 to the direct control of division headquarters, began arriving at its designated position in the sector formerly held by the 9th and 10th companies. Now the weak link in the cordon (the boundary between John's I.R. 135 and Kühlwein's I.R. 133), which Vinogradov had been able unwittingly to exploit, was reinforced. This was done just in the nick of time – darkness had just fallen, and von Pannwitz's soldiers were hurrying to deploy into their positions, when once again there was the sound of hurrying footsteps on the Trekharoch Bridge. The Russians were coming! This second attempt to break out across this bridge was even more bloody and unsuccessful than the first attempt – the crossfire of the machine guns permitted almost no one to reach the northern bank. V.S. Solozobov shares what he saw and heard: 'Shells were exploding, machine-gun bursts never fell silent, and flares were constantly lighting up the scene. However, this attempt also didn't bring the desired results: many of the men didn't even manage to swim halfway across the river.'

The resumed sound of fighting in the Citadel alarmed Galwitz, who even without this had been disappointed that the capitulation that he understood was scheduled for 1800 didn't in fact take place. Now, the gunfire that had flared up once again indicated that the remaining Russian defenders still hadn't lost heart and were continuing to resist. However, the *oberst* nevertheless hoped that the situation would be resolved by morning.

Among the reports that came in to the command post of the 45th Infantry Division at 0300 on 25 June, the first was from I.R. 133, which was holding the majority of the Citadel. On the coming day, Kühlwein's regiment had firm intentions to take full possession of it: 'In general, despite the desultory gunfire, the night passed more quietly. The Central, South and West Islands are firmly in the regiment's grip.'

At 0400 on 25 June, I/I.R. 133 launched an attack on Central Island by an assault group against an isolated building standing near the island's Northern Bridge, which was occupied by two Russian machine-gunners; the assault group included attached combat engineers with demolition charges. I.R. 133 announced that its seizure would signify the elimination of the last known remaining pocket of resistance on Central Island.

On North Island, III/I.R. 135, which now consisted only of two weakened infantry companies, which had been reduced by almost one-third by casualties, had been unable to reach their given objective, the Muchavec, everywhere. Nevertheless, it was anticipated that the 45th Reconnaissance Battalion with attached elements of III/I.R. 135 would quickly succeed in mopping up the final pockets of resistance on the island. Flame-throwers were being brought up to III Battalion, and groups of combat engineers were being attached to the assault groups. The isolated area that would be the target of the first assault was the Officers' House (the barracks of the 33rd Engineering Regiment and 75th Separate Reconnaissance Battalion near the Trekharoch Bridge).

Vasilii Solozobov, who almost hadn't had any sleep for several nights, again went down into the cellar, where the wounded were located. This was one of the gloomiest places in Fomin's sector of defense. The sufferings of the wounded were literally hellish – they'd been lying there without medications, food or water, and there wasn't enough bandaging material. Only the severely wounded were brought to the cellar – anyone who could still hold a weapon was on the upper floors. The screams and groans from the cellar, which were clearly audible to the soldiers, never ceased. L.A. Kochin recalls, 'Your hair stood on end from the human screams, but we were helpless to assist these unfortunates.' Two nurses and one doctor, Bardin, were staying with the wounded, but lacking even water, they couldn't do anything, and the wounded were dying one after another.

Having found a place a little quieter, the exhausted Solozobov instantly fell asleep. But soon he was being shaken awake by the pharmacist Vasilii Sukhoverkhov: 'Vasilii! Get up! Bardin has shot himself!' Solozobov leaped to his feet: the dead Bardin was lying nearby. He recalls, 'The wounded were quietly looking at him. We were also silent.' Fomin didn't approve of Bardin's suicide in a 'moment of spiritual weakness': 'To give up life pointlessly is a crime.' However, these events possibly explain why Fomin in fact ordered for all the women and severely wounded to be sent out of the building into German captivity.

At 0400, the fresh attack against the remaining pockets of resistance began – von Pannwitz's reconnaissance battalion assaulted Point 145, while Freytag's I/I.R. 133 tackled the Officers' House. He was attacking with Hurm's company and Loertzer's machine-gunners, and now *Leutnant* Schneiderbauer's 50mm anti-tank guns were in support; in addition, a group of combat engineers with demolition charges were standing ready. Leo Lozert also took part in the assault: 'Once again I had to lead the forward elements.'

The sounds of the anti-tank gun discharges and machine-gun bursts toward the Officers' House merged with the sound of heavy fighting on North Island, where the 45th Reconnaissance Battalion had gone on the attack. The fire from Schneiderbauer's guns was particularly effective – the explosions of the high-explosive fragmentation shells almost always generated casualties. A fire broke out on the second floor of the building, in the guardroom. However, initially it seemed that the attack against the Officers' House would falter just as happened the day before – the heavy fire from the defending Russians didn't allow Hurm the possibility to attack. Lozert:

> I again was the first to arrive at the church [Church of Saint Nikolai]; to my left and behind me was my 2nd Platoon of the 12th Company. Leutnant Hurm and his men continued to be pinned down under enemy fire to the right of the church and couldn't advance towards the casemates. My section of heavy machine guns, which had come up to join the riflemen, also couldn't enable a further advance.

Not even Schneiderbauer's guns were able to suppress the fire coming from the Officers' House. Rifle shots were coming from the most unexpected places. Schneiderbauer relates: 'Snipers made the enterprise extremely hazardous. A propaganda company officer, ignoring exhortations to be careful, was shot. Extricating the casualty degenerated into a lengthy and dangerous task.' However, the machine guns and anti-tank guns nevertheless did their job, and the defenders' fire began to slacken. *Feldwebel* Leo Lozert took advantage of this:

> Since now no one was eager to make the final bound and break into the casemate, I, on the contrary, abruptly broke into a run, and having come across an opening, stumbled into the casemate. In so doing, I collided with a group of armed Russians, who were completely grimy with gunpowder, and who immediately surrendered at my unexpected appearance. Since I wasn't firing, ever more Russians (soon there were around thirty of them) emerged from various recesses and were taken in by my soldiers, who had followed me.

Lozert had burst into the mess hall of the 33rd Engineering Regiment, which had recently been won back by Sergeant Lerman, through a door inside the Trekharoch Gate's eastern arch. For the defenders, a critical situation had arisen – continued possession of the mess hall's premises, which were adjacent to the bridge, allowed the defenders at least to consider the possibility of a break-out's success. But now having taken the mess hall in the west end of the barracks, the Germans could press the defenders back into a pocket, from which there would be nowhere to retreat. Access to the river was also important to the defenders: even prior to Lozert's success, it had been difficult to access the water, but now with the Germans in possession of the sectors of the Ring Barracks at the Trekharoch Gate, it had become impossible.

In a flash, along the entire perimeter of the Ring Barracks, the alarmed cries 'The Germans are in the end rooms!' flew from compartment to compartment. This news was especially frightening for the wounded. By this time, the wounded that were lying in the cellars had pecked holes into water pipes hoping to find at least a drop of water, and had excavated a pit that was a half-meter wide in the cement floor – but there was no water there either, only a fine, saturated sand that resembled a thin slurry. They attempted to filter it, but it was useless. All they could do was moisten their lips with the sand and wait for darkness – then one could hope that a few daring and enterprising men would be able to draw some water. Now even this hope was disappearing.

Hurm's soldiers, who had darted forward in Lozert's wake, were attempting to make a further advance along the Ring Barracks. Everything became jumbled – frenzied firing, grenade explosions, Russian swearing and German curses. Lozert continued to act: 'I went on ahead and having emerged out on the opposite side of the casemate, I spotted several German soldiers, who were attacking from the north, atop the walls across a water-filled ditch of the fortress.' These were elements of the 45th Reconnaissance Battalion. Caught in the pincers of the German attack, many of the casemate's defenders surrendered.

Lozert, though, was continuing to take fire from the right – from the direction of the eastern sectors of the 33rd Engineering Regiment's barracks, where the defenders were continuing to hold out. The fight for the Officers' House had only just flared up, however, and the situation that seemed to be going in favor of Freytag's battalion suddenly shifted in the opposite direction. A group of volunteers that had been quickly organized by Zubachev drove the Germans out of the Officers' House with grenades. At the same time it became apparent that far from all the defenders had surrendered at Point 145. Though practically out of ammunition, just as in the East Fort, the hold-outs had taken cover in its gorge barracks. Von Pannwitz's reconnaissance battalion had only seized the top of the wall, having taken the position from the north. To cross over to the southern side of the wall, in order to break into the casemates, promised heavy casualties. In addition to the fire from the defenders of Point 145, the reconnaissance battalion would also be taking flanking fire from the direction of the 33rd Engineering Regiment's sector of the Ring Barracks. However, von Pannwitz, just as did I.R. 135 on the previous day when it had seized the top of the inner wall of East Fort, mistakenly believed that he had captured the entire fortification. Likely, he had already hastened to report this. Later, it turned out that with the available forces, the objective couldn't be taken – but the report had already traveled up the line of command – to the regiment, to the division, and from there, to the corps.

As a result, at 1115 on 25 June, the command staff at the XII Corps headquarters, believing that the operation in Brest was finished, was pondering how best to employ the 45th Infantry Division next in the ongoing offensive. It was decided that Schlieper should leave behind small elements in the Citadel for the 'final resolution', while with his main forces he was to attack between Panzer Rollbahn No. 1 and Panzer Rollbahn No. 2.

By this time, the results of the 45th Infantry Division's operations were being summarized even in Berlin, at the OKH headquarters. At a morning conference with the OKH commander, Major von Below, who was a signals officer with Panzer Group 2, gave his impressions of the group's operations. Von Below's report confirmed Halder's impressions that the 45th Infantry Division had suffered heavy casualties in the area of Brest-Litovsk apparently to no purpose. It was decided to instruct General of the Artillery Brand first to assess the effectiveness of the Karl mortars' fire upon the Brest area, and second – to investigate the operations of the 45th Infantry Division there.

Meanwhile, Fritz Schlieper, who had personally traveled to corps headquarters at noon, was already seeing the situation differently than he had that morning. At the discussions that took place there, it became clear that the division would not be ready for a march prior to the evening of 26 June: 'Mopping-up has still not been completed (in the morning, several sectors were being swept and preparations were made for the final mopping-up of North Island).' However, such a situation couldn't continue for long – the XII Corps had already advanced far ahead to the east and was confronting major tasks. There was no sense in keeping an entire division to mop up a small territory in the rear. Probably, it was at this discussion that a decision was in fact taken – if the mopping-up operations in the Brest Fortress weren't completed within the next couple of days, and if no replacement for the 45th Infantry Division could be found, it would have to be dropped from the XII Corps roster.

Having seized the top of the wall at Point 145, the main thing that the reconnaissance battalion had accomplished was to make access to water much more difficult for Fomin's group. In addition, previous attempts to break out had all received some covering fire from the wall at Point 145 – now this possibility was gone. Finally, now the enemy had obtained a vantage point from where it could fire directly into the wide windows of the 33rd Engineering Regiment's barracks from the north. Now the Soviet soldiers, who'd been suffering from thirst and hunger for four days had nowhere to hide.

However, fighting continued; with the emergence of the reconnaissance battalion at the wall of Point 145, sniper duels had introduced a variety of problems in the sector. Remembers defender I. Dolotov:

> The Germans were using dummies in the fortress, which they were setting up in the grass and bushes on the walls beyond the Muchavec. The dummies were very skilfully made; they were moving them around and by their appearance, they made good imitations of living soldiers. Here, for the first time, I was convinced of the accuracy of sniper fire. A thin, freckled Red Army soldier with a chiselled nose was lying on a pile of mattresses at the edge of window and from time to time was taking aim with an ordinary rifle, which didn't even have an optical scope. After one shot he took off his forage cap, which had the red cap-band of an infantryman, and wiped his sweaty face with it. When I spotted a German who was nestled behind a thick tree atop the wall beyond the Muchavec, I pointed him out to the fellow. The German had carved a notch out of the side of the trunk just above ground level and had very successfully camouflaged himself, creating the possibility to fire without sticking his neck out from behind the tree. I wanted to get a demonstration of the sniper's accuracy and wanted to make sure the fascist didn't get away. I was worried that the Red Army man didn't have an optical sight, but he told me that at that range, he'd take him out anyway. When the chink in the tree trunk disappeared, the sniper fired. The German rose and

> then immediately collapsed. We were all stunned by his [the Red Army sniper's] skill, which in no way matched the dowdy appearance of this Soviet soldier.

The command of I.R. 133 wasn't burning with a desire to get involved in another battle inside the Ring Barracks, understanding that it could only lead to heavy losses. The mopping-up of the buildings, which yesterday had been considered already cleared of defenders, along with the simultaneously conducted assault against the Officers' House, demonstrated that those Russians who were prepared to fight to the bitter end were continuing to resist. Gerhard Etken:

> The remaining Russian units were continuing to fight stubbornly. It happened that from the buildings, the greater portion of which had been blown up, fire would immediately resume. The mopping-up was difficult, because individual Russians were hiding among the piles of rags and buckets, and even in the beds and ceilings, and they'd resume firing after a search of the building or rush at our soldiers with sharply-honed knives.

Convinced that the combat spirit of the defenders hadn't been broken, Kühlwein decided to employ the assets of combat engineers as well. *Oberstleutnant* Masukh, the commander of the 81st Pioneer Battalion, decided to lead the operation personally. Having climbed onto the roof of the Ring Barracks in one of its sectors that they'd seized, and using it to cross over the Trekharoch Gate, the engineers wound up above the barracks of the 33rd Engineering Regiment. They had brought along with them enough demolition charges to do what Lerman had done two days before with the Germans defending in the mess hall – blow holes into the ceilings and the walls, drive the enemy into a corner and force them to surrender. They decided instead to blow them up, dropping the charges down the chimneys.

However, the appearance of the German combat engineers on the roof didn't go unnoticed – Red Army soldiers located in the casemate of the wall at Point 145 began to shout to their comrades in the Officers' House that Germans were moving around on their roof. The defenders of Point 145 themselves couldn't fire – they didn't have any cartridges.

Leutnant Schneiderbauer recalls:

> Assault engineers got up onto the roof of the building block opposite us. In groups of six, they lowered explosive charges down with poles onto windows and firing positions, but only a few Russians gave up as a result. The majority sat it out in secure cellars and, despite the heavy artillery strikes, would take up the fire-fight again after the demolitions had exploded.

Schneiderbauer was mistaken; far from the majority was sitting in the cellars, and fire from the upper floors wasn't ceasing. With each explosion, the combat engineers were hearing screams and groans of the Russians, but they were continuing to fire back. Moreover, they decided to eliminate the threat from the German combat engineers. A group of defenders moved through the burned-out guardroom and clambered up onto the roof, where they began exchanging fire with Masukh's men. Two of the Red Army men were killed and two were badly wounded, but the Germans also took casualties – returning the Russians' fire, the commander of the 81st Pioneer Battalion *Oberstleutnant* Masukh himself was wounded. The operation had to be halted. The 45th Infantry Division was continuing to take intolerable losses – in the fight for the Officers' House, the commander of 14/I.R. 133 *Hauptmann* Dr. Watzek, who had distinguished himself the day before during the attack to free the encircled Germans in the church, was also killed.

From his command post, von Pannwitz submitted a report, which confirmed the optimistic assessment of the situation that he had made previously:

> Objectives and territory have been gained: the eastern portion of North Island of the Brest-Litovsk Fortress. Assessment of the enemy's situation: the enemy has been mopped up from the Citadel. At present only several scattered partisans are still located in the fortress, which are continuing to be eliminated. The battalion's losses: one killed, four wounded. Plans for the next day: at the order of Oberst John.

Unsuspectingly, von Pannwitz had triggered the next wave of reports about the fall of the Citadel. Probably prompted by the news from the division headquarters that the fortress had been taken, von Krischer issued Order No. 7, having wrapped up the work of the artillery around Brest and having initiated preparations for its further march to the east: '... No more combat tasks remain for the artillery of the 45th Division. It is preparing for further operations and is quickly beginning the necessary route march.' Thus, the division was now deprived of further support from heavy artillery of the OKH reserve.

At 1500, General Schlieper issued an order to I.R. 135 regarding the mopping-up of North Island (which was transmitted to its headquarters that afternoon), which subordinated the 45th Reconnaissance Battalion (minus its elements located in the city of Brest) to Friedrich John for this purpose, as well as II/I.R. 130, III/I.R. 133 and elements of the 81st Pioneer Battalion (at John's discretion). He was also promised additional assets – captured tanks, flame-throwers, etc. However, at the moment he still had only several groups of demolition engineers available.

Apparently, John initiated his attack immediately after receiving the order. Later in his memoirs, he would write:

> For the attack against East Fort we were given assault groups, equipped with flame-throwers [those that had previously been assigned to III/I.R. 133]. The entry to the horseshoe-shaped structure was inundated with the fire of anti-tank guns (firing over open sights), infantry guns, and one light field howitzer. However, it was impossible to bring the flame-throwers sufficiently close to be effective, because of the ferocious defensive fire of hostile small arms. Many 80mm mortars were deployed in positions beyond the northern walls, but the smokescreen placed by

> them on the East Fort didn't yield any results. However, we did seize a pillbox on the bank of the Muchavec.

The 'pillbox' mentioned by John was actually the gorge barracks of the Main Wall (Point 145), the seizure of which von Pannwitz had announced prematurely.

Thus, the Brest Citadel 'had fallen' once again. The commander of Army Group Centre Fedor von Bock couldn't help but trust his subordinates who had delivered this report. In his diary entry for 25 June 1941, he would write: 'Only now has the Citadel at Brest fallen after very heavy fighting.' However, already by 1550, in a joint report from Dettmer and the division's Ic von Rühling to the corps headquarters, which had just reported to Guderian about the capture of the Citadel, its 'taking' was already firmly forgotten. Dettmer reported on the continuing mopping-up of the fortress, which was entailing losses (especially officers); and von Rühling on the fact that there was no new information from the reconnaissance battalion whatsoever. Between 1630 and 1645 on 25 June, after the initiation of actions to mop up the fortress, I.R. 133 and I.R. 135 (with Kaehne's I/I.R. 135) almost simultaneously reported that the still-persisting pockets of resistance couldn't be approached by their infantry. Most likely, they had in mind Point 145 and the East Fort. Both commanders urgently requested tanks and flame-throwers. A report from *Oberst* Kühlwein, the commander of I.R. 133, also exists, in which he states that the mopping-up operation was again bogging down – neither the Northern Bridge nor the fortification adjacent to it had been taken. A new plan of attack was being worked out.

The daily report from John's regiment at 2050 on 25 June reports: 'Fighting continues against a cunning, diabolical and stubborn foe.' Later in his memoirs John confirmed his impressions of stubborn enemy resistance: 'Almost all the sections of the old buildings with their very thick brick walls had to be taken one by one, preparing them for this with explosives and hand grenades.'

The day of 25 June yielded I.R 135 few results. Its daily summary continues:

> Especially heavy fighting at the eastern fortification on North Island. Losses rather significant. After the enemy, as in the centre of the fortress, again rallied, even the fight for the fortification No. 145 became somewhat harder, the capture of which the reconnaissance had also reported. It was established that with the assistance of contemporary means, a fortification can be taken. For this a tank, a large flame-thrower and many demolition charges are necessary.

The report is referring to the *Flammenwerfer* 34 flame-thrower. It had a maximum range of 25–30 meters. With its larger tank, it also provided 45 seconds of uninterrupted work, enough on average for 35 discharges. The request for the *Flammenwerfer* 34 (with its greater maximum range than the *Flammenwerfer* 40) speaks of the great difficulty of approaching the defensive positions.

For all practical purposes, I.R. 135 had made no progress and continued to be stuck in its previously occupied positions. The remaining elements of 'Group John' were enveloping the remaining pockets of resistance. The plans for 26 June were to continue mopping up the Citadel and to assault East Fort after the arrival of special weapons designed to reduce fortifications.

Despite the fact that the Officers' House succeeded in holding out on this day, the conditions for the defenders inside it were nightmarish. The agonized screams of the wounded rising from the foul-smelling cellars, the corpses laying in the nooks, the occasional explosions of anti-tank gun shells within the casemates, and the bullets fired by snipers all became a familiar backdrop to something much more terrible on 25 June – thirst. On this day, when von Pannwitz's reconnaissance battalion reached the wall at Point 145, it reached a level that exceeded all the other torments – now there was no water at all. All the approaches to it were covered by German fire, and the bank of the Muchavec was strewn with the corpses of those who had nevertheless taken the risk to reach it. Sergeant N.A. Tarasov, a squad leader in the 84th Rifle Regiment's 7th Company:

> Here, in the fortress, I learned the value of water. I recall that I always had the vision of a geographical map in front of me. In my mind's eye, I saw enormous lakes and rivers, but here, in the fortress, we couldn't even slake our thirst; the air, filled with the stench of rotting corpses, made not only our mouths and throats dry, but seemingly everything inside us. It was very painful to look at the water flowing nearby, which was nevertheless almost totally inaccessible.

I. Dolotov remembers:

> It seemed to me that we were the only ones still defending in the Ring Barracks. The ability to comprehend and analyze dulled. It seemed that the war was endless, and there was no other life whatsoever. I wanted to eat and even more to drink. In the nightmarish intervals of drowsy slumber, I kept envisioning our family's large samovar, which I'd last seen fifteen years ago. I pictured removing the lid, tilting it, and gulping down the entire contents all by myself.

They tried to chew the damp sand, but often lacked the saliva in order to spit it back out. They were drinking urine and even their own blood. Men were losing their minds from the thirst and stench, but continued to meet any careless German movement with fire. On this day the only means by which to obtain water became the casting of flasks attached to weighted strings into the Muchavec, but they weren't able to pull all of them back. Moreover, almost all the water would spill out as the flask was being retrieved, leaving little to share among the terribly thirsty men.

The men dying from thirst conceived the most improbable plans for obtaining water – like digging underground tunnels to the Muchavec. Ivan Dolotov decided to attempt to use a more feasible method:

> It was still light when I proposed to Comrade Fomin to try to get water by what seemed to me to be a more reliable method. I had stumbled across a

> paint sprayer, which we used in the camouflaging platoon of the engineering regiment for camouflaging equipment. It seemed to me that if the end of the intake rubber hose was dropped into the Muchavec and the device itself was placed in the cellar, then this would become a water pump that would constantly supply water. The commissar approved my plan and ordered me to carry it out.
>
> Again with Gordon and with one other senior sergeant, we got to work. It was about 15 metres from the barracks to the water. Opposite a kitchen window and not far from the entrance to the boiler room in the cellar there was a rubber hose, which at one time had been used to wash potatoes. It was partially obstructed with brick fragments and dirt. Gordon and the senior sergeant ventured out and hauled it back down into the cellar. Since one end had been smashed flat by a collapsed section of wall, we had to cut a piece off. Having attached the hose to the atomizer, it was now necessary to drop the other end into the water. Now it was my turn. We sallied out only during artillery barrages, when everything was enveloped with smoke and ashes, and only by random chance was there a possibility to be caught in an explosion. We placed the device at the bottom of the staircase leading out of the cellar. We extended the entire length of the hose along the ground. When a barrage began, I darted across the road to the Muchavec with the end of the hose. Sliding down the slope of the riverbank to the Muchavec, I made a dash for the water – but lost the end of the hose within 2 metres of the water. I grabbed it and started to tug. The hose gave a little, but sprang back when I relaxed it. It turned out to be a little too short and I couldn't reach the water with it.
>
> On my way back, as I was clambering up the crumbling slope to the road, I felt a strong blow to the base of my skull, an explosion and …

Deafened by the explosion, Ivan Dolotov fell on the corpse-strewn bank of the Muchavec.

Observing the desperate attempts to obtain water and interrogating the haggard prisoners, the command of the 45th Infantry Division had full knowledge of the situation of the Citadel's defenders. Schlieper informed the XII Corps headquarters, 'I'm planning to encircle and take the pockets of resistance by attrition', noting that 'the attempt to crush the last two pockets of resistance in the Brest Fortress had failed because of the lack of tanks and flame-throwers; in the rest of the fortress, the situation is unchanged.' Tanks, large flame-throwers and a company of flame-throwing tanks had been requested by the division.

Apparently, around this time the matter of the division's assignment was being settled. Schroth had been unable to replace the 45th Infantry Division that was fighting in the fortress with a different division. In the XII Corps' daily order for 27 June, it is stated that the 45th Infantry Division had been withdrawn from the corps' roster as of 25 June 1941. It was decided that it would now be subordinate to the LIII Corps headquarters. The individual services were informed of this decision. There were almost no further communications with XII Corps headquarters.

In an order of the same day, 25 June, issued by LIII Corps headquarters, the division's task has been stated rather ambiguously: to be ready to move out no sooner than the afternoon of 28 June. However, it is clear that the division didn't have unlimited time – in essence, this was a directive to finish with the Citadel by the above-mentioned date.

The hardest day of the Officers' House was coming to an end. Its defenders, still capable of resisting, had very little left: hunger, the barrages and most of all, thirst, were striking down even the very strongest of them. The mood was depressed, but still many hadn't entirely given up hope. V.S. Solozobov:

> In the daytime it became known that once it grew dark that evening, the commanders of the headquarters and the lightly-wounded would make another break-out attempt. I was happy, if only to have a goal in reach: either break out from the cauldron, or be killed. The enemy shelling was intensifying with each passing hour. Shells were crashing through the ceilings of both floors.
>
> Evening arrived. We, about twenty men, were situated on both sides of a window. Just then Captain Zubachev stated that he was going to report to the commissar. Several minutes later he returned with Fomin. We waited for orders. Everyone was extremely tense. Our attention was focused on the window and the water. How long we stood there like that – ten, twenty minutes or perhaps even longer – I don't know. Then the commissar spoke up quite softly: 'Abandon the attack, comrades; everyone return to your former positions.' Everyone was depressed; a certain bewilderment was perceptible.

It was impossible to remain any longer, but to break out was also impossible ... Finally it grew dark, and dark silhouettes, indistinguishable against the backdrop of the bank of the Muchavec, were creeping toward the river, striving to be inaudible and freezing among the corpses whenever an illumination flare went up. Hundreds of people were waiting for their return with frantic hope. On the opposite riverbank, riflemen and machine-gunners were intensely peering into the shadows at the Muchavec, periodically firing a test burst, sending bullets into any seemingly suspicious shadow. Sometimes a 'shadow' emitted a dying scream – but ever more men, confronted with a choice between dying from thirst or a bullet, and who opted for the less agonizing way out, kept stealing toward the river.

In a report from the 45th Reconnaissance Battalion, which was sealing the Officers' House from the direction of the Muchavec, there is mention of the repulse of a break-out attempt that night, which had been undertaken in the battalion's sector. In the process, approximately twenty-five Russians had been killed. But was this in fact an attempt to break out from the Officers' House or from Point 145? Solozobov's recollections are sufficiently convincing to reject a break-out attempt by Fomin's entire group in the Officers' House. Perhaps this was some different, independent group, not under Fomin's command. It is fully possible that the riflemen of the reconnaissance battalion perceived the defenders of the Officers' House crawling toward the Muchavec to obtain water as an attempt to break out, and having opened fire at them, on the following day simply tallied up the corpses that were lying on the opposite bank of the Muchavec.

In the opinion of I.R. 135's adjutant *Oberleutnant* Haidvogl, '. . . the enemy is now definitely quite worn out, but is fighting with the courage of despair (since he believes that the Germans give no quarter). It is difficult to assess his losses; there are few prisoners.' A report from A.R. 98 supports Haidvogl's impression: 'The enemy resistance is gradually weakening.' I.R. 135's plans were still unclear – they depended on the allocation of special combat means to 'Group John'. The division headquarters was continuing to scour the area to find some – as a result, in the course of the night, 'Group John' received Somua S-35 tanks from Armoured Train No. 28 to support its mopping-up operations on North Island.

A new day dawned for the defenders of the Officers' House. Probably, now almost all of the defenders of the 33rd Engineering Regiment's sector of the Ring Barracks sensed that it would be their last. Both ammunition and strength had been exhausted. A military medical attendant of the 84th Rifle Regiment S.E. Mil'kevich recalls:

> Everyone knew that we could no longer expect help from anywhere; we were saying our goodbyes to each other, and strove to memorize home addresses, so that later, if one of us survived, he could inform comrades, families and the Motherland about the fate of those that didn't.

V.S. Solozobov, among the wounded men in the cellar, recalled:

> By morning the wounded men in the cellars probably knew everything by now and almost asked nothing of me; just the moans were a little softer, as if the men were nevertheless hoping to hear better. In order to cheer them up, I deliberately told them a lie: 'Our forces are attacking from the city of Brest towards the fortress.' The soldiers instantly cheered up. One of them uttered, 'That is quite likely, because our forces couldn't retreat far. If not today, then tomorrow they'll be here.' I myself was also hoping that these hopes became true. Exiting the cellar, I was almost overcome with fatigue. The commissar [Fomin] was sitting against a wall, his head in both hands. I decided to address him: 'Comrade Commissar, there's nothing with which to feed the wounded.' He tiredly replied, 'We must ascertain what we have available there; take a seat, we'll make a list now.' Fomin looked exhausted; he was wearing a soldier's combat blouse . . .

At 0840, Army Order No. 1 arrived. The 45th Infantry Division was being dropped from the roster of Walther Schroth's XII Army Corps and being added to the roster of General of the Infantry Karl Weisenberger's LIII Army Corps. Schroth said farewell to the 45th Division in the daily order for the corps No. 2 dated 27 June:

> ... [The division] in the course of a limited number of days under my command ... particularly distinguished itself by its courageous and energetic actions ... It is only reluctantly, but wishing that a soldierly good fortune be bestowed upon the division in the future, that I am striking it from my formation.

It is difficult to describe the final hours of the defense of the Officers' House and Point 145: there is hardly any information. Gerhardt Etken curtly noted this long-awaited success in the division's war diary: 'In the morning assault groups of I.R. 133 and A.A. [Reconnaissance Battalion] 45 take one more nest of resistance (Point 145 and the Officers' House), in the process of which groups of demolition engineers prove to be particularly suitable. A total of 450 prisoners were taken.' Just to be accurate, the taking of both pockets of resistance was completed only in the afternoon of 26 June. The final attack against the Officers' House, which began on the morning of 26 June, was not an infantry assault. Combat engineers got in on the action. Freytag's men only covered the detachment of engineers as they were preparing a 'large detonation' on the roof above the compartments adjacent to the Trekharoch Gate. Von Pannwitz was waiting for when they'd conduct the demolition of the wall at Point 145, which still had several dozen stubborn hold-outs in the casemates within the wall.

Just as before, gunfire was coming from the windows and embrasures of the fortifications – their defenders were not intending to surrender. One of the combat engineers was killed, and one was wounded. However, it was noticeable that the resistance was distinctly less; the message went out that 'the enemy is experiencing a severe lack of weapons.' Just before noon, a thunderous explosion shook the barracks of the 33rd Engineering Regiment. The 'large detonation', which had been carefully prepared by the combat engineers, succeeded – immediately, the walls that faced the interior of the Citadel on the upper floor of several casemates collapsed. In one of the sectors, the entire wall collapsed, together with the roofs, burying many defenders under the rubble.

The cave-in caught V.S. Solozobov as he was sleeping:

> When I came to, I couldn't understand what had happened to me: I couldn't see anything, my whole body was in pain, and I couldn't feel anything with my hands. At last I began to see light. From my joy I wanted to get up, but I was unable to do so, because I was piled with the rubble of the vault, which had collapsed from the explosion.

Those soldiers caught in the chambers that were subjected to the detonation's effects began to emerge from the rubble, surrendering to Freytag's infantry. The wounded in the cellars with their last remaining strength were also scrambling out of them. Numerous concussed, unconscious men were lying among the rubble. Approximately eighty men surrendered.

However, according to information from the assault engineers at 1415, Red Army soldiers were still holding out in the eastern portion of the Ring Barracks. They still had cartridges – and the defenders were continuing to fire at the Germans. Neither Zubachev nor Fomin were among them: both commanders were lying beneath the rubble. Mil'kevich, however, writes that Fomin received a serious concussion, but continued to direct the fighting – that is, he was only taken prisoner later.

Almost simultaneously, detonations were conducted on the wall at Point 145 as well. However, here, in the underground casemates, covered by the last rounds of ammunition that remained to the defenders of the Officers' House, the Red Army men didn't surrender. Moreover, the reconnaissance battalion was taking casualties. However, at 1345 the fighting ended at Point 145 as well. Here, fifty-four men surrendered to von Pannwitz.

What was happening in the last minutes of the Officers' House? The majority were preparing to make a choice – imprisonment or death. S.M. Kuvalin: 'Two soldiers took their own lives, preferring to take a bullet from their own gun than to be taken prisoner.' The Jew Abram Gordon, Ivan Dolotov's comrade, understanding that he wouldn't survive as a prisoner, hid in the ruins, hoping to wait until darkness. Others also sought some refuge – that night, when the Germans lifted their cordon, it would be possible to attempt to escape.

I.R. 135's summary report for 26 June announced: 'Because of the explosions, approximately sixty Russians ran out of the centre of the fortress onto North Island and surrendered. In their words, the remaining 200 found death from the explosions.' Thus ended the epopee of the Officers' House.

Excavation of the heaps of rubble of the barracks of the 33rd Engineering Regiment began almost immediately. Under the close watch of Freytag's soldiers, the recent defenders of the Officers' House labored to clear the rubble. V.S. Solozobov was one of them, having been extracted from the pile that had been covering him: 'There was a buzzing in my head. Suddenly I heard a cry nearby me: "Rus!" Two of our soldiers freed me from the bricks and rubble: Germans were standing right there . . .' Other groups of prisoners began to bury corpses; over these days, a multitude of them had accumulated on the battlefield. S.M. Kuvalin:

> The fascists searched us and took our personal things, and having divided us into groups of around twenty men each, ordered us to dispose of the corpses in this sector. We gathered and buried the fallen Soviet soldiers in the nearest shell hole without any scrutiny or registration. The corpses had putrefied and it was difficult to breathe. We laid the German soldiers in piles, removed all their personal documents, and turned the dog tag over to an officer, who was standing off to one side holding a bottle of eau de cologne.

Likely, it was thanks to the timely initiated removal of the debris that many defenders were saved, but they immediately became prisoners. Both Fomin and Zubachev were found here. They had both already been wounded by the time of the detonation, and when the roofs collapsed on them, they again were seriously injured.

Zubachev's skull was fractured, and the entire left side of Fomin's face was crushed. Neither commander of the Officers' House survived to liberation. Commissar Fomin, betrayed by conscripts, was executed that same day. Zubachev died of tuberculosis in the officers' prison camp in Hammelburg in 1944.

It is believed that Fomin was executed at the Kholm Gates, where there is now a memorial plaque. However, A.M. Fil', who was taken prisoner that same day, relying on the testimony of several of the fortress defenders, gives a different version of the Citadel commissar's death. According to it, E.M. Fomin was shot at the first fort across the wooden bridge that leads from the fortress to Terespol, at a prisoner collection point.

On this day Gerstmeyer's soldiers also entered the vegetable storage cellar, which had previously been the gunpowder magazine in the vicinity of the Main Wall. There, the 6-year-old Lenia Bobkov had been lying in a corner of the cellar since the morning of 22 June. He was so weakened that he couldn't even move when the door to the cellar was opened. The German soldier who had entered the cellar turned on a flashlight, and the young boy squinted. The German picked him up in his arms and carried him to an ambulance that was near an apartment building of the command staff, collecting the wounded. Here, he was the first to be bandaged, having seventeen wounds from shell fragments – only his head and right arm weren't bandaged. The son of Junior Lieutenant Bobkov was driven to the city hospital in Brest. He would spend fourteen months in hospitals until his discharge in the autumn of 1942, now under a different name.

* * *

After the war, when conducting various projects, 132 human remains were found in the vicinity of the Officers' House. With the exception of those found in the cellar of the White Palace (most likely, wounded men who'd been buried by the explosion of the shell fired by a Karl heavy mortar), these were bones of defenders of the Officers' House, who'd been buried after its capture by teams of military prisoners.

In March 1951, during a special military team's further excavation of the rubble caused by the 'large detonation', in addition to rusted weapons, the remains of thirty-four defenders of the Officers' House were found. There, the team also found among the brick rubble mixed with bones an Order of the Red Banner No. 12140, the silk banner of the 84th Rifle Regiment given to it by the Comintern (Communist International), and the regimental press. In addition, it uncovered a multitude of paper fragments – summaries, manuals, letters, and the three pages of notebook paper that later became known as Order No. 1 . . . but nothing remained of the defenders of Point 145.

Chapter 10

The East Fort

The loss of the Officers' House signified the end of the organized defense within the Citadel. The shots that still rang out on Central, South and West Islands primarily spoke more of the search for those Red Army officers and soldiers hiding in shelters than of combat operations. Only in East Fort did hundreds of soldiers continue to resist, cemented by the will of Major Gavrilov. Now, after the failure of the break-out attempt, their morale had fallen. However, the soldiers of 'Group John' didn't sense this – the fire of the Red Army men again and again was preventing any possibility to approach the casemates that they were holding and break into them. However, it still hadn't received the tanks and other equipment that had been promised to them.

After midday, I.R. 135 was given an assault group of combat engineers. With mortar fire and smoke-making equipment (smoke pots, shells and hand grenades), the regiment was trying to render the fort's garrison incapable of resisting. In fact, nurtured on the 'poisonous gas threat' of the 1930s, the defenders took the smoke as a poisonous agent. However, it had no effect on their resistance. Dar'ia Prokhorenko, a civilian woman trapped in East Fort, recalls, 'A smokescreen was released by the foe – everyone thought that they were releasing gas. The smoke was blue and had a bitter taste with the odour of a rotten potato. Political instructor Comrade Skripnik ordered the soldiers to put on gas masks; everyone was provided with one.' Vladimir Kaz'min, located in a chamber where the wounded were lying and who'd donned them with gas masks, recalls that a 'dense smoke' came crawling toward them from the inner wall. Grigorii Makarov wrote that 'grenades with long wooden handles' (the *Nebelhandgranate* 39 smoke hand grenades) came flying straight into the doors and embrasures. However, the response to the smokescreen was heavy return fire from small arms and machine guns from the loopholes. So John and Schlieper's main hopes rested on tanks.

At 1550, one tank trundled up to East Fort to support the mopping-up operation there, but most likely this was a captured T-38 tank. The division headquarters now knew that a lot of defenders were concealed within the fort. Von Rühling advised the units conducting the fighting that all the wells in the Brest Fortress should be poisoned without exception; it was necessary to announce this to all the subordinate elements. This would induce the garrison's soldiers to abandon their concealment and head to the rivers, where they could be killed or taken prisoner. One of the summary reports that arrived that evening stated, 'Quiet. The adversary as before is defending in isolated pockets of resistance in the Citadel. Nothing new is known about his disposition in the fortress.' Mopping-up inside the fortress actually collided not only with solitary defenders, but also groups that put up bitter resistance.

From the division command post, another rather laconic report went out to the LIII Corps headquarters: 'Except for one fortification, the Brest Citadel has been scrubbed of the foe. Within the Citadel and around it, it is still necessary to reckon with the appearance of isolated hostile riflemen . . .' Von Bock nevertheless had to find out that the 45th Division was still assaulting positions in the Citadel. He noted with some irritation in his diary entry for 26 June: 'All parts of the Citadel at Brest have still not fallen. The report of the 25th [June] was incorrect. Unfortunately casualties there are high.'

Things were becoming ever more serious for the defenders in East Fort. The remaining ammunition in the 333rd Rifle Regiment's stockpile at East Fort couldn't last for long – and the men's endurance had a limit. Primarily, as in all the other sectors, the lack of water was the foremost problem. Rather quickly it had been established that in one of the chambers of the inner wall, where the food storage facility was located, there were only barrels of fish, but in the cellar below them there was sawdust-covered ice. This gave them an opportunity to quench their thirst. However, it was running out – and moreover, it was becoming dangerous to dash between the outer and inner wall. They dug pits in the stables – at first it was impossible to drink the murky and repugnant water, but then it either became clearer or thirst overcame their aversion to it. However, at times there was only enough for a spoonful per person. Soldiers of the 393rd Separate Anti-aircraft Artillery Battalion sustained themselves with the dry rations they had received back on 18 June, and which fortunately, they had not turned over to the depot. Company quartermaster Sergeant Pavlenko had in reserve a sack of biscuits: it was sufficient for one biscuit per man per day, but then they also ran out. Yet in the casemates there were a lot of soldiers and other elements – they had to satisfy their hunger with oats and horse feed.

On 22 June an operating-room nurse of the 95th Medical-Sanitation Battalion Raisa Abakumova, who was living with her mother in one of the apartment buildings of the command staff next to East Fort, had found refuge in the stables of the 333rd Rifle Regiment in the outer wall of East Fort. Other family members of the command staff had also found shelter there: Lidiia Krupina (together with her two little girls, one of them just a year old, the other 2 years of age), Dar'ia Prokhorenko (with three children, including a year-old daughter), Efrosiniia Lisetskaia, Kseniia Kotova (with her twin 3-year-old daughters) and Mariia Borodich (with a daughter) . . . Abakumova was, first of all, a military servicewoman with a medical background. She had wound up in East Fort without even a first-aid kit – the few bandages that she had taken from the cottage housing the 125th Rifle Regiment's medical unit had run out even before she had found shelter in the stables. She began to bandage the wounded soldiers with strips of fabric torn from their undershirts. When he arrived at the fort, Gavrilov directed Abakumova to organize a medical unit.

The pupil of the 44th Rifle Regiment's band, then 15-year-old Vladimir Kuz'min recalls:

> Speaking personally, there wasn't any sort of medical clinic. There was simply a room where the wounded were placed, and it was simply one of the most ordinary two-three sections beneath the outer wall. The wounded were lying on the ground, on overcoats, but often not even on them ... They were dying in front of our eyes.

The ice was running out, and the filthy water from the 'wells' in the stable was not simply repulsive, but also unsafe. Chlorine tablets helped – they boiled the water and threw in some tablets. However, there were also year-old babies located in East Fort – it was impossible to sustain them on fodder and murky water. Dar'ia Prokhorenko:

> The first two days I had milk in my breasts, but then there was nothing to feed my baby. My daughter drew blood from me, but then there was not even that, and so she was crying wildly. For this Comrade Skripnik got angry at me, and the enemy shelled us more heavily. It seemed that our cellar together with us was being tossed skyward.

Next to her, the year-old daughter of Lidiia Krupina was also crying from hunger. Dar'ia Prokhorenko recalls, '25–26 June became bad for me; my baby daughter didn't stop crying, and the two older kids – a daughter and son – were begging me, "Mama, we want something to eat."' It seemed that by 26 June, the defenders of the East Fort had reached the limit of their agonies.

Schlieper's plans remained unchanged: further mopping-up of the Brest Citadel with the use of tanks. LIII Corps issued a deadline: on 29–30 June, the division was to move out on the march. It was necessary to finish the job by this time.

At 0100 on 27 June, Abram Gordon, who that evening had decided to make his way out of the Officers' House and flee the fortress, crawled under the Trekharoch Bridge. To his surprise, he encountered Ivan Dolotov, who was also trying to hide beneath the bridge – Dolotov himself, who was in a semi-delirium, didn't remember this. Dragging Dolotov under the bridge, Gordon tried to bring his comrade back to his senses. He succeeded. Dolotov recalls:

> I came back around from hunger and the chill. It was dark. Somewhere off to one side were the dashed lines of tracers from firing machine guns ... Gradually I realized that I had gone deaf, and I was upset that I had lost my main means of orientation. We were lying under the bridge opposite the Gate among the rocks and pilings of an abutment ... After some time with great difficulty, through flotsam of shattered boards and timber, we made our way across the river to a point close to the opposite bank of the Muchavec, then moved along it at a snail's pace up to our chest in water for concealment ... There wasn't the strength to move. We didn't abandon the rifle, the only one between the two of us. For some

> reason, up to this point we had always thought that it would be best of all to break out from the fortress in the direction of the Kobrin Gate; obviously, this was guiding us even now. From Gordon I dimly understood that things in the barracks were somehow very bad.

This night, I.R. 135, which was blockading the East Fort, had a major stroke of luck – one of its defenders, a political instructor, fell into their hands that night and provided it with information that 20 officers and 360 soldiers were still in it, with 10 light machine guns, 10 submachine guns, 1 quad-mounted machine gun and 1,000 hand grenades. There was food, and a source of water had been dug. The plans for surrender were not known.

According to many indications, the political instructor was S.S. Skripnik, the commissar of the East Fort. The circumstances of his capture are unknown – did he deliberately cross over to the enemy, convinced of the pointlessness of further resistance, or, having argued with Gavrilov, was he trying to escape from East Fort and reach units of the Red Army? Finally, it is possible that on that night of 27 June, a second attempt to break out through holes created in the floor of the stables and the thick wall was undertaken. Having broken out, some of the soldiers might have been captured, Skripnik among them. His further fate is unknown.

Further interrogations of the political instructor disconcerted both John and Schlieper – it was becoming clear that the matter was going to be prolonged. The size of the fort's garrison was equivalent to that which had been holding out in the Officers' House, but the conditions in which they were situated were much more tolerable. The only thing that made the fort vulnerable, noted Gerhardt Etken in the division's war diary, was the fact that the defenders were nevertheless suffering from the shortage of water. As a result, in Order No. 12/41 on the division's actions for 27 June, there is no mention of a final defeat of the Russians – only that the siege of East Fort would be continued.

While planning was under way in the 45th Division headquarters for the coming day, Gordon and Dolotov, making their way along the Muchavec with frequent stops, reached the fork in the river – and at the same time, the 'eastern walls', the German fire from which had inflicted so many casualties on the garrison of the Officers' House. Here, completely exhausted, they decided to rest. Here they were also taken prisoner:

> I was lying next to a tree, when suddenly figures with rolled-up sleeves and submachine guns materialized and were looming over me. Soon more Germans walked up to us together with two of our guys with filthy bandages and dark, grizzled faces. Holding onto Gordon and one other of the prisoners, we moved towards the Kobrin Gate. The fascists followed behind us. They brought us to a long, wide trench, which had been dug before the war in the earthen wall for rifle marksmanship training (and which extended to the left when coming out of the fortress through the Kobrin Gate). They placed us in front of a board, upon which previously targets had been posted. About ten paces away some sort of officer or

> feldwebel (we still didn't know their ranks) was standing together with a half-dozen submachine-gunners. By now, we were also seven or eight men.
>
> After some command from their leader, the submachine-gunners formed a row. Conversation stopped. It seemed that they were planning to shoot us. On the faces of our soldiers (we were glancing around at that moment), I didn't see any fear; they were all serious or even indifferent, and their faces were tired and dull. I also didn't have any sense of fear or some sort of despair. When Gordon and I exchanged farewells, there was a feeling of sorrow and pain that everything was going to end at any moment, then a sudden upsurge of despairing rage at the figures standing in front of us. Just then everything changed. An officer walked up and shouted something at the unteroffizier. He walked over to us and, approaching each of us, took a long look at our faces. He asked something of Gordon. I couldn't stand up any longer and took a seat with my back against the board.
>
> Soon they brought us two or three small loaves of bread, and a woven bag full of dried Caspian roach. One of our guys, escorted by a submachine-gunner, left and soon returned, carrying a bucket of water.

Several hours later, the group of prisoners was loaded aboard a truck that was slippery with blood, which took them to a field surrounded by barbed wire – Biala Podlaska. There Dolotov met Lerman and Iakimov, who were thought to have been killed during Vinogradov's break-out, and he learned of Fomin's death. Lerman and Gordon disappeared in August, in a separate camp block, into which all the Jews had been gathered. But Ivan Dolotov, having passed through the camps in Biala Podlaska and Lillehammer (Norway), lived a long and in general happy life. However, my effort to meet with him in 2006 was unsuccessful. Regrettably Ivan Dolotov was ill and couldn't chat with me ...

At 1000 on 27 June, two tanks (one a captured French tank and the other a captured Russian tank) arrived on North Island, as well as another captured Russian tank with an engine that kept failing. After noon, as Schlieper watched, the tanks began to hammer East Fort from point-blank range, having moved right up in front of its fortifications. Return fire continued to come from within the fort. John announced that because of the tank fire at the loopholes and windows, the Russian fire diminished substantially – but no white flag appeared. In the 45th Division's daily report to LIII Army Corps headquarters, it was forced to note that at the given moment, the tank's action (only one tank was mentioned), like the continuing fire at the gun ports, hadn't achieved any results. However, the intentions remained the same: to continue to wear down the enemy strength with the armor and to pry the defenders out of the fortifications. Mopping up the rest of the Citadel of the isolated, concealed Russians that were firing from the most inconceivable hiding places, like trash cans and piles of rags, was continuing.

The elements that were taking in prisoners began the processes of clearing away the rubble in the Citadel and of burying the German corpses in the common cemetery in Brest. By 27 June, the 45th Infantry Division's losses were 28 officers and 251 non-commissioned officers and soldiers killed; 31 officers and 619 non-commissioned officers and soldiers wounded; and a rather large number of missing-in-action (the majority of which were KIAs that hadn't yet been found), 2 officers and 206 non-commissioned officers and soldiers. It isn't clear why so many hadn't been located, if apparently nearly the entire fortress was now in German hands. Perhaps the fire was still so heavy that it made it impossible to collect the bodies? As a result, the 45th Infantry Division's total irrecoverable losses [killed and missing-in-action] thus far were 30 officers and 457 non-commissioned officers and men. The losses were heavy – but the fighting was still continuing.

* * *

By the evening of 27 June, there was bustling in the stable below the inner wall – although the wall was shaking from shell explosions, yet another attempt to break out was being prepared here. Understanding that an escape across the grounds of the fort was impossible, the defenders decided to make an unexpected attempt – having broken through the casemates' ceilings or walls, they intended to burrow through the earth covering the wall and, catching the enemy by surprise, to make a break for it in the darkness and smash through the German cordon. Approximately 200 people were ready to take part in this attempt.

However, the soil proved to be sandy – sand kept refilling the tunnels. Nevertheless, in several places they were able to break through the ceiling, erect ladders and dig their way up to the surface. One soldier after another clambered up the ladder and emerged on the surface. However, they were spotted – machine-gun bursts and shell explosions forced them to drop prone or try to seek shelter in the tunnels again. Many failed in the attempt – one of the tunnel exits caved in when a shell landed on it just as the first soldier emerged from it. Machine-gun bursts that now and then struck the wall forced other soldiers to forego the digging of more tunnels. Altogether, approximately fifty men were killed or wounded during this break-out attempt. Soldiers gloomily dug fresh graves directly in the stable, while Abakumova and her assistants sought to tend to the wounded as far as they were able to do so. Now they also had nothing left to do but wait. By this time, Dar'ia Prokhorenko's and Lidiia Krupina's year-old daughters had both died.

On the morning of 28 June, an assault gun now joined the tanks that were shooting up the East Fort. An 88mm anti-aircraft gun – the largest caliber that the artillery could now contribute – was also employed against the fort. However, it seems that the additional weapons weren't bringing about the desired result, so *Oberst* John drove off to the airfield at Terespol in order to seek air support. The former chief of staff of the II Fliegerkorps (Air Corps) Paul Deutschman (who was a colonel in 1941), recalled:

> The commander of one of the regiments of the 45th Division arrived at the air corps' command post in Biala Podlaska and asked for assistance in

> taking a Red Army commissar school in Brest (it was steadfastly resisting and preventing an advance) that his elements had encircled, in order to support Panzer Group 2.

Of course, the defenders within the gorge casemates of East Fort had no way of preventing forward movement along the *rollbahns*. However, some sort of weighty reason was needed in order to get the *Luftwaffe*'s commitment and employ such powerful bombs.

John learned that he could get air support, but for this it would be necessary to pull his own units back to West Fort. He was able to reach an agreement with a bomber unit (according to some sources, 6 Staffel [flight]/KG [Kampfgeschwader, or Combat wing] 3, which was equipped with Ju-88 bombers) staging from the Terespol airfield, to bomb East Fort that evening.

At 1145, a discussion took place between Armin Dettmer and the 1a of the LIII Army Corps headquarters regarding the order governing the division's departure, which still hadn't been put into effect. Losing patience, Dettmer sent a radio message to the LIII Corps headquarters, requesting authorization to move out in trail behind the 52nd and 167th divisions in the event of a departure in march column. He stressed, 'We request a prompt decision.' However, the corps headquarters was initially silent. Eventually, a reply came: the 45th Infantry Division's departure from Brest was cancelled. Weighing all the circumstances and realizing that the 45th Division was still needed in Brest, Weisenberger decided to part with it. The 45th Division left the roster of the LIII Corps and was made subordinate to a temporary command, Höh.Kdo.z.b.V. XXXV. That evening a Fourth Army order arrived, according to which the division was presumably supposed to become part of the OKH reserve and be directly subordinate to Fourth Army headquarters. However, the dispatch of a reinforced regiment to Kobrin that was indicated in the order was cancelled – probably because by this time units of the division had already been diverted to guarding airfields.

The renewed firing on the East Fort by tanks and the assault gun failed to bring results. In the course of the afternoon of 28 June, the withdrawal of the committed elements from East Fort to the cordon line began. It was conducted with intensive fire cover, so that the defenders would not use the withdrawal to make another break-out attempt. Elements of III/I.R. 135 and the 45th Reconnaissance Battalion pulled out of the fortress entirely – for them, the fighting was over. Only 5/I.R. 135 and Hartnack's II/I.R. 130 remained on North Island. Everything was now ready for the bombing of East Fort – in order to mark the target, white sheets were laid down on the outer edge of the ditch. However, approaching heavy cloud cover forced a cancellation of the mission. It was revealed at 1915, though, that the regiment still didn't know about the reason for the air-raid's cancellation. Now Hartnack's battalion was forced to re-establish the tight cordon around East Fort quickly.

With the dawn on 29 June, Hartnack's companies were again pulled back from East Fort. The weather promised to be fine, and by 0800, the drone of aircraft engines approached from the west. A white signal flare soared into the sky, and five Ju-88s dove on the target with a howl, releasing high-explosive fragmentation SD-500 bombs. Six direct hits were obtained, two missed the target, and two bombs failed to explode (one of them fell inside the Citadel, near one of the gates). The effects of one of the hits are still visible today on the western side of East Fort's outer wall. The casemates didn't suffer – even *Oberst* John wrote about this, and any visitor today who desires to do so can go for a walk around them and not see any traces of collapsed walls or debris. Then once again, gunshots rang out from the windows and embrasures during an attempt to attack: its defenders were not contemplating surrender.

John obtained an agreement for another bombing mission that afternoon. The II Fliegerkorps command opted again to use medium bombers, one of which would be flown by a select crew, which was to drop the single 1,800 kilogram bomb (the SC-1800) available at the airfield on the fort. In addition, if the enemy still didn't surrender after the second bombing mission, a new approach was being prepared for 30 June – the attackers would roll numerous fuel barrels up the slope of the glacis in front of the three inner gates and windows, before igniting them all. Since the windows of the gorge barracks of the inner wall faced the ditch (the interval of space between the inner and outer walls), it was fully conceivable to drive out its defenders by this method. The goal was just the same as it had been now for several days: to destroy the garrison without taking excess casualties. For this operation, Hartnack requested 8,000 liters of an enriched fuel mixture (petrol and oil from captured stockpiles).

Immediately after 12:00 noon, the defenders said farewell to the members of the command staff's families that were still taking cover in the casemates of East Fort. Dar'ia Prokhorenko recalls:

> All the cellars were smashed; only ours remained intact, where the children were located. Then someone spoke up for the women and children to leave, or else the children would starve to death. We all got ready to leave, and there was now nowhere to fight; everything was demolished.

Major Gavrilov remembers, 'I'll never forget the tears of my combat comrades as they escorted the women and children out of the fort.'

At 1500, several white flags appeared: emaciated and haggard refugees were coming out of the East Fort and moving toward the positions of Hartnack's battalion. They told the Germans that 'the commanders don't want to surrender, but the privates, on the contrary, are ready to do so.'

Meanwhile, the cordon was again pulled back from the fort – the designated time for the planned air-strike was approaching. At 1730, seven Ju-88 bombers appeared overhead: one was carrying the SC-1800 bomb; the others, SC-500 general-purpose bombs. 'Everyone get down, take cover! They're about to begin!' – the commands of the German non-commissioned officers were forcing the most curious to get under cover. However, there was a crowd of observers, many with cameras, atop the walls and casemates and even in the several intact patches of woods. There was also a film crew from the German *Deutsche Wochenschau*, the official newsreel production company. Military prisoners, who were removing corpses and clearing away rubble in the Central Citadel, also gazed at the bombers above the East Fort with anguish.

The first six Ju-88s carrying the SC-500 bombs dove on the target. The thunderous explosions, which shook the East Fort, were audible in Brest as well – the ground quaked throughout the city. Rising columns of smoke and dust concealed the fort – was anyone there still alive? As was discovered a half-hour later, most of the bomb releases were generally on-target, but of the twelve bombs, the two that fell closest to the target failed to explode.

The solitary Ju-88 carrying the SC-1800 bomb slowly circled above the fortress, probably receiving final instructions over the radio before going into its dive on the target. These were the final hours of East Fort. V.Ia. Sisin:

> The right flank had been entirely demolished. Bricks were flying, dust, stench, nothing was visible. There were a lot of killed and wounded. I was together with Gavrilov, Kasatkin and Domienko, and there were soldiers here too – Valiannik, Arkhipov, Vovchenko. Then Gavrilov went somewhere. He returned. He was gripping two hand grenades in his hands. I asked, 'Comrade Major, what are we to do?' He had tears in his eyes. He said nothing to me in reply, turned, and entered a casemate.

Again Hartnack's soldiers watched as deserters came running out of East Fort through the clouds of dust, waving white rags – but this time there were only thirty of them. Perhaps the rest were ready to surrender? However, when the Germans attempted to approach the stables, again they were met by several shots from inside them – this was the depleted response of the East Fort.

Circling, the solitary *Luftwaffe* bomber climbed higher and higher – and at 1800 it went into a dive. Thousands of pairs of eyes watched as the distinctly visible pale blue bomb separated from the fuselage . . . The blast wave struck everyone on North Island who out of curiosity hadn't taken cover. The city rocked – in many of the buildings, the window glass shattered and the entire population saw the enormous columns of smoke and dust that rose above the Citadel. However, when the smoke and dust cleared away, no white flag appeared above the fort.

'The enemy it seems has still not been sufficiently ground down,' states the summary report of 29 June issued at 1930. 'Nothing indicates his surrender – an operation has been scheduled for 30 June to burn the defenders out with petrol and overnight there will be a barrage on East Fort, which will further attrite its defenders.' It seems that both the regiment and the division had already reconciled themselves to the fact that despite the impressive air-strikes and the audible, raging fire inside the fort that was sweeping over the ammunition supplies, the attempt to seize the East Fort had again failed. So the next message from 'Group John' was all the more unexpected – the Russians were beginning to surrender! At 2030 there were already 160 of them. Likely, after all the premature reports of the recent days, Schlieper and Dettmer still didn't believe in success. However, at 2100, 'Group

John' now reported 220 prisoners. Could it be? By 2200, 384 prisoners had come in. The East Fort commander was not among them. The prisoners were saying that he was going to shoot himself.

The circumstances surrounding the capitulation of East Fort will likely never become known – in the 'Account of the taking of Brest-Litovsk' there is the statement, 'The Red Army men received permission to surrender from their leader, a major. They were not at all shellshocked, appeared strong and well-fed, and gave the impression of being well-disciplined.' However, judging from the fact that the surrender took place over the course of two hours, only the final group to come out of the fort received permission for it. It is important to note that the report states that the defenders of the East Fort surrendered with the permission of its commander. However, those who knew that Gavrilov was the commander of East Fort believed he'd been killed. Perhaps that is why the scrutiny of the Soviet state security services in fact never fell upon Major Gavrilov later.

The news of the capitulation of the last fortification of Brest-Litovsk instantly flew around the entire 45th Division. For it this meant not only the long-awaited victory, but also the need to prepare for a march. The fall of East Fort was reported as well to higher headquarters but neither the corps nor the Fourth Army gave the division any fresh assignment. The darkness that had fallen, filled with the smoke and glare of the fires above East Fort, forced a postponement of its final mopping-up until the morning.

Back on the prior evening, when it was becoming clear that the East Fort would soon fall, Gavrilov had ordered Junior Sergeant Rodion Semeniuk, who was in charge of the 393rd Separate Anti-aircraft Artillery Battalion's ammunition depot, to bury the battalion's banner, which Semeniuk had retrieved from the guards' tent at Shramko's order back on 22 June and had brought back to the headquarters. On the night of 29 June, Semeniuk and two soldiers wrapped the banner in canvas, placed it in a canvas pouch, and then in turn placed the pouch in a lead bucket that had been used for feeding horses. Then they buried the bucket in one of the casemates on the right-hand side of the outer wall. They refilled the half-meter-deep pit that they'd dug, firmly tamped down the dirt, and covered it with trash to conceal it. On 27 September 1956 Rodion Semeniuk, the only one still alive of those who had buried the banner, brought several officers and soldiers of the military unit then stationed in the fortress to the location, and in front of their eyes dug up the banner of the 393rd Separate Anti-aircraft Artillery Battalion, which was turned over to the Museum of the Defence of the Brest Fortress.

Meanwhile Gavrilov, whom many believed had been killed and were arguing over whether he'd shot himself or blown himself up with his last grenade, found a refuge in one of those same tunnels that the defenders had dug when trying to escape to the outer wall, together with a Border Guardsman who'd always been by his side during the siege, serving as his adjutant. Having climbed into the tunnel, the Border Guardsman and Gavrilov began to dig through its walls in opposite directions – Gavrilov to the left, the Border Guard to the right. The loose sand easily yielded, and now situated between the inner brick wall of the casemate and the outer earthen wall, they dug their ways to a point a meter or two to either side of the exit tunnel that had been previously dug by the soldiers.

The search of East Fort began the next morning. Gavrilov could easily hear it when German troops entered the barracks. Stopping at the tunnel entrance, they consulted a bit, before one of them approached the opening and fired a submachine-gun burst into it. Then the group went on ahead to search other casemates.

During the sweep through the East Fort, several wounded Russians were evacuated from it, and the bodies of dead Germans that were lying in front of it were recovered. Quite a bit of ammunition was found, which spoke of the fact that the defense might have continued for some time. They squirted several compartments that they could not search with flame-throwers. In the summary report of the 45th Infantry Division to the Fourth Army command dated 30 June, there was an announcement regarding the capture of East Fort on the afternoon of 29 June (which just as before got somewhat ahead of the real state of affairs). In Dettmer's opinion, the morning and afternoon air-strikes on 29 June made a substantial contribution to the success. He wrote, 'The fortification has been taken by our elements; nevertheless, it is still burning in places. In the process 386 prisoners were taken, after several women and children had been released by the garrison just after midday.' Noteworthy is the fact that on the evening of 29 June, 384 prisoners were reported; on 30 June – 386 prisoners; and in the 'Account of the taking of Brest-Litovsk', the number of prisoners grew to 389. This confirms the fact that even after the surrender of the main garrison, several Red Army men remained within East Fort.

The seizure of East Fort, in Dettmer's opinion, signified the elimination of the last remaining resistance. 'From this moment,' he emphasized, 'the entire Citadel and city of Brest-Litovsk are firmly in the grip of the 45th Division.' The further plans of the division were to ready its main forces to move out. However, simultaneously several elements were given the order to continue mopping-up and searching the Citadel. As they understood in the headquarters of the 45th Division, the fall of East Fort signified only the end of the last of the more significant pockets of resistance, and the beginning of a new chapter in the history of the defense – the semi-partisan resistance by solitary men and small groups that were roaming the emptied barracks that were permeated with the smell of gunpowder. The 45th Infantry Division didn't have the slightest desire to be written into this chapter in any way. As of 0000 on 1 July, the 45th Division again became subordinate to the headquarters of LIII Army Corps. At 0600, its forward detachment marched out of Brest.

Epilogue

On 1 July, a ceremony took place at the South (Semenov) Church in Brest-Litovsk at the new, just-completed cemetery for the fallen men of the 45th Infantry Division. Almost 400 of the division's dead were commemorated. This is the number as reported by the division's quartermaster that can be found in its war diary. However, Dr. Gschöpf wrote that 482 (thirty-two of them officers) were buried in the division's cemetery, which was the first German war cemetery in the Soviet Union. The 'Account of the taking of Brest-Litovsk' reports that 453 officers and soldiers were killed or missing-in-action (thirty-two of them officers), which fully corresponds with the quartermaster's figures, since more than fifty men still hadn't been found by 1 July. Dr. Gschöpf's data are close to General of the Infantry von Greiffenberg's data for 27 June 1941 – 487 killed and missing-in-action.[1] Possibly, Dr. Gschöpf made a mistake – later he writes about more than 1,000 wounded, which is a figure almost twice that given by the 45th Infantry Division. Otherwise, one is left to speculate that the number of wounded indicated by the headquarters of the 45th Infantry Division is a significant understatement.

It was decided to give the name '45th Infantry Division' to one of the city's streets. Every unit of the division sent representatives to the burial ceremony. What would happen next? The number of killed-in-action in the division's very first battle in Russia, whose bodies were buried here at the Russian church, was comparable to the number killed in the division's entire campaign in France in 1940. The Austrians could only hope that the fate of the Eastern campaign had already been decided – news from the front allowed them to assume so. The only troubling fact was that there were still quite a few Russians hiding in the Citadel that had no intention of surrendering. At night and sometimes in the daylight hours as well, there were occasional gunshots and fleeting figures visible in the distance. What were they wanting, why didn't they surrender or flee?

The 45th Infantry Division spent two more days in Brest – it is interesting that the 854th Artillery Battalion was placed back under Hipp's command for several hours and returned to the city; similarly Gerstmeyer's III/I.R. 133, which was preparing for the march to the east, was detained in Brest for a day (from 5 July to 6 July). On 6 July Hipp's artillery also received the order to leave the city. The 45th Infantry Division's last trucks pulled out of Brest – the motorized column and horse-drawn carts headed to the east through Kobrin and Antopol'. The division's heavily wounded were moaning in the city hospital in Brest, while its fallen men in the new cemetery there were silent. The postal service still hadn't delivered the death notices to the towns and cities of Upper Austria. Having left Brest, the division remained eternally as part of its history. Partially obscured in clouds of dust, Hans Hartnack's trucks signified the completion of the assault on the Citadel – but within it, scattered defenders were continuing to resist.

In the darkness of the cellars, Red Army men, now gaunt after two weeks of what already seemed like an endless war, were warily harking to the silence which had settled over the Citadel after a steady rumble of trucks and armor. One after another, that night they began to slip out of the fortress. Many exited through the veterinarian clinic of the 333rd Rifle Regiment, which was located next to the Main Wall. Once over the wall, covered by the wall of a caponier, they crossed the ditch and, striving to keep to the fringes of fields, they would disappear into the Malorita woods. In the middle of July, another figure crept out of the East Fort and stealthily made its way into the veterinarian clinic – the fort's commander, Major Gavrilov. He had five grenades left and cartridge clips in two weapons: a TT pistol and a Mauser 712 machine pistol. Gavrilov was hoping to slip out of Brest and escape into the Bialowieza Forest.

Having slaked his thirst, Gavrilov crossed the ditch, but bumped into some army tents of some German unit that was positioned next to the ditch. He had to return to a casemate. Inside it, next to a door that faced the ditch, was a large pile of manure left over from stable cleanings. Having dug into it and leaving only a small slit for observation, Gavrilov decided to wait for a pre-dawn hour when the coast was clear. In his cover, he could hear Germans walking along the ditch, and once as they passed through his casemate. Not all the Germans had left – at night Gavrilov drank water from the ditch, and during the daytime he sustained himself on feed concentrate for horses, hoping to hold out for as long as possible. However, a sharp pain in his stomach that started on the sixth day grew so intense that the commander of the East Fort slipped into a state of semi-consciousness. He woke up to the sound of voices. Through the slit in his shelter, Gavrilov saw two Germans quite nearby, inside the casemate next to his pile of manure. The major released the safety catch on his Mauser, and just in time: these two Germans began to probe his shelter with their feet. Gavrilov squeezed the trigger, which had been apparently set on fully-automatic fire; the Mauser began to bark and immediately fired off the entire clip ... The Germans, who hadn't been hit, ran off, but several minutes later the commander of East Fort was involved in his final battle: having fired five bullets from his Tokarev TT pistol, he began to throw grenades. When hurling the second one, probably failing to consider his weakened state, he tossed it in such a way that he was caught by the ensuing explosion. Concussed, he was taken prisoner.

Having survived his years in prison, Major Gavrilov's Party membership was not initially restored to him. Only in 1956 did he again obtain his Party membership card, and in 1957 he received the highest honor, the title of Hero of the Soviet Union. He passed away in 1979 in Krasnodar, and according to his last will and testament, he was buried in the garrison cemetery of Brest.

In addition to Gavrilov, there were also others in his situation. Helmuth K., a 19-year-old driver of the Reich Labour Service, wrote a letter on 6 July 1941 to his parents, informing them that 'the Citadel is still holding out', and that there were still pockets of resistance: 'Twice, the "Reds" raised a white flag, and each time, when an SS company was sent forward, the doors were slammed in their faces.' Once, moving in the Citadel together with another truck, Helmuth narrowly avoided death during a Stuka diving bombing run to punish a pocket of defenders. The bomb fell just 300–400 meters away from Helmuth's vehicle: 'If I speak openly, I pissed my pants a little,' he acknowledged. On 11 July, two German officers were shot on the streets of Brest. The following day, Helmuth wrote his parents again:

> There are underground tunnels that stretch for 3 kilometres from the Citadel to the barracks: Russians are still sitting in them. Our unit is in the barracks. The streets are often strewn with nails. More than once already we've had to change our tyres.

Of course, Helmuth might have exaggerated the danger of his 'heroic workdays'. A Stuka air-strike in July against hidden defenders seems far-fetched – however, there is other evidence that the Junkers in July struck targets around the Citadel. Perhaps someday an explanation for these air-strikes will be found. However, it is incontrovertible that there still remained quite a few defenders within the Citadel in July. Why hadn't they abandoned it? Perhaps these weren't remnants of the garrison, but escapees from surrounding military prison camps. Gaining concealment in its abandoned ruins and scrounging a weapon there, they'd disappear into the Malorita woods.

It is possible, though, that the final defenders of the fortress were in fact soldiers who had been defending it in June, who'd been in hiding inside it ever since the destruction of Fomin's, Gavrilov's or Bytko's groups. They were hoping for the approach of the Red Army, and of course, it was also likely not an easy task to escape the fortress. For example, at the end of July the Germans had in Brest 'two security battalions, an engineering battalion on R&R, signals elements, motorized columns, a large vehicle repair shop, large military hospitals, transportation units for moving up supplies, a radio telegraph centre, and forming march echelons of soldiers and tanks.' It can't be excluded that with these units, the Germans were able to maintain a tight cordon around the Citadel, as well as to patrol Brest and its environs. Thus in July 1941 quite a few of the defenders of the fortress were continuing to hide in it. Again, energetic measures for its next 'mopping-up' were necessary.

On 30 July 1941, General of the Infantry Walther von Unruh arrived in Brest-Litovsk as its new commandant. Brest was in ruins. However, von Unruh was struck by the fact that more than a month after the conclusion of the assault, the city's Citadel still remained a source of danger:

> It was totally demolished by gunfire and shells, and only the gates remained standing. In general, it is constituted of desolate piles of rubble,

> smoking and malodorous, which are still the sources of small-arms fire and machine-gun fire from the remaining Soviet soldiers.

In order to re-establish road traffic through Brest, it was necessary to mop up the fortress once again. Von Unruh began this process right away, and already within several days, at the beginning of August, the last Soviet soldiers in the Citadel were captured – a small group led by some unknown commander. Unruh states, 'The officer and his soldiers were promised that they could calmly eat, drink and smoke until they were carried away.' Probably, it was precisely this group that I.V. Ivanov and other military prisoners of the camp at Biala Podlaska talked about with S.S. Smirnov:

> Four men from the Brest Fortress were brought in. They wound up in this camp straight from the fortress ... Their final attempt to escape to the Bug together with others didn't succeed. Caught in a security sweep, the soldiers returned fire as long as they had bullets, and then ran down into a cellar, where they were trapped and surrendered.

Ivanov writes that as a sign of respect, the Germans took off their helmets in front of them. He continues,

> The appearance of the prisoners was horrifying. They all were in rags, with bloodied, filthy bandages, emaciated and grizzled. All the time they were coughing and wiping their eyes – apparently the effects of tear gas. They were so weakened that they could hardly stand on their feet and were supporting each other.

However, several Russian soldiers were still continuing to sit in a 'fort to the south of Brest that was encircled by a water-filled moat.' This author is certain that this comment is in reference to Fort V – this fort had refused to surrender to the 45th Infantry Division in June. But we have no concrete sources about this episode. A cordon didn't allow them to escape, but no one had any intention to take them by storm – the commanders of the German units occupying the area had heard about the lessons of the Citadel. At this time a search of the remaining forts was under way – they were full of ammunition and equipment, which were gradually brought to the Citadel for subsequent transportation. Incidentally, Hitler during his visit to the fortress was shown ordnance that was not there in the Citadel on 22 June, which is to say that the fortress had become a depot for captured equipment.

Only at the end of August 1941 did the commandant of Brest-Litovsk Walther von Unruh announce to the army commander that Brest and the deep rear had been pacified: 'There is no firing anywhere. Once again happy faces are seen. There are no more partisans. One can move around unarmed. Order and security have been established.'

By then, the parents, wives and families in the towns of Upper Austria had already received the death notices. Between 22 June and 30 June, 524 officers and 8,362 non-commissioned officers and soldiers had been killed on the Eastern Front.

This meant a daily average of 987 men killed-in-action. Considering that according to Rudolph Gschöpf's data on the irrecoverable losses of the 45th Infantry Division for 22 June (21 officers and 290 non-commissioned officers and soldiers, for a total of 311), it turns out that more than 30 percent of the *Wehrmacht*'s total irrecoverable losses for the first day of the campaign in the East were in fact those of the 45th Infantry Division from Lintz, Austria.

This division's history ended in June 1944 in the cauldron of Minsk. Its last commander, *Generalmajor* Joachim Engel, was captured. By this time, few of the officers of the 45th Infantry Division were veterans of the assault on Brest-Litovsk: on 22 September 1941, *Hauptmann* Gerstmeyer, whose III/I.R. 133 had held the 'eastern walls' was killed; on 26 September, *Oberleutnant* von Schilling, the commander of the 1st Company in the battalion of Zahn's, then Wetzel's *panzerjägers*, was killed, followed soon thereafter (on 18 October 1941) by one of those who had planned the assault – the division's Ia Armin Dettmer; on 8 December 1941, *Oberleutnant* Wetzel, who had commanded the division's *panzerjäger* battalion at Brest after its original commander *Oberstleutnant* Zahn fell on 23 June, himself was killed. Yet then the war was only beginning . . .

Note

1. General of the Infantry Hans von Greiffenberg was the Chief of the General Staff of Army Group Centre for Operation Barbarossa. He would later write his account of the war's first year, which was translated into English under the title *Battle of Moscow 1941–1942*.